The Sea

1 *Aspronisi, "the White Island," west of Thira (Santorini).*

The Sea

A Philosophical Encounter

David Farrell Krell

BLOOMSBURY ACADEMIC
LONDON • NEW YORK • OXFORD • NEW DELHI • SYDNEY

BLOOMSBURY ACADEMIC
Bloomsbury Publishing Plc
50 Bedford Square, London, WC1B 3DP, UK
1385 Broadway, New York, NY 10018, USA

BLOOMSBURY, BLOOMSBURY ACADEMIC and the Diana logo are trademarks
of Bloomsbury Publishing Plc

First published in Great Britain 2019

Cover design: Irene Martinez-Costa
Cover image © Benjamin Lee/Getty Images

A catalogue record for this book is available from the British Library.

A catalog record for this book is available from the Library of Congress.

ISBN: HB: 978-1-3500-7671-6
        PB: 978-1-3500-8053-9
        ePDF: 978-1-3500-7672-3
        eBook: 978-1-3500-7673-0

Typeset by RefineCatch Limited, Bungay, Suffolk

To find out more about our authors and books visit www.bloomsbury.com
and sign up for our newsletters.

For Davidcito and Vanessa,
and for two who have recently made
the immense sea journey,
Isabel Salomé and Luca David

Malachi Mulligan to Stephen Dedalus:

— *God, he said quietly. Isn't the sea what Algy calls it: a grey sweet mother? The snotgreen sea. The scrotumtightening sea.* Epi oinopa ponton. *Ah, Dedalus, the Greeks. I must teach you. You must read them in the original.* Thalatta! Thalatta! *She is our great sweet mother. Come and look.*

JAMES JOYCE, *ULYSSES*

Η ΘΑΛΑΣΣΑ ΕΧΗ ΤΑ ΔΙΚΑ ΤΗΣ

"The sea will have her way."

EVANGELIA MATSADOU

Which is the best of Shakespeare's plays? I mean in what mood and with what accompaniment do you like the sea best?

JOHN KEATS, *LETTER TO JANE REYNOLDS*, SEPTEMBER 14, 1817

Here lies one whose name is writ in water.

EPITAPH OF JOHN KEATS

Contents

Preface x

Key to the Principal Sources Cited xiv

Introduction xxvii

1 Let Ourselves Be Cradled 1

2 *Amniotica* 37

3 Forwards and Backwards—Catastrophe? 83

4 Full of Gods 117

5 The Tears of Kronos 163

6 These Drowning Men Do Drown 199

7 Waves and Drops of Time 255

   A Concluding Word 297

Index 303

Preface

Friends who volunteered to read this book in manuscript urged me to say something "up front" about its strange itinerary. And the itinerary *is* strange, if only because it sets out from two very different points of departure.

The first starting point of the book was my reading—decades ago now—of Sándor Ferenczi's *Thalassa: A Theory of Genitality* (1924). That remarkable book expanded Freudian psychoanalytic theory in the direction of what Ferenczi called *bioanalysis*. I was gripped by the main theme of bioanalysis, which is what Ferenczi called "the thalassic regressive undertow." By that he meant that the sea, celebrated by poets and scientists alike as the original site and source of life, eventually draws all life back to itself. All that lives ends by drowning, as it were, in what Hegel called "the universal element." Ferenczi also reflected on the way in which the gestation of the mammalian fetus in amniotic fluid, the saline solution in which we humans too spend our initial months, can be understood in phylogenetic terms as the need to find an ersatz for the sea. These early months continue to have effects on the remainder of our lives, he argued; sleep and sex, for example, cannot be understood apart from our having been cradled in the amnion. And what Freud after 1920 called "the destruction-and-death drives," Ferenczi added, may be interpreted as the sea's imperious summons to return whence we came.

Love, death, and the sea? It was difficult for a young philosopher not to be interested.

Yet the present book has a second starting point, if it is possible for beginnings to double in this way. Although I was born in a landlocked state, I soon traveled to the seashore, and like many human beings I never stopped going there. I did what everybody does at the sea: I swam, sunbathed, collected sea wrack, explored the shoreline, ate ravenously, and slept soundly. Often enough, when the sea allowed it, I simply floated on my back and let sundry thoughts and lines of poetry drift across my mind. In later years I came to appreciate what Herman Melville meant when he said that meditation and water are "wedded for ever."

Meditation? An old-fashioned word. The dictionaries say that *to meditate* is "rare," at least when it means "to contemplate, ponder." Yet they accept as more current the meaning "to dwell in thought, to muse, to reflect, to cogitate." My own form of meditation is not so well-structured—my friends assured me of that—and it is tied to no belief or religious practice. It is, I must admit, highly associative and intuitive, responsive rather than argumentative, perhaps even "passive," as passive as floating on one's back. In recent years a number of French thinkers—Merleau-Ponty, Levinas, and Derrida among them—have stressed the importance of such passivity, however. In this they may have been following the lead of Heidegger's *Being and Time*, which emphasizes that existence is "moved" rather than self-moving: *Bewegtheit*, rather than *Bewegung*, is the guiding concept of fundamental ontology.

My own meditation on the sea reflects this passivity, but also my resistance to it, a resistance that takes the form of research and analysis. Yet no amount of strategic reading or painstaking research and analysis can explain precisely why the thinkers and writers who appear in my book are the only ones who appear there. Why Ferenczi rather than Jung or Rank? Why Schelling and Hegel rather than Kant? Why Hölderlin and Nietzsche of all the thinkers and poets of the sea? Why Melville rather than Conrad? And why, of all her novels and essays, Virginia Woolf's *The Waves*?

I find no ready answers to these questions, to my friends' and my own chagrin. Except to remark that one of the clearest signs of human finitude, a sign that is seldom read, is the set of choices we all make in what is after all our very limited reading. It is as though we do not choose those works we read; rather, they choose us. No amount of research or scholarly discipline can alter very much the way these choices go. They follow submarine currents and undertows. All I can hope is that the works that have chosen me in this encounter with the sea prove to be rich resources for my readers as well.

I will defer detailed discussion of the chapters of this book until the "Introduction," but let me add a word about the styles of the book, which, conforming to the double starting point, are at least two. I allow myself the old-fashioned and rather puffed-up words *philosophical encounter*, *meditation*, and *reflection* in order to describe one of the styles of the book, a style that reflects more my personal experiences at, on, and in the sea than any wish to write a scholarly work. And yet some of the chapters, such as those on Ferenczi, are purely expository, if only because the ideas developed in them are so difficult. Some of the chapters, such as the first, "Let Ourselves Be Cradled," reflect a style that Maurice Blanchot described as "fragmentary writing." Here the waves of writing are not as predictable as they are in expository writing, and readers may well have the feeling that they are as adrift as I am. Yet both the expository and the fragmentary styles serve the same purpose, hoping to develop styles of meditation that do justice to the sea, which will have her way, not ours. To repeat, Melville tells us that meditation and water—and he means principally the salt sea—are "wedded for ever," and no doubt he chose his verb quite carefully.

Philosophers have increasingly abandoned the sea to marine biologists, adventurers, and poets, preferring the security and the logic of the lee shore. Poets, occasionally joined by psychoanalysts, take us back to the sources, however; that is, to the sources that feed the sea, the sea that evaporates to cloud, the cloud that releases rainfall, and the stream that rushes to the sea, the source of all sources.

My thanks to Alexander Bilda, who helped me find so many books that were hiding in undersea grottoes, but who above all offered friendship and scintillating conversations; to the wise Eva Matsadou and her wonderful family at the Carlos Pansion in Akrotiri, Santorini, where much of this book was written; to Walter Brogan, Dawne McCance, Paul North, Charles Scott, and the insightful and generous readers of the manuscript for Bloomsbury Academic Press, readers whose names I do not know but who made many insightful corrections and suggestions concerning the final form of the book; to the entire editorial and production staff at Bloomsbury, especially Liza Thompson, my generous editor at the Press, who read the earlier drafts of the book and encouraged the book's publication, as well as to Paul King for his astute copy-editing, and to Merv Honeywood for his diligent work on the production of the book; and finally to Salomé M. Krell who refined the photos that she and I have taken over the years at Balos Bay. Photos 2, 3, 4, 5, 10, 11, 16, and 25 were taken by her, the rest by the author.

D. F. K.
Carlos Pansion, Akrotiri
Strobelhütte, St. Ulrich

Key to the Principal Sources Cited

Note: When the context makes the source clear I do not cite the code but simply the volume and page number in the body of my text. I have tried to list all my sources here, even when I have merely alluded to works and not made a specific page reference to them.

Works by Derrida

BS I, II *Séminaire: La bête et le souverain, Volume I (2001–2002).* Ed. Michel Lisse, Marie-Louise Mallet, and Genette Michaud. Paris: Galilée, 2008. Translated by Geoffrey Bennington as *The Beast and the Sovereign*, Volume I. Chicago: University of Chicago Press, 2009. *Séminaire: La bête et le souverain, Volume II (2002–2003).* Ed. Michel Lisse, Marie-Louise Mallet, and Genette Michaud. Paris: Galilée, 2010. Translated by Geoffrey Bennington as *The Beast and the Sovereign*, Volume II. Chicago: University of Chicago Press, 2011. Because the French pagination appears in the margins of the English translation, there will be no need to cite the English pages, but only the French.

EA *États d'âme de la psychanalyse: L'impossible au-delà d'une souveraine cruauté.* Paris: Éditions Galilée, 2000.

Translated as "Psychoanalysis Searches the States of Its Soul: The Impossible Beyond of a Sovereign Cruelty," in *Without Alibi*, edited and translated by Peggy Kamuf. Stanford: Stanford University Press, 2002.

ED *Écriture et la différence*. Paris: Seuil, 1967. Translated by Alan Bass as *Writing and Difference*. Chicago: University of Chicago Press, 1978.

G *De la grammatologie*. Paris: Minuit, 1967. English translation by Gayatri Chakravorty Spivak. *Of Grammatology*. Baltimore: Johns Hopkins University Press, 1976.

PM I, II *Séminaire: La peine de mort*, 2 vols. Volume I contains the seminar of 1999–2000. Paris: Galilée, 2012. Volume II contains the seminar of 2000–1. Paris: Galilée, 2015. Translated by Peggy Kamuf and Elizabeth Rottenberg for the University of Chicago Press, 2014 and 2017. Here too the French pagination appears in the margins.

Works by Ferenczi

Sándor Ferenczi, *Versuch einer Genitaltheorie*. In Sándor Ferenczi, *Schriften zur Psychoanalyse*, 2 vols. Ed. Michael Balint. Frankfurt am Main: Fischer, 1972, 2:317–400; cited simply by volume and page in the body of my text. The *Versuch* essay has been translated by Henry Alden Bunker, M.D., as *Thalassa: A Theory of Genitality*. New York: W. W. Norton, 1968, reprinted in later years in multiple editions. I have translated all the passages from Ferenczi's works myself, but I make reference to the English translation of the *Versuch* (i.e., *Thalassa*) after the slash solidus in the body of my text. Page references to the German edition appear before the slash solidus.

Works by Freud

GW 1–17   *Gesammelte Werke*, 17 vols. Ed. Anna Freud et al.
London: Imago Publishing Co., Ltd., 1952.

Works by Hegel

I cite the published works of G. W. F. Hegel simply by volume and page
number in the body of my text, according to the following edition:
Werke in zwanzig Bänden. Theorie Werkausgabe. Ed. Eva Moldenhauer
and Karl Markus Michel. Frankfurt am Main: Suhrkamp, 1970. I have
compared the material in vol. 9 of this edition (Part Two of Hegel's
Encyclopedia of Philosophical Sciences, Philosophy of Nature) with
Hegel's early Jena lectures, cited below.

JS 1–3   *Jenaer Systementwürfe I: Das System der spekulativen*
Philosophie. Ed. Klaus Düsing and Heinz Kimmerle.
Hamburg: Felix Meiner Verlag,1986; *Jenaer*
Systementwürfe II: Logik, Metaphysik, Naturphilosophie.
Ed. Rolf-Peter Horstmann. Hamburg: Felix Meiner
Verlag, 1982; and *Jenaer Systementwürfe III:*
Naturphilosophie und Philosophie des Geistes. Ed.
Rolf-Peter Horstmann. Hamburg: Felix Meiner Verlag,
1987. This inexpensive paperback edition of the Jena
system, volumes 331–3 of the Meiner "Philosophische
Bibliothek," is based on the new historical-critical edition
of Hegel's *Gesammelte Werke*.

Works by Heidegger

BW   *Basic Writings from* Being and Time *(1927) to* The Task
of Thinking *(1964)*. Second edn. San Francisco:
HarperCollins, 1993.

EGT   *Early Greek Thinking.* Second edn. San Francisco: Harper
         & Row, 1984.

H   *Holzwege.* Frankfurt am Main: V. Klostermann, 1950.

Hk   *Heraklit.* With Eugen Fink. Frankfurt am Main:
         V. Klostermann, 1970.

NI, NII *Nietzsche,* 2 vols. Pfullingen: G. Neske, 1961.

Ni 1–4   *Nietzsche.* The English translation is in four volumes.
         Second edn. San Francisco: HarperCollins, 1991.

SZ   *Sein und Zeit,* 12th edn. Tübingen: Max Niemeyer, 1972.

US   *Unterwegs zur Sprache.* Pfullingen: G. Neske, 1959.

VA   *Vorträge und Aufsätze.* Pfullingen: G. Neske, 1954.

W   *Wegmarken.* Frankfurt am Main: V. Klostermann, 1967.

WhD?   *Was heißt Denken?* Tübingen: M. Niemeyer, 1954.

29/30   *Die Grundbegriffe der Metaphysik: Welt—Endlichkeit—
         Einsamkeit.* Martin Heidegger Gesamtausgabe vol. 29/30.
         Frankfurt am Main: V. Klostermann, 1983. English
         translation by William McNeill and Nick Walker, *The
         Fundamental Concepts of Metaphysics: World, Finitude,
         Solitude.* Bloomington: Indiana University Press, 1995.

65   *Beiträge zur Philosophie: Vom Ereignis.* Martin
         Heidegger Gesamtausgabe vol. 65. Frankfurt am Main:
         V. Klostermann, 1989.

96   *Überlegungen XII-XV (Schwarze Hefte 1939–1941).*
         Martin Heidegger Gesamtausgabe vol. 96. Frankfurt am
         Main: Vittorio Klostermann, 2014.

97   *Anmerkungen I-V (Schwarze Hefte 1942–1948).* Martin
         Heidegger Gesamtausgabe Band 97. Frankfurt am Main:
         V. Klostermann Verlag, 2015.

Works by Herman Melville

Throughout the book I cite the Northwestern University/Newberry Library Edition of Melville, edited by Harrison Hayford et al., by code letter and page number in the body of my text.

9   *The Piazza Tales and Other Prose Pieces 1839–1860.* Evanston and Chicago, 1987.

CM   *The Confidence-Man: His Masquerade.* Evanston and Chicago, 1984.

IP   *Israel Potter: His Fifty Years of Exile.* Evanston and Chicago, 1982.

M   *Mardi, and a Voyage Thither.* Evanston and Chicago, 1970.

MD   *Moby-Dick, or The Whale.* Evanston and Chicago, 1988.

O   *Omoo: A Narrative of Adventures in the South Seas.* Evanston and Chicago, 1968.

P   *Pierre, or The Ambiguities.* Evanston and Chicago, 1971.

R   *Redburn: His First Voyage.* Evanston and Chicago, 1969.

T   *Typee: A Peep at Polynesian Life.* Evanston and Chicago, 1968.

W   *White-Jacket, or The World in a Man-of-War.* Evanston and Chicago, 1970.

Works by Merleau-Ponty

N   *Nature: Course Notes from the Collège de France.* Ed. Dominique Séglard. Translated, with Notes, by Robert Vallier. Evanston, Illinois: Northwestern University Press, 2003.

S   *Signes.* Paris: Gallimard, 1960.

V   *Le visible et l'invisible.* Ed. Claude Lefort. Paris: Gallimard,
           1964. Translated by Alphonso Lingis as *The Visible and
           the Invisible.* Evanston: Northwestern University Press,
           1968.

Works by and letters of Nietzsche

J   *Jugendschriften 1861–1864.* Ed. Hans Joachim Mette.
           Munich: Deutscher Taschenbuch Verlag, 1994 [first
           published by C. H. Beck Verlag, 1933–40].

KSW   *Kritische Studienausgabe der Werke*, 15 vols. Ed. Giorgio
           Colli and Mazzino Montinari. Berlin and Munich: Walter
           de Gruyter and Deutscher Taschenbuch Verlag, 1980.

KSB   *Kritische Studienausgabe der Briefe*, 8 vols. Ed. Giorgio
           Colli and Mazzino Montinari. Berlin and Munich: Walter
           de Gruyter and Deutscher Taschenbuch Verlag, 1986.

Works by Plato

I cite wherever possible (that is, wherever they exist) the Schleiermacher
translations, referring always to the Stephanus pagination, in *Sämtliche
Werke in zehn Bänden.* Ed. Karlheinz Hülser. Greek and German (Édition
Les Belles Lettres for the Greek text and Friedrich Schleiermacher et al.
for the German translation). Frankfurt am Main: Insel Verlag, 1991.

Works by the Pre-Platonic Philosophers

DK   Hermann Diels and Walther Kranz, *Die Fragmente der
           Vorsokratiker*, 6th edn, 3 vols. Zurich: Weidmann, 1951.

KRS   G. S. Kirk, J. E. Raven, and M. Schofield, *The Presocratic
           Philosophers: A Critical History with a Selection of Texts*,
           2nd edn. Cambridge, England: Cambridge University
           Press, 1983.

Works by Schelling

I/7, II/2, etc.	*Sämmtliche Werke.* Ed. Karl Schelling. Stuttgart and Augsburg: J. G. Cottaʼscher Verlag, 1859. Schellingʼs *Freedom* essay, *Abhandlung über das Wesen der menschlichen Freiheit und die damit zusammenhängenden Gegenstände* (1809), appears in vol. 7 of the first division (i.e., I/7) of the Karl Schelling edition. The third (1815) version of the *Weltalter* also appears in this edition, section I, vol. 8 (i.e., I/8), as *Die Weltalter, Erstes Buch.* Volume 8 also contains "Über die Gottheiten von Samothrake" (1815). Schellingʼs *Philosophy of Mythology* (1842) appears in vol. 2 of the second division (i.e., II/2). An inexpensive paperback selection of Schellingʼs writings appears as *Ausgewählte Schriften* in 6 vols. Ed. Manfred Frank. Frankfurt am Main: Suhrkamp, 1985. Schellingʼs *Philosophy of Mythology* appears in vol. 6; I cite the pagination of the Karl Schelling edition (II/2, with page number), which Manfred Frank provides in the inner margin of his edition.
WA	The first two versions of *Die Weltalter* appear in F. W. J. Schelling, *Die Weltalter Fragmente: In den Urfassungen von 1811 und 1813.* Ed. Manfred Schröter. Nachlaßband to the Münchner Jubiläumsdruck. Munich: Biederstein Verlag und Leibniz Verlag, 1946.

Other works cited by code

AL	Albin Lesky, *Thalatta: Der Weg der Griechen zum Meer.* Vienna: Rudolf M. Rohrer Verlag, 1947.
BE	Wilhelm Bölsche, *Entwicklungsgeschichte der Natur*, 2 vols. Neudamm, Germany: J. Neumann Verlag, 1894–6.

BL   Wilhelm Bölsche, *Das Liebesleben in der Natur: Eine Entwicklungsgeschichte der Liebe*, 3 vols. Leipzig: Eugen Diederichs Verlag, 1900–3.

CHV, 1–3 *Friedrich Hölderlin Sämtliche Werke und Briefe*, 3 vols. Ed. Michael Knaupp. Munich: Carl Hanser Verlag, 1992.

E   Alphonso Lingis, *Excesses: Eros and Culture*. Albany: State University of New York Press, 1983.

EG   *The Epic of Gilgamesh*. Tr. N. K. Sandars. Harmondsworth, England: Penguin Books, 1974. I have also referred to *Das Gilgamesch-Epos*. Tr. Albert Schott, ed. Wolfram von Soden. Stuttgart: Philipp Reclam, 1988.

GM   Gabriel García Márquez, *Cien años de soledad*. Buenos Aires: Editorial Sudamericana, 1967. Translated by Gregory Rabassa as *One Hundred Years of Solitude*. New York: Harper & Row; and London: Jonathan Cape, 1970.

HP 1, 2 Hershel Parker, *Herman Melville: A Biography*, 2 vols. Baltimore and London: Johns Hopkins University Press, 1996 and 2002.

KU   Immanuel Kant, *Kritik der Urteilskraft*. Ed. Gerhard Lehmann. Stuttgart: Philipp Reclam, 1966, reproducing the second (B) Preussische Akademie edition.

OR   Otto Rank, *Das Trauma der Geburt und seine Bedeutung für die Psychoanalyse*. Giessen, Germany: Psychosozial-Verlag, 2007, originally published in 1924.

RC   Roberto Calasso, *The Marriage of Cadmus and Harmony*. Translated by Tim Parks. New York: Alfred A. Knopf, 1993. I cite the English translation, which is excellent, but always check the original: Roberto Calasso, *Le nozze di Cadmo e Armonia*, 9th edn. Milan: Adelphi

Edizioni, 2002 [1988]. When two page numbers appear after a quoted passage, the first refers to the Italian edition, the second (after the slash solidus) to the English.

RG   Romain Gary, *La promesse de l'aube*. Paris: Gallimard Folio 373, 1980 [1960].

U   James Joyce. *Ulysses*. Revised edn, London: Bodley Head, 1969; originally published in 1922.

WG   W. K. C. Guthrie, *The Greeks and Their Gods*. Boston: Beacon Press, 1950.

WW   I cite Whitman's poetry by line number from Walt Whitman, *Leaves of Grass*. Ed. Sculley Bradley and Harold W. Blodgett. New York: Norton, 1973.

Works cited or alluded to without code

I cite Virginia Woolf's *The Waves* simply by page number in my text, according to the following edition: Virginia Woolf, *The Waves*, with an Afterword by Sam Gilpin. London: Collector's Library, CRW Publishing, Ltd., 2005; originally published in 1931.

For references to Novalis see Friedrich von Hardenberg, *Werke, Tagebücher und Briefe*, 3 vols. Ed. Hans-Joachim Mähl and Richard Samuel. Munich: Carl Hanser Verlag, 1987.

For "The Oldest Fragment Toward a System of German Idealism," which appears to have been co-authored by Schelling, Hölderlin, and Hegel, see Christoph Jamme and Helmut Schneider, eds *Mythologie der Vernunft: Hegels "Ältestes Systemprogramm" des deutschen Idealismus*. Frankfurt am Main: Suhrkamp, 1984.

I cite the Bible in the following edition: Dr. Martin Luther, *Biblia, das ist die gantze Heilige Schrift*, 3 vols. Ed. Hans Volz, Heinz Blanke, and Friedrich Kur. Munich: Deutscher Taschenbuch Verlag, 1974, based on the last edition during Luther's lifetime: Wittenberg, 1545.

For references or allusions to Homer, see Homer, *Ilias*. 5th edn. Tr. Hans Rupé. Darmstadt: Wissenschaftliche Buchgesellschaft; Munich: Tusculum, Heimeran Verlag, 1974; Homer, *Odyssee*. 4th edn. Tr. Anton Weiher. Darmstadt: Wissenschaftliche Buchgesellschaft; Munich: Tusculum, Heimeran Verlag, 1974.

On Greek mythology in general my principal sources are: Robert Graves, *The Greek Myths*, 2 vols. Harmondsworth: Penguin Books, 1955; Carl Kerényi, *The Gods of the Greeks*. London: Thames and Hudson, 1951; and *Der kleine Pauly: Lexikon der Antike in fünf Bänden*. Ed. Konrat Ziegler and Walther Sontheimer. Munich: Deutscher Taschenbuch Verlag, 1979.

For references to Hesiod and the Homeric Hymns, see *Hesiod, The Homeric Hymns, and Homerica*. Tr. Hugh G. Evelyn-White. Loeb Classical Library. Cambridge, Massachusetts: Harvard University Press, 1982 [1914].

I cite Sophocles' tragedies according to the following edition: *Sophokles Dramen: Griechisch und Deutsch*. Ed. Bernhard Zimmermann. Tr. Wilhelm Willige and Karl Bayer. 4th edn. Düsseldorf and Zurich: Artemis & Winkler, 2003.

For references to Lucretius, cited by book and line of verse, see Lucretius, *De rerum natura*. Tr. W. H. D. Rouse, rev. M. F. Smith. Loeb Classical Library. Cambridge, Massachusetts: Harvard University Press, 1992.

I cite Goethe's *Faust* by line, from Johann Wolfgang von Goethe, *Faust*. Ed. Erich Trunz. Munich: C. H. Beck, 1972.

I refer to Yeats's poetry according to William Butler Yeats. *The Collected Poems of W. B. Yeats*. New York: Macmillan, 1956.

Finally, for oceanographic materials, see the splendid volume, *Ocean: The Definitive Visual Guide*. 2nd revised edition by Peter Frances et al. London: Dorling Kindersley, Ltd., 2014.

2 *The black cliffs on the south coast of Thira near Mavro Vouno.*

Introduction

> *The legends of well-nigh all the ancient peoples report
> that humankind came from the water and that the soul is
> a puff of air. Remarkably, science has determined that the
> human body consists almost entirely of water. One is reduced
> in size. Having got off the train, by which they had crossed
> through the compact network of European energies, and still
> jumpy from the motion that had hustled them along, the
> siblings stood before the tranquillity of sea and sky not
> otherwise than they would have stood a hundred
> thousand years ago. Ag[athe's] eyes welled up,
> and A[nders] bowed his head.*
>
> ROBERT MUSIL, *NACHLASS*

Numberless songs hail "the seven seas," but there is only one sea, or at least only one *source* of the sea. The Greeks called it Ὠκεανός. They thought of it as a vast river, but whether river or sea *Okeanos* courses without interruption about the Earth. The various land masses of the planet, the continents that drift this way and that on their tectonic plates, are not so much obstacles to the singular source as dust to be washed away from one shore and piled onto another. Of course, the land does stretch beneath the sea and forms its bed. And beneath it all, as the allusion to shifting plates already tells us, flows liquid fire. For fire is as much beneath the earth as above it in the form of our sun.

Were it not for subterranean fire and magma, where would all the jutting continents come from, to say nothing of all the flora and fauna of land and sea?

It will not do to be a Neptunist anymore, since the Vulcanists long ago won the laurels. Or did they win simply because they themselves were land animals who needed a place on which to assert themselves? In any case, this is a book about the sea. Not the sea of the Neptunists, nor principally of stormy Poseidon, nor of the brave mariners who sail it, but the sea of Leukothea, the radiant sea goddess. But that would be the sea from which one may need rescue. The story of Leukothea, originally named Ino, is not so well known. But is that not the reason why books are written?

On the way to Leukothea, the present book visits some early Greek thinkers who are joined by Hölderlin and Nietzsche, Goethe, Schelling and Hegel, Melville and Woolf, along with the psychoanalyst Sándor Ferenczi. The structure of the book may be described as follows: chapters 1, 2, and 3 pursue what in the Preface I called the two starting points of the project, chapter 1 developing my more personal relation to the sea with the themes of cradling, floating, and passivity, chapters 2 and 3 offering an exposition (by way of close reading) of Sándor Ferenczi's 1924 *Versuch einer Genitaltheorie*, called in its English and French translations *Thalassa*. Chapters 4 through 7 are also expository, although bioanalysis is not their theme. Chapter 4 turns to the early Greek philosophers' encounters with the sea; chapter 5 takes up the meaning of the sea in F. W. J. Schelling's 1842 *Philosophy of Mythology*; chapter 6 reads Herman Melville's *Mardi* and *Moby-Dick* on the general theme of human finitude in relation to the sea; and chapter 7 reads Virginia Woolf's *The Waves* in search of a new kind of temporal manifestation of human finitude. "A Concluding Word" returns then to the more personal aspect of this philosophical encounter with the sea.

Allow me now a more detailed word about each of the chapters. Chapter 1, "Let Ourselves Be Cradled," takes its title from one of Hölderlin's late hymns, "Mnemosyne," in which the sea plays an important role. One of the inspirations of the present book comes from some lines in that poem, lines that run through my mind especially when I am swimming (or floating) at a small bay on the southwestern shore of Thira, today's Santorini. After reflecting on the human being's drive to mastery and his or her desire to attain the infinite or unbounded, Hölderlin says,

> But forwards and backwards we will
> Not want to look. Let ourselves be cradled, as
> On the swaying skiff of sea.

The sea is strangely elided here with the skiff or barque that floats on the sea. Its cradling, *wiegen*, which we experience passively, as the verb "to let," *lassen*, tells us, is the theme of the chapter. The human body— in this case my own body, floating on its back in Balos Bay—seems itself to be that swaying skiff as it drifts weightless in the sea. Although it is no more than a personal experience, one that anyone might have, the *passivity* of this cradling seems to me to be philosophically important.

The chapter then turns to the final scene of the "Homunculus" episode of Goethe's *Faust II*. There the Aegean Sea is celebrated as the element that will grant the human spirit the body that it craves. For up to now that spirit has been housed in a glass retort. Goethe writes,

> Till now the glass alone bestows his weight,
> Yet he'd be delighted to incarnate.

ll. 8251–2

In this final scene of the "Classical *Walpurgisnacht*," set in "A Rocky Cove of the Aegean Sea," it is the first philosopher, Thales, who understands the solution to Homunculus's plight, and it is a saline solution: the sea is the erotic seedbed of humankind, and Homunculus will have to plunge into it in order to undergo a long and complex evolution. Thales' insight is all the more remarkable when we note that the early Greeks had no word for *sea*: θάλασσα is a non-Hellenic word of unknown origin. It is as though when the early Hellenes emigrated from the Hyperborean north to the southernmost point of the Balkans they confronted the vast expanse of saltwater in wordless astonishment. Nietzsche hears that very silence when in his book *Daybreak* he contemplates the Bay of Genoa at eventide.

Hölderlin, he too born in a landlocked state, did not encounter the sea until he walked from his home in German Swabia to Bordeaux in December and January of 1801–2. After crossing the forbidding Auvergne in the dead of winter, he arrived at the hillside vineyards from which he could see the Dordogne and Garonne rivers, joined as the Gironde, emptying into the Atlantic. His poem "Remembrance," *Andenken*, sings his astonishment at the sight. There are no known reports of his having bathed in the sea, as after him Nietzsche was so fond of doing, but since he left Bordeaux and walked home already in May–June of 1802 that would have been difficult. Even so, Hölderlin is the poet of "the swaying skiff of sea."

Not long after him, Melville's *Redburn* reflects on the *swells* of the sea, "a certain wonderful rising and falling of the sea." Melville, who will return in chapter 6, "These Drowning Men Do Drown," dedicates his literary life to "the poetry of salt water," and chapter 1 now meditates on the cradling motion of poetry and of the Chopin *barcarolle*, of which "the swaying skiff of sea" might almost be a translation.

However, the sea often shows a very different face, the face of catastrophe. The geological history of ancient Thira is one of repeated volcanic eruptions, earthquakes, and tsunamis. Chapters 2 and 3 will find Ferenczi invoking the sea as the scene of catastrophe. Meanwhile, if "cradling" seems to be a desire for utopia, a wish for Atlantis, Atlantis itself is a tale of catastrophe. Freud's skepticism concerning what Romain Rolland called "the oceanic feeling," which he (Rolland) took to be the source of all religions, therefore seems quite justified. My own encounter with the sea therefore has to recognize these two very different faces of the sea, which will have her ways. Admittedly, all those ways are in grave danger today, and chapter 1 cites the particular disaster ecologists call "the Plastic Isles." The willful neglect and active ruination of the seas moves apace as I write and it is difficult to know what might stop it. Musing on barcarolles will not clean up the plastic trash, some of my readers will surely complain, and I join in the complaint. Yet every activism needs to replenish its energies. How? Perhaps on the model of Alphonso Lingis's "Rapture of the Deep," with which chapter 1 closes. Lingis's rapture remains realistic about the dangers of the sea, dangers it in fact courts. Yet it also respects a certain necessary passivity: "I drowned the will to move myself," writes Lingis, remembering the powerful surges that shunted him this way and that. Lingis's principal inspiration for "The Rapture of the Deep," in addition to his own experiences as a diver, is Sándor Ferenczi's *Thalassa*, to which chapters 2 and 3 of my own book now turn.

Chapter 2 sets out to understand in a critical way Ferenczi's speculation that the symbol of the fish, which has varied significance in dream-life as interpreted by psychoanalysis, may actually involve a phylogenetic "memory" of us land-dwelling mammals. Even though, among those mammals, the human being leads only nine months of something like a marine existence, those months are decisive for its later life in ways that even today are scarcely understood. Comparative embryology has long since convinced us that the human embryo develops through stages that are at least reminiscent of earlier life forms, even if they are not exact replications of those forms. Ferenczi's hypothesis is that at some point in evolutionary history a catastrophic drying up of the seas forced some forms of aquatic life—represented today by the Amazonian or African lungfish—to strike out on a path that would culminate in species that form an amnion for their young. Amniotic fluid would replace the now lost saltwater environment, and birth would be the repetition of that original catastrophe, sudden desiccation. In this respect, Ferenczi is strongly influenced by the work on birth trauma by his colleague and friend Otto Rank.

When, where, and how such a marine catastrophe may have occurred, however, Ferenczi is unable to say. Nor is he able to demonstrate anything convincing about this phylogenetic catastrophe with regard to the specific development of *female* sexuality and the *female* reproductive organs. Yet two arguments based on comparative embryology and morphogenesis bolster his speculation, which otherwise smacks of science fiction: first, it is the land-dwelling animals alone (with the possible exception of the cetaceans) that develop a protective organ filled with amniotic fluid for their young; second, by contrast, embryos belonging to animals that do not develop such an ersatz for the sea do not reproduce sexually. Thus bimorphic genitality, sexual reproduction, gestation in a womb, and the menace of desiccation constitute "an indissoluble biological unity."

In Ferenczi's view, however, the sea is not only the origin of life but also its end, insofar as it exerts a pull on all life, especially mammalian life, to return to it. Ferenczi calls this "the thalassic regressive tendency," which is the undertow, as it were, in which all life is caught. This admittedly daring idea of a "universal striving toward an existence in the sea that has been lost in primeval time" is Ferenczi's interpretation of the Freudian death drive. Indeed, if the sea is both a life-spawning pool and a death-dealing undertow, then it may claim to be, as Melville's Ishmael calls it, "the ungraspable phantom of life" and the "key" to life's mystery. Such a "life" must now be written as *lifedeath*.

Yet what about the precise when, where, and how of the putative thalassic catastrophe? Chapter 3 takes up this bedeviling question or set of questions. The history of science, as far as I have been able to determine, does not yield a reliable source for Ferenczi's idea of the drying up of the seas. The "catastrophism" of Georges Cuvier in the eighteenth century, for example, does not seem to be directly linked to the catastrophe of marine desiccation. To be sure, seas do dry up: the Aral Sea today has all but vanished, its fish having long since expired because of the dwindling pool's excessive salinity, and ages ago the Mediterranean and Aegean seas became deserts when volcanic eruptions and shifting tectonic plates closed the Straits of Gibraltar. Yet, as Kant says, no one has ever *witnessed* an aquatic species transforming itself into a land-dwelling species on account of such catastrophic desiccation. A number of early Greek thinkers apparently feared that all the seas would eventually evaporate, and that this would mean the end of world—a watery interpretation of what the Stoics came to call ἐκπύρωσις. Aristotle scolds these early thinkers for their lack of confidence in the cycle of evaporation, cloud formation, rainfall, fresh water streams, and the replenishment of the seas. In chapter 4 we will examine some of the early Greek thinkers more closely on this and other aspects of the sea.

Meanwhile, the final phylogenetic chapter of Ferenczi's *Thalassa* poses still more undecidable questions, questions that he does not hesitate to call "philosophical." Among these questions are the following: (1) Can there be a biology based not on the use-function of organs and organisms but on the pleasure and unpleasure to which organs and organisms respond—can there be what Ferenczi himself calls "a supplemental biology of pleasure," *eine lustbiologische Ergänzung*? (2) Would not such a supplement in fact have to be an *Unlustbiologie*, a biology of unpleasure, if in fact catastrophe and regression mark the development of life at every stage? (3) Yet *do* the destruction-and-death drives prevail always and everywhere on the scene of life, or are there hard-won pleasures that counteract catastrophe—is there something like a *resistance to* or a *biological censoring of* the thalassic regressive undertow? (4) Finally, is the drive to regress to an earlier state—Freud's famous death drive—invariably about the *demise* of life?

In response to this last question, Ferenczi notes the way in which the common sea urchin, even in a severely deteriorated state, uses its own necrotic tissue in order to regenerate itself. He wonders whether Nietzsche is right when he totally recasts the usual way we think of life and death. Ferenczi cites Nietzsche as follows: "All inorganic matter originates from the organic; it is dead organic matter. Corpse and human being." The sense of the last phrase is chronological: *first* corpse, *then* human being, as though we were all still living in the Age of Kronos as described in Plato's *Statesman*, where time runs in reverse. Ferenczi concludes that the very question of the beginning and the end of life would have to be dropped or at least entirely reformulated. The organic and the inorganic would be in "a constant to-and-fro tidal flow" between death and life. In the face of such tides we would have to think Nietzsche's "thought of thoughts," the eternal recurrence of the same, which is the thought of *tragic affirmation*. This would be a second reason—the first being the *cycle* of sea, evaporation, and rainfall—to turn to the Greek thinkers of the tragic age.

Chapter 4 considers five of these thinkers: Thales and Anaximander of Miletus, Heraclitus of Ephesus, Xenophanes of Colophon, and Empedocles of Acragas, all of whom take up the sea as a vital theme. For Thales, all things are "full of gods," and preeminent among these things is water. For Anaximander, the sea may be closely associated with the "unlimited," the boundless expanse from which all that is comes to be; human beings too, with their long gestation and latency periods, come to be by way of some form of aquatic life. For Heraclitus, "the first of fire's turnings is the sea"; the Λόγος and the lightning-bolt that steers all things are best reflected in the sea. For Xenophanes, the constant cycle of earth sliding into the sea and the sea depositing that earth on other shores is the key to the catastrophic history of humankind. For Empedocles, as perhaps also for Anaximander and Heraclitus, it is the paradox or oxymoron of unchanging change, the steadfastness of the perpetual flux in all things, that most needs to be thought. And it needs to be thought by the heart's blood, which is yet another saline solution, inasmuch as all thinking is pericardial, not cerebral. The supreme thought for Empedocles is the *tragic* thought that both Hölderlin and Nietzsche espied in him; that thought and its affirmation are the principal inspirations for the thought of eternal recurrence. At the center of that thought, as at the center of the Empedoclean "sphere," Queen Kypris rules; not Zeus or Kronos or even Ouranos, but Kypris Aphrodite alone, foam-born of the sea.

Can the gods of Greece be subordinated to their goddesses in such a way? Schelling thinks so. Chapter 5, "The Tears of Kronos," studies Schelling's 1842 *Philosophy of Mythology* from the point of view of the sea, which the Greeks interpret as the salty tears of the great Titan. Schelling argues that Kronos's son Poseidon differs from his rigid and self-centered father in that he begins to *flow*. Poseidon's mother Rhea, after all, is flux itself. Poseidon's task is to move to the periphery in order to find a goddess of and in the sea, and to find her in a way that is less brutal than the way his brother Hades has found Persephone. Although Schelling does not say so, I argue that the most likely queen for Poseidon is Ino Leukothea. An unlikely goddess, perhaps. One of the four daughters of Cadmus and Harmony, Ino does not shy from homicide and blasphemy. Zeus nevertheless asks that she nurse the infant Dionysos after her sister Semele's terrible death, and Ino agrees to nurse and protect the god. However, driven mad by the jealous

Hera, Ino boils the infant in a cauldron, then takes the lifeless flesh of the god in her arms and leaps into the sea. She drowns. Thereupon Zeus restores both his son and his son's nurse to life, and he convinces his brother Poseidon to accept Ino as a sea goddess. From that point on she is called Leukothea, "the radiant goddess," and she rescues endangered sailors and sea voyagers: hers is the purple veil or sash that Odysseus wraps about himself—as though he were an initiate into the rites at Samothrace—when his raft founders in the sea.

For Schelling, deity as such requires, in the words of Clement of Alexandria, that the father god "become woman." This is the central theme of Schelling's lecture course, and there is no more fitting backdrop for that theme than the sea. For the salt tears of Kronos, who weeps because his day is done, can bear and sustain the entire weight of a human being afloat on his or her back. The entire weight of a human being, however, is its mortality. The second major theme of Schelling's lectures—the feminization of deity being the first—is the tragic destiny of deity itself. For the history of mythology is pervaded by a sense of the ultimate futility of all cult and the inevitable transience of all gods, "the feeling of the finitude of these gods." What is tragic about mythology is that in it even the gods are caught in an "undertow of profound dejection." Hence the tears of Kronos, the bitter brine into which, centuries later, Melville's Pip sinks and loses his wits.

Chapter 6 takes Herman Melville to be the great American thinker of human and divine finitude. The chapter focuses especially on the transition that Melville's sea stories undergo in the writing of *Mardi, and a Voyage Thither* (1849), which is well on the way to *Moby-Dick* (1851). The narrator of *Mardi*, joined by a poet and a particularly loquacious philosopher, spend much of their time while adrift in the Pacific discussing the nature of art and religion, the problem of free will and necessity, and above all the nature of nature and of a markedly finite human nature. It is in *Mardi* that we see Melville's reading of Milton and Shakespeare, Dante and the Bible, Voltaire and Laurence Sterne bearing fruit, the fruit of a remarkable self-education. Among the most revolutionary of the interlocutors' themes is the preeminence of the human body over the mind, anticipating Nietzsche's proclamation in *Thus Spoke Zarathustra* that the body and not the soul is the "great reason" in humankind. Near the end of this vast two-volume novel, which, predictably, did not do well, a Mardian priest reflects on the sadness that pervades cosmic space in a universe where "tranquillity" is "the uttermost that souls may hope for."

By the time he is writing *Moby-Dick*, Melville has cleansed himself of many if not most of the illusions of his time and birthplace. He is left with two wrinkled brows affronting one another on the high seas, those of Ahab and the white whale. And the sea itself? The sea's magnanimity consists in the fact that it "will permit no records," so that when all collapses the sea rolls on "as it rolled five thousand years ago." Every name and every deed, including the deed of a meditation on the sea, is therefore "writ in water" and remains "but a draught of a draught." And yet. If there be "a metaphysical professor" in the vicinity, he or she will ineluctably lead you to water, and water will eventually guide you to the sea and all its ungraspable phantoms. Even if the journey is arduous, "either in a physical or metaphysical point of view," what Melville's Ishmael calls "the universal thump" descends on all alike, so that "all hands should rub each other's shoulder-blades, and be content."

None of the characters in Virginia Woolf's *The Waves*, or the single character into which she says they coalesce, finds contentment. Chapter 7, the final chapter of the book, takes up the theme of temporality—that of waves crashing on the shore or of a drop slowly forming on the stalactite of a cavern. This would not be the ecstatic temporality of Heidegger's *Being and Time*, which marks the time of suddenness, but the more embodied and more slowly forming and intermittently releasing temporality of the drop. It would be closer to the temporality that Heidegger describes as the "banning" and "binding" of time, both of these expressed in the same German phrase, *die Bannung der Zeit*. Yet for none of Woolf's characters does time have a binding power. Rather, *The Waves* records the repeated failure of what Heidegger calls "resoluteness," "the moment of decision," and "authenticity." The embodied temporality of the drop calls for a revised ontology of Dasein.

My own book, an encounter with the sea, cannot float such an ontology, if only because its response to the sea is less willful and less adventurous than that. "A Concluding Word" thus returns to the theme of *cradling*, Hölderlin's "Let ourselves be cradled, as / On the swaying skiff of sea," which is one of the book's two inspirations—and in the end its primary inspiration.

3 *The Caldera, or "cauldron," of Thira, viewed from the lighthouse.*

1

Let Ourselves Be Cradled

. . . And always
Our longing soars into the unbounded. But much is
To be kept close. And we need loyalty.
But forwards and backwards we will
Not want to look. Let ourselves be cradled, as
On the swaying skiff of sea.

FRIEDRICH HÖLDERLIN, "MNEMOSYNE"

Perhaps I may be forgiven for reproducing a note from a recent journal of mine, written during one of my many stays in the southern portion of the ancient island of Thira, today's Santorini, which is the *topos* of this entire book:

On my back, floating in the sea at Ormos Balos, feeling the waves ripple beneath my head, back, and limbs, I have the sense not that I am swimming or sinking but that I am levitating, rising out of the watery element into the aerian. The feeling is enhanced when I close my eyes. Weightlessness, as though Hölderlin's "bobbing barque" or "swaying skiff" has become a space capsule. The land that can be so rough on our feet, ankles, knees, and hips, so jarring and jolting to our joints, gives way to weightlessness. On our backs in the sea, when it's not too rough, it's a little bit like dreams of flying, without looking ahead or behind to see what is making the psychoanalysts smile so contentedly—their couch itself having now become the bobbing barque or swaying skiff of our bodies.

As unspectacular as the note is, if only because it has to do with touch, not spectacle, it is the inspiration for my entire meditation. I confess to being embarrassed about it. On my back, floating on or in the sea? It seems so unadventurous, so unheroic, so utterly passive. Embarrassed? In Spanish that means pregnant.

The Aegean Sea plays an important role in Goethe's *Faust II*, in a scene Goethe worked on toward the very end of his life. At the culmination of the second act, in a scene set in a "Rocky Cove of the Aegean Sea," the Tritons and Nereids prove that they are more than mere fish by swimming off to the isle of Samothrace in order to fetch the Cabirian gods. Why? They hope that these ancient gods, the "Great Gods," as they are called on Samothrace, will be able to help one of the central figures of Act II, namely, Homunculus, the "little human" or the "seed of humankind," to become a full-fledged human. For Homunculus, who is all spirit and no body, hovers ghostily in an alchemist's retort; yet he, or it, would love to become embodied and thus fully human. Some say that modern Western humanity, for all its science and philosophy, and for all its technical achievement and redoubtable power, is precisely in the position of Homunculus—a feisty spirit encapsulated in a glass container.

The Nereids and Tritons, returning from Samothrace, announce that they have brought these Samothracian gods to the rocky cove not only to help Homunculus incarnate but also to celebrate the sea in a festival of peace. It is as though all the warships that plow the waves of the historical Aegean are now to be demobilized, and as though peace is the deeper meaning of the deep.

Homunculus, meanwhile, is underwhelmed by the sight of the Cabirian gods, who are, as Schelling says, dwarf-like gods of yearning and mourning. How could the languorous, languid, languishing deities of Samothrace, consumed as they are by their own longing and apparently powerless to help themselves, help him get a body?

> They're all ill-shapen, seems to me,
> Botched clay pots is all I see;
> Yet now the wise men gather round
> And crack their pates on what they've found.

> ll. 8219–22

Strange words, impertinent words, from an upstart spirit in a bottle. Indeed, the spirit of humankind, amoeba-like, itself seems ill-shapen, or to have no shape at all. When Proteus first espies Homunculus, he cries, "A little dwarf that glows in the dark!" (l. 8245). The word *Zwerglein* is the clue to Goethe's motivation for calling on the Cabirian gods to help with his homunculean task. For among the most telling characteristics of the Cabiri is their pygmy-like size. In Goethe's play, the Telchines arrive from Rhodes and the Daktyls from Mount Ida, to join forces with the Cabiri of Samothrace—all the dwarfish smithy gods of Greece who guard the secrets of technology descend on that rocky cove of the Aegean.

Yet in the end it is the wisdom of Thales, the Neptunist philosopher, that prevails: the only way Homunculus will be able to inherit a body is to immerse himself (itself?) in the fecund sea, in order there to assume and pass through all the myriad forms of organic life, to evolve through eons of time in the direction of a still remote humanity. At the end of the scene, the radiant beauty of Galatea, who suddenly appears on Venus's half-shell, captivates the spirit of humankind, who is now all afire, himself (itself?) all *Sehnen* or longing. All the elements, melting now into the elemental brine, combine over vast ages of time to provide Homunculus, the spiritual seed of humanity, the body that it craves. "For thus rules Eros, who began it all!" (l. 8479).

What could have been more natural for Goethe than to identify the erotic beginnings of humankind with the sea, and the sea with the ancient Greek Aegean? It comes as a bit of a shock to learn that the ancient Greek language has no word for sea. W. K. C. Guthrie explains that the original Achaean Greeks were so landlocked in the Hyperborean north that "the sea" meant nothing to them (WG 97). The word θάλασσα, in the Attic Greek dialect θάλαττα, which gives Buck Mulligan his shout, is in fact a non-Greek word of unknown origin. "Confronted with the Mediterranean," writes Guthrie, "the Greeks called it 'the salt element' (ἅλς)," which, by Freudian-Abelian inversion gives us our word *salt* (ibid.). Other words employed by the Greeks were "the flat expanse" (πέλαγος), which is equivalent to the Latin word *aequor*, and πόντος, meaning "the way across," which is reflected in the Latin *pons*, "bridge," πόντος being reminiscent of the Greek πόρος, "narrow strait," that which enables a maritime crossing (ibid.).

It may be that Guthrie has learned some of this from Albin Lesky's classic work on the subject, *The Greeks' Path to the Sea*. Lesky recounts the history of the early invasion of Greece by Achaean Hellenes, an Indo-Germanic people from the South Balkans, around 2000–1800 BCE, followed some six hundred years later by the Dorian invasion from even farther north. In both cases, writes Lesky, "the sea confronted the invading Greeks with an entirely new and exciting element of the world; they had to deal with it and accommodate themselves to it" (AL 6). According to the linguists that Lesky has been able to consult, only two ancient languages, namely, *das Albanesische und Hellenische*, are missing the *Urindogermanisches* word *mari*, which gives the German its *Meer* and the Latin languages their *mare* (AL 7). In spite of exhaustive research into the word θάλαττα, all one can say is that it belongs to "a pre-Hellenic people" (AL 8–9). Even the great god Poseidon, whom the Hellenes brought with them, is originally a god of lakes and streams, while the Tritons and Nereids are related to sweet Melusine and Undine, all of them figures that the northern freshwater peoples carried with them as they came south and discovered the sweeping expanse of brine (AL 98, 121, 129–30).

Because our histories of Greece usually begin with maritime battles against the Persians, and our histories of Greek philosophy with Ionian Miletus and Ephesus on the southwestern coast of Turkey, we assume that the Greeks are at home on, in, and with the sea. Nothing could be more natural, in our view, than Thales' exclamation that water is the source of all things, or Anaximander's speculation that human beings emerged from thorny fish, or Empedocles' insistence that he himself was at one time a fish.

How should one enter into a topic as vast as the sea? Precisely as one enters the *topos* of the sea, at least at Balos Bay on Thira, which is to say, *carefully*. My feet cannot find purchase on these rolling lucky stones; no toes are long enough or strong enough to grip these shifting rocks tossed by the waves as though they were pingpong balls. I struggle to keep my balance, my arms the wings of a frantic butterfly. And, unlike the Caribbean Sea, the Aegean is never quite warm

4 *Balos Bay near Akrotiri, Thira.*

enough. This is no bathtub. Once I am in over my knocking knees, I dip my hands and arms into the chill water, as the cardiologists have urged. Summoning something like courage, and giving up entirely on my fragile feet, I take the plunge. My head "it simply swirls," my ears hear naught but bubbles, my eyes open on the wonderworld below, and I am surprised to find myself in motion—slow motion—as the stones and pebbles give way to sand and clumps of luxuriant seaweed. After the initial shock, the sea is already warming up, or perhaps I am growing more cold-blooded. Progressing by regressing, Heraclitus would say; drawn by the thalassic regressive undertow, Ferenczi will say.

Nietzsche, though he loves the mountains of the Maderan Valley and Sils-Maria, craves a life close to the sea. "I must live near the sea!" he exclaims over and over again in his books and letters. And when the summers grow too hot and he must head for the hills, he laments, "I am so unhappy to leave the sea" (KSB 6:180). Of his book *Daybreak* he says that it took shape by sunning itself on the rocks near the Bay of Genoa; its every word, he says, reflects "intimate converse with the sea" (KSW 6:329).[1] A passage from *Daybreak* (no. 423) depicts the Bay of Genoa at eventide, when the sea invites—or commands— silence:

> *In the great silence.* – Here is the sea; here we can forget the city. True, the bells are still noisily tolling their *Ave Maria*—it is that lugubrious and foolish yet sweet sound at the crossroads of day and night—but it lasts only a moment! Now all is silent! The sea lies there, pale and shimmering, and cannot speak. The sky puts on its evening mime, forever mute, with red, yellow, and green colors,

---

[1] See also Krell and Bates, *The Good European: Nietzsche's Work Sites in Word and Image* (Chicago: University of Chicago Press, 1997), ch. 4.

and cannot speak. The low-lying cliffs and rows of boulders that march into the sea as though to find there the place that is loneliest, none of them can speak. The vast taciturnity that suddenly befalls us is beautiful and terrifying; our hearts swell with it.—Oh, the deception of this taciturn beauty! How well it could talk, and how wickedly too, if only it wanted to! The happy misery on its tongue-tied face is a deceit; it is there to mock the compassion you feel for it!—But let that be! I am not ashamed to be mocked by such powers. Indeed, I feel compassion for you, nature, because you must remain silent, even if it is only your malice that binds your tongue: yes, I feel compassion for you on account of your malice!—Ah, it grows even quieter, and once again my heart swells: it is terrified by a new truth, *for it too cannot speak*, it mocks me too whenever my mouth cries something out into this beauty; my heart too enjoys the sweet malice of its silence. Speech and even thought are despicable to me: do I not hear behind every word of mine the raucous laughter of error, hallucination, and the spirit of delusion? Must I not mock my compassion? Mock my mockery?—Oh, sea! Oh, eventide! You are treacherous mentors! You instruct human beings to *cease being human*! Should they give in to you? Should they become as you are now, pale, shimmering, mute, monstrous, resting contentedly upon themselves? Elevated sublimely beyond themselves?

KSW 3:259–60

Here there is something of that "oceanic feeling" that Freud refuses to recognize in himself, perhaps because no grown-up psychoanalyst wants to confuse his or her active life with those months spent in the mother's belly. Yet Nietzsche's is no perfect identification with the infinite, no subterfuge of a moralizing sublimity, no ultimate comfort, but only silence—and something like a treacherous silence, or at least a disquieting taciturnity. Yet there are other very different passages on the sea in Nietzsche's works, precisely because the sea is not always so silent. A rough surf, with huge waves pounding the shore, has a powerful undertow, and in that undertow the rocks sound like horses' hooves being chased by a horde of hissing pebbles. One of the earliest references to the open sea in Nietzsche's works occurs in the first section of *The Birth of Tragedy from the Spirit of Music* (KSW 1:28). It is a quotation from the first volume (book IV, section 63) of Schopenhauer's *World as Will and Representation*, and it features a variation on that swaying skiff of Hölderlin's: "As a boatman sits in his skiff, entrusting himself to his fragile vehicle, while the sea, boundless on every side, rages and howls, its mountainous waves rising and sinking, so in the midst of a dolorous world the individual human being calmly sits, supported by and trusting in the *principium individuationis*." [2] And one of Nietzsche's own most remarkable passages on the sea appears a decade later in the book that follows *Daybreak*, namely, *The Gay Science*. Aphorism number 60, which is still about hearing and the ear, but which claims to be all about "Women and Their Action at a Distance," I will reserve for a later chapter—indeed, the last.

Meanwhile, a story about Nietzsche swimming. When the manuscript of the book by Don Bates and myself, *The Good European: Nietzsche's Work Sites in Word and Image*, went off to the University of Chicago Press, my work with an extraordinary copy-editor, Margaret Mahan, began. She worked through the text carefully, saving Don and me

---

[2] Arthur Schopenhauer, *Die Welt als Wille und Vorstellung* (Cologne: Atlas Verlag, n.d.), originally published 1819, 2nd ed. 1844), 392.

from a thousand errors and improving the style of the book immensely on every page. During one of our meetings, she challenged something in the manuscript that I had not really noticed:

– Aren't you making too much fuss about Nietzsche *swimming*?
– Swimming? I replied.
– It's all over the book—swimming as a pupil at Pforta in the Saale River, bathing on the beaches at Rapallo and Sorrento, dipping into the lakes at Sils. You've got him swimming all over the place.

I checked, and of course it was true. I began to wonder whether I was projecting or whether indeed Nietzsche was an aquatic beast. To this day I remain unsure. It isn't that Nietzsche was an Olympic swimmer. He barely survived his high school swimming test in the Saale. And at Rapallo it was winter and the sea was stormy; at Sorrento, due to Emerson's law of compensation, he met a beautiful woman on the beach. It is usually his books, not their author, that are sunbathing like lizards on boulders bordering the sea. His eyes, so sensitive to the reflection of sun on snow that he had to forbid himself the high mountains and their glaciers, would have reacted strongly to the brine as well, and they certainly would not have withstood the blinding power of sun on sea. He does not tell us how he withstood these challenges, as far as I can recall, but I worry about it.

Yet Nietzsche, after the Greeks and Montaigne, is arguably the first philosopher of the body, at least in my reading experience, and so he has to be a swimmer. He has to surrender to the water. And it is he after all who writes about the amphibian's imbroglio of having to lug about an ungainly body on land—and worse, the hominid horror of having to stand up and walk. It is entirely natural that we should locate Nietzsche off the vertical axis and on the horizontal and the horizonal axis of the sea.

And so I insisted on Nietzsche the Swimmer. Margaret acquiesced. I wonder if she too is still worried about it?

When did *Hölderlin* first see the sea? We have to imagine that his first vision of the Atlantic Ocean, or of the wide mouth of the Gironde that empties into it, occurred when he crossed the wild hills of the Auvergne in the winter of 1801–2. He was walking from his home town, Nürtingen, near Stuttgart, to Bordeaux—a walk that took two months of the darkest days of December and January. He wrote about his first vision of the sea in *Andenken*, "Remembrance." Here are some extracts in translation:

> But go now and greet
> The lovely Garonne
> And the gardens of Bordeaux,
> Where along the sharp line of shore
> The narrow walkway winds, and into the stream
> Steeply plummets the brook, while above
> Gaze down a noble pair
> Of oaks and silver poplars;
>
> I think of that now, and of how
> The broad peaks and their elm wood
> Bend over the mill down below,
> Where in the courtyard a fig tree grows.
> There on holidays the brown women walk
> On silky soil
> In the month of March,
> When night and day are equal,
> And crossing meandering walkways,
> Laden with golden dreams,
> Breezes sway and cradle. . . .

There on the windswept peak
Of mountain vineyards, plunging down,
The Dordogne comes,
And together with the splendid
Garonne, as broad as the sea,
Their stream spreads wide. But it takes
And gives memory, the sea,
And sedulous love too fastens our eyes,
But what remains, the poets found.

CHV 1:473–75

One interpreter of the poem, as I recall, could not resist the temptation to think of those "swaying breezes," *einwiegende Lüfte*, the breezes that rock the cradle, as *wiegende Hüfte*, the "swaying hips" of the women, the well-tanned women of the south who on days of rest saunter across the silky soil of the courtyard and tread the nearby paths. Swaying hips or no, such "cradling" reminds us of another series of lines by Hölderlin, lines that also have to do with the sea that takes and gives memory. In a poem that has memory in its very title, *Mnemosyne*, Hölderlin thinks back to the Aegean Sea and its heroes of yore, who seem to him now to be haunting undersea grottoes. He ends the poem in this way:

. . . And always
Our longing soars into the unbounded. But much is
To be kept close. And we need loyalty.
But forwards and backwards we will
Not want to look. Let ourselves be cradled, as
On the swaying skiff of sea.

CHV 1:437

Our longing soars into the infinite, will not be checked. Yet we need to hold onto things, keep them close, be true to them, and not merely yearn for what is distant. What does that mean—to be true to things, to be loyal or faithful to them? That sounds like the language of resoluteness, if not of *ressentiment*, and that would not be Hölderlin's language. Not to gaze ahead, nor to linger on the past, Hölderlin says, but to "let ourselves be cradled." As though in the bed of our infancy, or perhaps in someone's arms. Perhaps even in the womb of our mother, back to which and to whom we gaze again and again, whether we are aware of it or not. Cradled in someone's arms or someone's belly—here the infinite arms and swelling belly of the sea. As though the best of life were floating, being afloat, being a "float forever held in solution," as Whitman says in "Crossing Brooklyn Ferry" (l. 62).

Floating? How strange the word sounds, and how memorable, as though the sea really does give memory. Recall Merleau-Ponty's remarkable passage in *The Visible and the Invisible*, translated by Alphonso Lingis, on "floating in being" with another human being:

> For the first time, the body no longer couples itself up with the world, it clasps another body, applying itself to it carefully with its whole extension, forming tirelessly with its hands the strange statue which in its turn gives everything it receives; the body is lost outside of the world and its goals, fascinated by the unique occupation of floating in Being with another life, of making itself the outside of its inside and the inside of its outside. And henceforth movement, touch, vision, applying themselves to the other and to themselves, return toward their source and, in the patient and silent labor of desire, begin the paradox of expression.
>
> V 188–9/143–4

Is not Hölderlin saying something similar? He contracts the image of the sea and the skiff or barque, *der Kahn*, in a very strange way. Normally, a skiff or barque would be rocked by the sea; yet here the skiff is conflated with or identified as the sea itself. The sea *is* the bobbing barque or swaying skiff that sustains our body. What sort of *aprosdoketon* is this? How are we to hear the strange elision in the phrase *auf schwankem Kahne der See*? It is a metaphor, obviously, since the sea is here the vehicle that transports the sense; but also a metonymy, synecdoche, and even an odd kind of prosopopoeia, the sea itself having metamorphosed into the skiff upon the sea, rocking as the waves rock, the sea therefore becoming a metonymy of the skiff, or vice versa, each a persona of the other, as though each is floating in being with another life. Yet what is the use of looking forward or back for the proper figure of speech when the point is to let ourselves be cradled?

A second oddity in Hölderlin's lines: he does not invoke *einen* schwankenden *Kahn*, a rocking or bobbing boat, as we expect him to—and as Nietzsche, referring back to Schopenhauer, himself writes (KSW 1:40); rather, Hölderlin writes the words *auf* schwankem *Kahne der See*. Now, *schwank* is an adjective, rarely used, which means "thin and flexible," most often referring to fields of high grass, grain, or reeds swaying in the wind. The word most often designates a *weak* reed, used figuratively to describe an unsteady and insecure person. To be sure, the sea is never fragile and insecure; the sea, even at its calmest, is no weak reed. "The sea will have her way," as the Greeks still say today. Yet the sea in Hölderlin's line keeps us afloat without the aid of any sort of vehicle. The sea keeps us close, on the very edge of inundation, while every now and then a wave slops over our face and goes up our nose—a cleansing and chastening experience. However, for the moment at least, flat on our backs, there is a kind of fidelity we feel, a kind of loyalty in the sea and in ourselves. True, we have to overcome our quite justified fear of drowning, of "dissolving into the universal element," as Hegel says. We still have to *give ourselves over* to the sea, as it were.

Such giving-over is the German *Hingebung* or *Hingabe*, which is something like "devotion," but more physical, something closer to "surrender." Hegel knew that phenomenology requires such giving-over to the phenomena, but he also hated and feared *Hingebung* because it unmans the philosopher. That is why, in his view, only the concept, but not poems, can be trusted. Poems do cradle us, however, especially poems that sing like barcarolles, out of the cradle endlessly rocking. And what English-speaking reader can fail to hear in Hölderlin's cradling lines Walt Whitman, the Whitman who so maddened and entranced D. H. Lawrence? Stories too cradle us, and so do novels such as *The Waves*, which we will read much later in the present book, even if Woolf's are rough seas.

And if by now I have been writing page after page and have merely mentioned but not yet cited Herman Melville, then I am a complete dunce. I will not yet cite *Moby-Dick*, that immense poem of the sea, which would require a chapter all its own, but a passage from *Redburn*, written in the spring of 1849, and unfortunately not much read today. This is Redburn's first voyage, and he is more boy than man, and certainly no poet: his diction is unsophisticated and there is no barcarolle to his prose. Yet Melville is the writer here, and he has Redburn meditate on the swell of the sea:

> As I looked at it so mild and sunny, I could not help calling to mind my little brother's face, when he was sleeping an infant in the cradle. It had just such a happy, careless, innocent look; and every happy little wave seemed gamboling about like a thoughtless little kid in a pasture; and seemed to look up in your face as it passed, as if it wanted to be patted and caressed. . . .
>
> But what seemed perhaps the most strange to me of all, was a certain wonderful rising and falling of the sea; I do not mean the waves themselves, but a sort of wide heaving and swelling and sinking all over the ocean. It was something I can not very well describe; but I know very well what it was, and how it affected me.

It made me almost dizzy to look at it; and yet I could not keep my eyes off it, it seemed so passing strange and wonderful.

I felt as if in a dream all the time; and when I could shut the ship out, almost thought I was in some new, fairy world, and expected to hear myself called to, out of the clear blue air, or from the depths of the deep blue sea. . . .

Then was I first conscious of a wonderful thing in me, that responded to all the wild commotion of the outer world; and went reeling on and on with the planets in their orbits, and was lost in one delirious throb at the center of the All. A wild bubbling and bursting was at my heart, as if a hidden spring had just gushed out there; and my blood ran tingling along my frame, like mountain brooks in spring freshets.

Yes! yes! give me this glorious ocean life, this salt-sea life, this briny, foamy life, when the sea neighs and snorts, and you breathe the very breath that the great whales respire! Let me roll around the globe, let me rock upon the sea; let me race and pant out my life, with an eternal breeze astern, and an endless sea before!

R 64, 66

A year before writing and publishing *Redburn* Melville wrote a review of two sea books for *The Literary Review*. He opened the review with this: "From time immemorial many fine things have been said and sung of the sea. And the days have been, when sailors were considered veritable mermen; and the ocean itself, as the peculiar theatre of the romantic and wonderful. But of late years there have been revealed so many plain, matter-of-fact details connected with nautical life that at the present day the poetry of salt water is very much on the wane" (9:205). If my own little book has a purpose, it is perhaps to restore a bit of poetry to the science of the sea.

To repeat, poems cradle us, especially poems that sing like barcarolles. And Hölderlin's lines of poetry (along with Melville's lines of prose) do read like a Chopin barcarolle, specifically, the Barcarolle in F sharp major, Opus 60. On the evening of November 15, 1983, I heard for the first time a recording of that barcarolle at the precise moment I was reading aphorism number 160 of Nietzsche's "The Wanderer and His Shadow." My own readers will think I have made this synchronicity up and contrived it all, but I have not, I swear it—:

Chopin's Barcarolle. – Practically all states and modes of life possess a *blessed* moment. Fine artists know how to fish *that* moment out. Even a life on the sea-strand has such a moment—even a life that plays itself out in proximity to the noisy and greedy crowd, a life that is otherwise boring, dirty, unhealthy. Chopin brought this blessed moment to sound in the barcarolle, indeed in such a way that the gods themselves may have craved to lie back in a skiff over long summer evenings.

KSW 2:619

The finest recording of that Chopin barcarolle I have heard is by my dear friend Hélène Grimaud.[3] (She does not know that we are dear friends—we met only once and she would not remember—but that does not matter, since I and thousands of other music lovers are her dear friends.) Grimaud says of this piece that it is "a transfigured and idealized nocturne," and "possibly the most richly charged and all-encompassing miracle he ever created, sensual and colorful, and nostalgic for something he imagined might have taken place but never did." And she advises us how to listen to it: "If you let the piece

---

[3] Deutsche Grammophon no. 00289 477 5325. In what follows I cite the accompanying booklet, which contains an interview by Michael Church with the artist. It comes as no surprise that Hélène Grimaud's most recent recording for Deutsche Grammophon (no. 00289 479 3426) bears the title "Water."

wash over you, that's what it communicates with its matchless melodies, innovative harmonies, poignant modulations and—beneath the charm and brilliance—so many deep and mysterious currents of passion, waves of sadness and longing that speak directly to the human heart."

Hölderlin's lines too let our selves be cradled in the rolling barque and barcarolle of the sea, at least if we repeat those lines aloud in the original:

> ... Und immer
> Ins Ungebundene gehet eine Sehnsucht. Vieles aber ist
> Zu behalten. Und Noth die Treue.
> Vorwärts aber und rükwärts wollen wir
> Nicht sehen. Uns wiegen lassen, wie
> Auf schwankem Kahne der See.
>
> CHV 1:437

Such being cradled—whether by Hölderlin's verse and Melville's prose or by Chopin's barcarolle—may suffer a rude awakening, however. Eva Matsadou, who lives and works on Santorini, says that all indigenous Thirans bear on their faces the scars of all the earthquakes, volcanic eruptions, and tsunamis that have made and unmade the island since time immemorial. Of the sea she says, writing her words out for me in capitals, Η ΘΑΛΛΑΣΣΑ ΕΧΗ ΤΑ ΔΙΚΑ ΤΗΣ, translated perfectly (except for the neuter possessive pronoun) by Stubb in Melville's *Moby-Dick*: "The sea will have its way." Melville, visiting Rome, was struck by Keats's epitaph: "Here lies one whose name is writ in water." Remembered in water, forgotten in water, since the sea, like writing, both takes and gives. Later we will hear Melville's Ishmael say that the magnanimity of the sea consists in its permitting no records.

There is a fairly reliable record of the rude awakenings that have occurred on Thira, or Santorini, over the centuries.[4] Sometime between 1654 and 1500 BCE, this island, which the Greeks called "The Round Island" (*Strongyle*) and "The Loveliest Island" (*Kalliste*), literally exploded, blew up, surrendering three-quarters of its mass to the sea. It was the most destructive volcanic explosion in recorded human history, more powerful than the explosion of Krakatoa (between Sumatra and Java) in 1883, which killed 36,000 people. Remarkably, no one died in the horrific explosion of the ancient island: earthquakes and minor eruptions had warned the Cycladic settlers of what was coming and they fled to safety. The ash pillar resulting from the explosion, which left only a narrow crescent of the once "round" island intact, rose some forty kilometers into the ionosphere. Heavy ash fall occurred across the Aegean and stretched from Egypt to the Black Sea; lighter ash fall extended to the Pacific Northwest of America and to the Greenland ice bank. How to account for such a disaster?

The volcanic cone at the center of "The Loveliest Island" spewed so much molten material into the air that it gradually hollowed out; the crust of the volcano then collapsed and allowed the surrounding sea to rush in and form a *caldera*, or cauldron, where the bulk of the island used to be. A tsunami of waves fifteen meters high (some fifty feet) devastated fleets and ports at Crete and on the coast of

---

[4] The material in the next several paragraphs first appeared in Salomé M. Krell's and my "Why Santorini? A Response in Two Voices," in *Mosaic: A Journal for the Interdisciplinary Study of Literature*, 44:1 (March 2011, a special issue on Kristin Linklater and the Santorini Voice Symposium of 2009), 199–208. See Georges Vougioukalakis, *Santorini: "The Volcano"* (Santorini: Institute for the Study and Monitoring of the Santorini Volcano, 1995), supplemented by a report in *The New York Times/Süddeutsche Zeitung* for October 29, 2003.

5 *Cliffs above Balos Bay.*

Turkey. Some archaeologists speculate that the explosion and the tsunami spelled the end of the great Minoan civilization on Crete. In any case, the sky must have blackened over several growing seasons, destroying crops and all hopes of harvest for years. An explosion of such magnitude, volcanologists tell us, occurs only once in every ten thousand years of earth history.

It is therefore fitting that legend locates the mythical "Atlantis" precisely here, on Santorini, the Greek Thira, even though Plato, our sole source for the legend, locates the island far to the west of Gibraltar, in the Atlantic that received its name from the legend. Even so, much of Plato's physical description of the island in the incomplete dialogue called *Kritias*—the isle of Atlantis being round and encircled by multiple waterways—suits in many respects the ancient Thira, at least in the form it had some 18,000 years ago. Since Plato wrote, an entire literature has agglomerated like a coral reef about the ancient utopia and its catastrophic end, all the way down to Donovan's "Hail, Atlantis!"

Eruptions have continued to occur in this area throughout human history, well beyond the times of myth and legend. At what might have been the very center of the Cycladic-Minoan explosion, subaquatic eruptions began to form a new islet starting at about 197 BCE. The geographer Strabo reports that "between Thira and Thirasía [a fragment of the original Strongyle to the northwest of the main island] flames leapt from the sea for four days, making the sea bubble and blaze, and gradually, as though by leverage, raising above the surface of the sea an island of some 2,300 square meters, composed of incandescent masses." Major eruptions, with lava flow gradually building up the islets today known as the Old and New "Chimneys" (*Palea Kameni* and *Nea Kameni*), occurred in 46–7 of our own era, and then again in 726. The chronicler Theophanes reports on the latter eruption:

In the summer of that same year, 726, steam, as from a fiery furnace, bubbled up from the depths of the sea between the islands of Thira and Thirasía for several days, and in a short while, after it had increased and hardened by the furious heat of the blazing fire, the smoke began itself to seem like fire, and, on account of the thickness of this solid matter, large pumice stones were spewed out all over Asia Minor and Lesbos and Abydos and towards those parts of Macedonia which overlook the sea.

Theophanes was not exaggerating. Today you can climb a high hill southwest of the village of Akrotiri and discover, perched on the white tephra and pozzuolana that constitute the top layer of the soil, a huge, glistening black boulder. It shines like obsidian. No one carted it up there. And yet you are at least five kilometers as the crow flies from the volcanic center of Strongyle. Volcanologists call these huge boulders *bombs*.

Another major eruption occurred in 1570–3, another in 1707–11, another in 1866–70. Between 1925 and 1928 the islet of Nea Kameni increased by about a third of its former size. More lava flowed between 1939 and 1941, and the most recent eruption occurred in 1950. The most recent earthquake, in 1956, caused half the population of the now crescent-shaped Santorini to flee. Not many returned, although in the intervening years others have come. There is therefore something distinctly odd about the hordes of tourists who invade the island each summer. And the increasing number of hotels built into the ash at the very edge of the cliff—to get the view of the sea—testify to the human craving for the unbounded and the desire to tempt fate.

When you visit Nea Kameni (the "New Chimney") today you must wear good shoes. You walk on clinkers and you pause to examine cautiously the fumaroles releasing steam and sulfur just shy of the boiling point. From the top of the Old and New Chimneys you gaze across the Caldera—incredibly blue because incredibly deep, almost four hundred meters (over 1,200 feet) down to the restless seabed—to the scarred walls of what used to be lovely and round. Today it is perhaps more sublime than beautiful. Or, if the layers of black basalt, red scoria, and white ash *are* beautiful, that beauty, once again, is hard-won. Seen from here, the villages and towns are tiaras on the head of a rough-and-tumble queen: Oia to the north, the most picturesque of the towns; Fira, the busiest; Akrotiri, the least adorned and hardest working; and farther south, at the very tip of the crescent, Pharos, the lighthouse, warning the approaching ships from Crete to keep their distance.

Your own boat, as it returns to the mainland from the Chimneys, will pause and shut off its engines until the sun sets. It will rock gently, cradled on the leaden sea. After the red egg sinks into the sea on that molten horizon, as though reversing the direction and the sequence of events that brought the island and its fragments forth in the first place, night comes on quickly. The tranquillity of the evening and the night belies the violence of all those volcanic cataclysms of former days—and of the impending future, since the tectonic plates below, the Libyan subducting the Eurasian, are not yet at peace.

About that "oceanic feeling" of which Freud declares himself perfectly innocent. In *Civilization and Its Discontents* (GW 14:421–2), Freud tells us a story that shows how he would impugn everything this first chapter has said thus far. He tells of sending his book, *The Future of an Illusion*, to a friend—whom he soon reveals to be Romain Rolland. To Freud's thoroughgoing critique of religion, which his friend can only affirm, Rolland nevertheless objects that Freud has ignored the *source* of religious feeling. That source would be, in Freud's reading of Rolland's words, a "special feeling that never abandons him [Rolland], one that many other persons have confirmed to him, and one that we may suppose millions of human beings have experienced" (GW 14:421). The feeling in question is "a sensation of what one might call 'eternity,' a feeling as though of something unlimited, unbounded—an 'oceanic' feeling, as it were" (GW 14:422). Even after all the dogmas and liturgies of institutionalized religions have been expunged, says Romain Rolland, one may still call oneself *religious* "on the basis of this oceanic feeling alone" (ibid.).

Rolland's objection gives Freud a great deal of trouble, principally because, as Freud famously writes, "I myself cannot discover this 'oceanic' feeling in me" (ibid.). If Freud is anxious to avoid philosophy, and he is, always and everywhere, he certainly will not embrace anything as vaporous as "oceanic feeling." He doubts whether such a feeling could be reduced to its physiological components, so that as a psychoanalyst he would be reduced to associating whatever notions or representations might occur to him when he hears the word. What occurs to him, rather strangely, is a historical novel about Hannibal, who, immediately before his suicide, as a comfort and a consolation, avers that "one cannot fall out of the world." Freud interprets Hannibal's consolation as "a feeling of indissoluble confederation, of belongingness to the totality of the outside world," a feeling that may accompany certain thoughts, especially thoughts of a grand scope; but again he confesses that he cannot convince himself of the "primary nature of such a feeling" in his own person. Of course, he cannot deny that others may be possessed of this "oceanic feeling," but he doubts whether such a putative feeling could be the *fons et origo* of all "religious needs" (ibid.).

My interest in writing the present book is not, I hope, such religious needs, but only the oceanic feeling itself, or an entire set of oceanic feelings, some of them cradling, others catastrophic, but all of them having a very salty sense. However, if all things are "full of gods," and if water is a privileged thing, as Thales seems to have said, then "religious" feelings may not be so readily banished. Whether Thales would take such feelings to mean worship of Poseidon or Leukothea or water cucumbers remains a question. Those old oceanic feelings, in a very salty sense, will in any case be my theme throughout.

Should one demand that anyone who dares to write about the sea be a mariner, an adventurer who plies and plows the ocean waves, an explorer or a naval officer, indeed, an officer of the bridge? Karl Jaspers and Martin Heidegger both suffered lifelong self-doubt because ill-health prevented them from serving in the armed services on either land or sea in the First World War. Heidegger, declared unfit for combat and sent to a weather station at Verdun, seems to have been more affected by this failure to serve than Jaspers. During the dark days of the Second World War, clearly not on one of his own better days, Heidegger wrote: "For the spirited man of action [*den geistigen, handelnden Mann*], there are today only two possibilities: either to stand out there on the command-bridge of a minesweeper or to steer the ship of uttermost questioning in the face of the storm of beyng" (MHG 96:160). The puerility of his gesture, proclaiming himself the officer of the bridge on the good ship *Thinking*, should be enough to assure us that a less militant approach to the sea is justified. Especially when in a later note Heidegger admits that his brave ship is sinking: "Thinking is the *sinking ship* on the sea of beyng. Only when the rats abandon ship does the proper time arrive for the ship—for *if it sinks*, it belongs to the element, beyng itself. The only one who is left, and he quite alone, is the one to whom the ship is entrusted. And he sinks along with it" (MHG 97:112). Every reader of *Moby-Dick* takes the sinking ship seriously. Every reader also identifies at least in part with Ahab. Also with Starbuck, Stubb, Pip, and Ishmael. Not necessarily with a whaler or a minesweeper, however.

Epi oinopa ponton, cries Buck Mulligan, reciting a refrain from Homer for Stephen Dedalus, who unfortunately knows even less Greek than I: "upon the wine-dark sea" is the usual translation. Such a strange color to choose for the sea! Yet Paul Valéry and Maurice Merleau-Ponty make the sense clear: the wine-dark sea is a sea so blue that only wine is more red. Except that when the sun shines mightily on the sea all is white gold. Not only to the eyes but also to the touch. In his *Ages of the World*, Schelling cites gold, oil, and balsam as the three elements or substances in which mind and matter, spirit and stuff, conflate to the point of absolute identity. He might just as well have written *the sea*, which combines all three elements. If men and women love the feel of gold against their skin, it is because gold, especially in the form of unpolished nuggets, possesses the sleek skin of the sea, and both are balsam to the flesh. That is why whenever men and women go to an island on a beach holiday, to an island on which no gold may be found in nature, there will always be a jeweler who specializes in gold, and the sea worshipers will buy gold jewelry so that they can take the sea with them back to Kansas City or Zürich. As for oil and balsam, Schelling is thinking of soothing medicinal unguents and resins such as the Balm of Gilead, unguents that provide the base for many perfumes and healing agents. And even if the trees and shrubs that produce balsam, or the blooms that yield etherial oil, occur in the deserts of the Near East, the sea was once there too, and there is something in the *skin* of brine that still has a viscous and healing quality about it. Loren Eiseley tells the story of the immense journey of calcium from the coral reefs of the sea to the human skeleton; every bit as immense is the journey of the skin of the sea, with its gold, oil, and balsam, to the human endo- and epidermis.[5]

We forage for trash at the seaside, "seaspawn and seawrack," as Dedalus says (U 45), because of the soothing, smoothing action of the sea on everything it spews onto the shore. The rugged-looking tree trunk, when we touch it, turns out to be velvet. And what can one say about those shards of frosted glass that have spent years in the workshop of the sea? Years ago an angry ignoramus smashed a beer bottle against the rocks and years later the sea renders it a poem. In retrospect the ignoramus becomes an artisan. Nietzsche once thought of sea wrack as a demonstration of the eternal return of the same, indeed, as a *consoling* demonstration of that idea:

> A certain emperor always kept in mind the transience of all things in order not to take them *too seriously* and to remain calm in their midst. To me, on the contrary, everything seems much too valuable to be allowed to be so fleeting: I seek an eternity for everything. Ought one to pour the most costly unguents and wines into the sea?—And yet my consolation is that everything that was is eternal:—the sea spews it forth again.
>
> KSW 13:43

Those who have read Nietzsche's many meditations on eternal recurrence will remember that he is quite critical of the thought of the "same." He is rather the thinker of the eternal return of the *different*. Given the difference that the sea makes, the consolation is all the greater.

---

[5] Loren Eiseley, *The Immense Journey* (New York: Vintage Books, 1959 [1946]), passim.

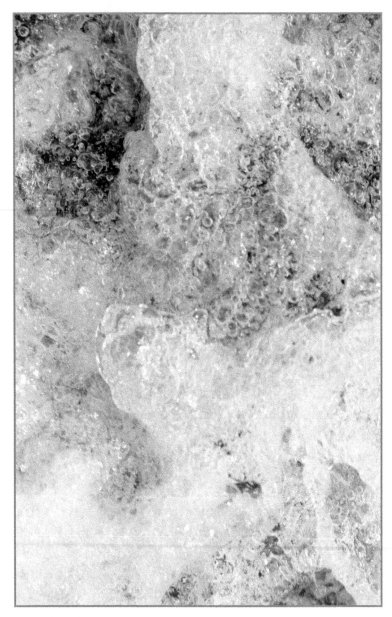

6 Gischt, aphrós, *or sea spume, at Balos Bay.*

Yet now that we are surveying the shore for sea wrack and sea spawn, it is time to observe the foam that slowly sinks into the sand. The spume of the sea, what the German, imitating the sound of the sea, calls *Gischt*, demands its own poem. Endless stanzas of foam bubble and vanish on the shore as soon as the sea declaims them, sinking away to silence.

Sea wrack, we were saying. It is impossible to talk of foraging for sea trash on the beaches without mentioning the monstrosity of *human* trash. If the ancients spoke of the Isles of the Blessed, we in the age of globalization have to speak of the Isles of Plastic. On the island of Santorini, where fresh water has to be shipped in, and shipped in by way of plastic bottles, a walk along the shoreline will present an astonishing and disheartening spectacle of plastic trash. Yes, the old washing machines that were dumped off the cliffs, the old rubber tires, and the detritus from centuries of fishing and shipping still plague the eye. Yet now it is plastic that dominates the scene, plastic sacks from the markets and plastic bottles from everywhere.

The problem of plastic trash has become critical in certain parts of the Atlantic and the Pacific, where vortices or gyres compress the trash in particular areas. Sometimes the trash is slightly submerged, sometimes it is in full view on the surface. The areas involved are often compared to the size of states in the United States, and not the smaller states. Seabirds cannot resist the temptation to nest on these unblessed isles. Their young do not flourish on the bits of trash they consume. For what the fowl and the fish eat in these areas contains polymer molecules that never break down, molecules that eventually poison them and may some day do the same to us, when the trash comes home to roost. The sun exerts photodegradation on them and the churning sea breaks up the plastic into very tiny fragments, but those fragments do not dissolve. It is one of the best examples of physical change that does not undergo chemical change. Some fragments, even most, sink to the bottom—if they are not consumed on their way down—while some remain on or near the surface.

For readers who have robust stomachs and are stronghearted, I recommend examining various websites for accounts of the Isles of Plastic. The very rubrics under which one may pursue the research are horrifying enough: the Great Pacific Garbage Patch, the Pacific Trash Vortex, and ditto for the Atlantic, Photodegradation, Microplastics, Marine Debris, Marine Pollution, "Ghost Fishing." Whereas one applauds the collective efforts of conservationists and mariners to clean up these areas, for which no country accepts responsibility, one also has to take seriously the remark of one expert who notes that a thorough cleanup would bankrupt the nation that attempted it. Finally, plastic debris is but one of the many pollutants that are killing the seas: deep sea mining and drilling, oil spills, untreated sewerage, industrial waste, agribusiness runoff, ballast water discharged from ships, lost containers, underwater noise pollution, the undersea deposits of nuclear waste, which all the "advanced" nations deny they have deposited—the list is long and more than discouraging.

I am aware that in this first chapter of the book I am helplessly adrift among passages from poems and novels and treatises on psychology and volcanology. One expects of a philosopher a certain amount of seamanship, a modicum of navigation skills. Yet I have never written about the sea before, and I am greener about the gills than Melville's Redburn, greener than any landlubber that ever sought to write about the sea. May Thales come to my rescue and shunt slippery Proteus aside!

It is time to bring some order to this fledgeling meditation, lest it disintegrate entirely into scattered sinking polymer fragments. An appreciation of Sándor Ferenczi's *Attempt at a Theory of Genitality*, the English and French *Thalassa*, not itself the most orderly of meditations, will be my first effort. Yet chapters 2 and 3 may best be introduced here by Alphonso Lingis's "The Rapture of the Deep." Lingis chooses as his epigraph those extraordinary words of Ariel's "ditty" in act 1 scene 2 of Shakespeare's *The Tempest*, words so uncanny that they make us wonder whether any play with the title *The Tempest* could be a comedy:

> Full fathom five thy father lies;
>   Of his bones are coral made;
> Those are pearls that were his eyes:
>   Nothing of him that doth fade,
> But doth suffer a sea-change
>   Into something rich and strange.

Lingis writes about the compulsion to travel even in an age when television and film take us closer to the world than the naïve traveler can ever hope to get. The same is true of underwater "specials" that give us edited versions of the best of the sea. Lingis cites Ferenczi's *Thalassa*, which identifies the sea and our return to the sea as "the libido itself" (E 4). And yet the libido is connected in some mysterious way with death—therefore with anxiety and fear—and Lingis's chapter will end by confronting the shark. Yet that is to anticipate.

Laden with air tank, regulator, gauges, I went into the sea. The belt of iron weights dropped me through the strong current of the surface. Below there was no current, but there was surge, water compressed to three atmospheres throwing me back and forth thirty feet, so that I fought it violently to stabilize myself, afraid of being dashed agains the coral cliffs. . . . I drowned the will to move myself, consigned myself to the movement of—what? Equatorial storms that had not been visible on the surface, that were raging or had raged perhaps hundreds of miles away? Earthquakes or volcanic cataclysms breaking the floors of the abyss? The movement of the moon swinging in its orbit two hundred and forty thousand miles away? And then the bliss came, as though in being suspended in this cosmic movement and losing the motility that comes from taking a stand and taking hold, I had found what I went down in the sea to find.

E 5

Surrendering the erect stance, giving up the hold on things, letting himself be cradled—these are the keys to Lingis's rapture. The rapture itself responds to the *excesses* in things, which will not be reduced to our vertical, domineering gaze or our categorial knowledge project. Yet such excesses are not about profundity. "The deep is all in surface effects" (E 7). These surface effects—extravagant colors, inexplicable shapes, uncanny movements—are not to be known. Rather, "they delight" (ibid.). The logic of science is "impeccable," no doubt, and oceanographers have learned vast amounts about undersea life. Yet science fails to explain "the lengths to which they go," "they" being the corals and the fish that exhibit "the most flamboyant colors, the most intricate patterns, as though their combat fatigues had been, between one Ice-Age season and the next, redesigned by Milanese haut-couturists with minds empty of everything but frivolity" (E 8). What gets surrendered in "The Rapture of the Deep" is the *functional* approach to life. There is "a logic of ostentation" above and beyond every logic of use and survival-value:

The color-blind *octopus vulgaris* controls with twenty nervous systems the two to three million chromatophores, iridophores

Thank you

for shopping with Speedyhen.com

One of the UK's largest media retailers.

Our customers say we're **Excellent** ★★★★★ ★ Trustpilot

Need help?
Scan here!

and leucophores fitted in its skin; only fifteen of these have been correlated with camouflage or emotional states. At rest in its lair, its skin invents continuous light shows. The sparked and streaked coral fish school and scatter as a surge of life dominated by a compulsion for exhibition, spectacle, parade. The eye adrift in the deep finds itself in a cosmos of phenomena and not of noumena, a theatrics and not a teleological engineering, a depth of *doxa*, opinion or glory, and not of truth and dissimulation.

E 9

At the limits of Sándor Ferenczi's bioanalysis we will confront a very similar rejection of *functional* thinking. In his case the rejection will have to do with the imbrication of libido and what Freud identifies as the destruction-and-death drives. In Lingis's case, the excesses that one confronts in the sea are equally outside or beyond the logic of function—beginning with the surrender of the vertical posture and the acceptance of a not very functional horizontality:

Denuded of one's very postural schema, of one's own motility, swept away and scattered by the surge, one does nothing in the deep. One takes nothing, apprehends nothing, comprehends nothing. One is only a brief visitor, an eye that no longer pilots or estimates, that moves, or rather is moved, with nothing in view.

For the eye moved by the thalassa complex the deep is an erotogenic zone. The eye adrift in the deep is not penetrating, examining, interrogating, surveying, gauging. It passes over surface effects, caresses.

E 10

The word *caress* dominates the rest of Lingis's chapter. Having surrendered the gaze that seeks to conquer the unbounded, the eye of the diver caresses and is caressed by the "surface effects" of an alien domain. "It is seeking the invisible" (E 13). Yet if the erotic drive somehow, at its limit, encroaches on the death drive—or if the latter encroaches on the former—then it is not surprising that fear sometimes strikes the diver. Lingis introduces the theme of fear by mentioning a night spent in a small boat under the full moon, "watching the sharks coming in across the white sands below to feed in the estuary" (E 14). The vision is one of beauty, excessive beauty, perhaps sublimity: "The incontrovertible ugliness of the shark on the laboratory table or in the tank is not the perfect beauty of this shadowy arabesque under the breakers" (ibid.). But then there is the diver's inevitable daytime confrontation with the shark and with the fear that is not entirely unforeseen. Indeed, Lingis says, "The one that goes down to the deep goes for the fear" (E 15). He continues:

> Off Hikkaduwa, the wreck was sprawled out at 120 feet. There was no way of determining, by looking at these scattered ribs encrusted with spiney urchins, what dock had once built it and what flag it once flew. . . . In the iron caves of its hull black coral grew like ferns, scorpionfish and stingrays waited in the soft white sands the sea scattered, picked up, scattered, over its floors. Looking up, there was the shark. A white-tip, poised like a torpedo circling the ship it had exploded. It turned slightly, its color and contour vanished, and the eye that had been on the lookout was detached from its look, from the seas, caressed by the cold look of the monster.
>
> Ibid.

That is where Lingis's chapter ends, but it is not where the story ends. Not long after *Excesses* was published, Al was a house guest of ours in England. Over the years, whether in Germany, England, or the United States, he had always been a welcome guest—also our most trusted babysitter. One evening in Wivenhoe, England, at about the time for the three children to head for bed, they sat on Al's lap, all three of them, and demanded a story. He told them about diving near a wreck and he described the beautiful creatures that had attached themselves to the hull. The three were wide-eyed, rapt to the tale. Then he told them how, when he swam slowly to the bow of the sunken ship, he saw a shark, a very large shark, stretched out over the hull. The shark, luckily, was asleep. Al described how you can tell when a shark is sleeping, how the eye has one eyelid above but also another below, and that when the eyelids meet in the middle that means the shark is asleep. "But then," he said, "the lower lid went down and the upper lid went up."

In the case of the three rapt children, rapt to the rapture of the deep, the eyelids went up, very high. They waited for Al to continue, but he said nothing more. The story was over. The oldest child reasoned that if Al was there in the living room, recounting now his adventure, all must have turned out well; the two younger ones had no such advantage. Perhaps in order to rescue her younger siblings, the oldest asked Al, "But then what happened?"

Another long pause. Finally, Al said in a very quiet voice, "That's when I learned how slowly human beings swim."

7 *The south coast of Thira near Messa Pigadia.*

2

Amniotica

When we watch the seals glide up and down the rocks and into the sea, we feel the tedium of the bodies we had to evolve when we left the ocean. A hundred seventy pounds, of salty brine mostly, in an unshapely sack of skin: what a clumsy weight to have to transport on our boney legs! We can certainly understand the dolphins and whales, mammals that evolved on land but long ago returned to the ocean.

ALPHONSO LINGIS, *DANGEROUS EMOTIONS*

By early December 1882 Nietzsche is residing in the Albergo della Posta in Rapallo on the sea's edge. It is not an easy time for him. The Lou-affair has left him emotionally exhausted and bitterly at odds with his meddling mother and sister. His hotel room is cold; the sea is unrelievedly stormy. And yet it is one of Nietzsche's most creative periods. He begins to gather a large number of fragments from his earlier writings for a work he will call *Thus Spoke Zarathustra*. Number 258 in this series of notes reads: "How heavy the world was to me then—as it was for the animal that had lived in the sea and now had to live on land: how was it to lug its own body around?" (KSW 10:217). In the second section of Zarathustra's Prologue, words like these are placed in the mouth of the old saint in the forest: "As though in the sea you lived in solitude, and the sea carried you. Alas, you would climb onto land? Alas, you would once again lug your own body around?" (KSW 4:12). Two years later, writing notes for what will become *Beyond Good and Evil* and *On the Genealogy of Morals*, Nietzsche ends one long jotting with this: "Like everyone else, I was born a land animal; nevertheless I *must* now become a sea animal!" (KSW 11:550). Nietzsche's portion or lot, in that case, would be that of the seal or dolphin or whale. Or perhaps that of a very different sort of aquatic creature.

In the mid-1950s children and impressionable adults thrilled to a sequence of three Universal-International horror films featuring "the Gill-Man." The first of these was *The Creature from the Black Lagoon* (1954), directed by Jack Arnold, screenplay by Harry Essex and Arthur A. Ross, story by Maurice Zimm. The film stars Richard Carlson (good scientist, gentle lover), Richard Denning (aggressive scientist, brash lover), and Julia Adams (neophyte scientist, beloved of both the gentle and the brash). Who will ever forget Adams, in her white double-strap bathing suit swimming gracefully across the lagoon as the Creature backstrokes beneath her in terrifying proximity? We spectators are all in terror of the Gill-Man, a scion of the dark who fears and despises the light. We are all in terror—even if the Creature clearly is smitten, helplessly and hopelessly in love, and not with Richard Carlson. We marvel at Carlson's empathy with the monster, however, and we are content when Richard Denning's ambition and aggression meet a horrific underwater end. Even after the Gill-Man abducts Julia Adams and carries her down to his secret lair in the depths of the lagoon, a lair luckily supplied with a cavernous air pocket, Carlson still takes pity on the monster. His cohorts shoot the beast multiple times; he is badly wounded; but Carlson allows him to escape into the brackish waters of the Black Lagoon. The last we see of the Gill-Man, he is lying motionless in deep water. Is he dead?

In the first sequel, *Revenge of the Creature* (1955), directed by Jack Arnold, screenplay by Martin Berkeley, story by William Alland, the Creature does not want revenge, despite the film's title, but only love. Again he falls for the scientific assistant of the new biology professor who wishes to plumb the Gill-Man's secrets. She, the assistant, delights in calling herself an *ichthyologist*, which she struggles to pronounce well, but she will show little interest in or sympathy for the Gill-Man. She, her professor, and the Creature find themselves at a Florida marine entertainment facility, where "Flippy" the Dolphin jumps through hoops. Presumably, the locale has been chosen as an example of the mutually beneficial cooperation between rigorous science and the popular entertainment industry. (As with all sequels, the deterioration in the quality of the story, the screenplay, the direction, the acting, the photography, and all else is excruciatingly evident.) The Creature escapes, as any sensible person would, and abducts the ichthyologist. Will she requite his love? Or, once again, will she only care about looks? The Creature does have looks of a certain kind, but all the assistant can do is scream, loud and long. In the end the professor rescues his assistant and the assembled police and army troops fire on the Gill-Man as he escapes into a river. The final shot (of the camera) shows him motionless in the brackish water. Is he dead?

In the second and final sequel, *The Creature Walks Among Us* (1956), directed by John Sherwood, story and screenplay by Arthur A. Ross, we see the transformation of the Gill-Man into a land animal and his eventual death by drowning. It is clear by now that the Gill-Man is a male, even though the full frontal views disclose no genital. He appears to have been a protohominid, air-breathing, and with an epidermis, but only a quasi-hominid, one that during the Late Devonian age regresses from the mammalian to the amphibian stage. He develops gills and his lungs shrink to vestigial organs; a spiky armor of scales covers his epidermis. He becomes the "thorny fish" that Greek Anaximander

thought gave birth to humankind. And for reasons that are unclear—
for we never meet the Creature's parents or grandparents—he ceases to
evolve. And so we meet the recessive, regressive monster at story time,
uncannily alone and with dubious evolutionary credentials.

After he is badly burned by a lantern that he smashes in his rage
against the light, the scientists operate to save him. A tracheotomy
resuscitates the vestigial lungs, and, by virtue of the wizardry that only
physicians possess, the Creature's metabolism is artificially enhanced.
As a result, his "evolution" is dramatically forwarded, as though in
a fast-motion film: the cold-blooded amphibian suddenly becomes
a warm-blooded mammal. "We *are* changing a sea creature into a
land creature!" cries the mad scientist, his beady eyes blazing. The
Creature—no longer a Gill-Man—is transmogrified: his claws are
transformed into hands with webbed fingers. Perhaps not *hands*,
Heidegger would insist, since this is no *Dasein*, and not even a *Mensch*,
but prehensile organs. Yet the movie-goer, even at the age of twelve,
can see that the Creature is rapidly approaching *Dasein*, crossing the
putative abyss of essence that separates animality from humanity and
encroaching on the openness of being *as such*. The Creature does not
speak yet, but there is nevertheless indisputable proof of his budding
humanity: the scientists feel constrained to clothe him.

Held captive for research purposes in an electrified sheep pen,
which is no real improvement over the marine entertainment facility,
the transformed Creature, shuffling awkwardly on his new-formed
hominid feet, rescues the lambs from the predations of a puma. He is
violent against violence, violence committed against the lambs and—
against women. For once again he has fallen in love with a human
being. He loves and wants to protect the mad scientist's wife from his
(the scientist's) predations; she, however, is as terrified of her champion
as of her cruel husband. The Creature, once again misunderstood, his
love unrequited, escapes from his human captors and lurches to the

edge of the sea. He pauses atop a sand dune. Earlier in the film he has tried to escape from his captors by leaping into the sea; his thrashing in the brine, as he clasps his chest in desperation, is surely the most horrific scene in the film. Evolution has betrayed him. He is recaptured.

In the end, at the end, the Creature kills the misogynist scientist, who by now is fully psychotic. The heroic Creature, however, remarking the widow's unrelenting revulsion, once again heads for the coast. We see him pause atop that dune, remembering thinking knowing. Remembering what? The thrashing, the gasping, the crushing chest pains. Thinking what? "Fear death by drowning." Knowingly, however, he walks into the sea that can no longer sustain and nurture him. Knowingly and thinkingly he regresses to the inorganic state that he finds preferable to the insanities of ambition and aggression that are the human interpretations of life and love. For, as Ishmael says, "there is no folly of the beasts of the earth which is not infinitely outdone by the madness of men" (MD 385).[1]

Heidegger, who would not lend the Creature a hand, also says that we who are possessed of a hand and who are thus capable of thinking

---

[1] I am indebted to Stefan Sumser of St. Ulrich for his research and his insights into the Gill-Man films. He also informs me that the Gill-Man later appears in a delightful episode of "The Munsters" during the 1965 season; there he appears under the pseudonym of "Uncle Gillbert." And in 2009, at Universal Studios, the Gill-Man starred in a *musical* version of "The Creature from the Black Lagoon." The story-line of the musical? At long last the female assistant to the scientist, fulfilling a prophecy, falls in love with the Creature. Which prophecy? In mid-February 2017 at the Hôtel de Caumont in Aix-en-Provence, which featured an exhibition titled "Marilyn: I Wanna Be Loved by You," I happened to see a film clip from "The Seven-Year Itch" (1955), which is the film that contains the "iconic" scene of Marilyn gracing a subway grate. More iconic, however, and truly prophetic is the fact that she and Tom Ewell's character have just been to see "The Creature from the Black Lagoon." Marilyn will not say that the Creature is good-looking. "But," she says, "he wasn't really all bad. I think he just craved a little affection—you know, a sense of being loved and needed and wanted."

should never go to the movies. Perhaps he is right. Let us begin more earnest work. Sándor Ferenczi's 1924 *Attempt at a Theory of Genitality*, called in its English and French editions *Thalassa*, argues that phylogenesis is in effect *coenogenesis*, that is, the development at the embryonic stage of structures that are not found in earlier forms of the species, structures that seem to be adaptive responses to changes in the environment. The new structure in vertebrates that particularly impresses Ferenczi is the amniotic sac, in which mammalian young are protected from desiccation, concussion, starvation, sepsis, and death. Why the need for this particular sort of protection? Because the history of the earth is one of catastrophe. Why, specifically, the need for the amniotic sac and its outer membrane, the chorion? Because when the seas dry up—for that is the recurrent catastrophe—fish need a place to swim and spawn and survive. And, as counterintuitive as it may seem, the catastrophe threatening *all* sea creatures as it does, this is the fraught beginning of a differentiated genitality and of the gendered and sexed species that we are. Differentiated initially into two, male and female, even though each of the two confronts the same catastrophe and faces the identical need for protection, so that the genital bimorphism of mammals—and of many other animals before them—remains a mystery. Who knows, perhaps as the human genders develop, so may their genitalities, albeit over considerable time? But then nature has oceans of time. In any case, for the moment it seems to be a story of a two evolving out of a one, a one that is endangered—the original endangered species—by an entire series of catastrophes.

The story of this catastrophic evolution of sexed creatures begins in chapter 6 of Ferenczi's *Versuch einer Genitaltheorie*, "The Phylogenetic Parallel." The chapter does not make for smooth sailing, for there are methodological maelstroms and gusting headwinds of weird conceptuality along the way. If Freud, in the fourth chapter of his *Beyond the Pleasure Principle*, confesses to "speculation," Ferenczi here confesses to "fantasy." Scientific fantasy, to be sure—perhaps a serious kind of science fiction rather than science fiction of a more dubious, B-movie sort. Allow me to present a simplifying précis of Ferenczi's three difficult chapters on phylogenesis, coenogenesis, and what Ferenczi will call *bioanalysis*.

After apologizing for his foray into a scientific field that is doubtless familiar to him—he is after all a physician—but in which he is no specialist, Ferenczi announces his principal "idea." He is on the search for "a kind of historical parallel to the individual catastrophe of birth and its repetition in the act of sexual intercourse" (2:357/44). At the very outset, then, we are reminded of Ferenczi's years of close collaboration with Otto Rank, whose *Trauma der Geburt* was published during the same year that saw Ferenczi's *Versuch*, namely, 1924. That is also the year of Freud's "Economic Problem of Masochism," one of the master's most important elaborations of the "destruction-and-death drives" that were postulated in his 1920 *Beyond the Pleasure Principle*.

Ferenczi begins by noting that his incursion into evolutionary biology is motivated by the role of *symbolism* in psychoanalytic theory and praxis. It is noteworthy that Ferenczi's decipherment of symbols employs the vocabulary developed by Friedrich von Hardenberg (Novalis) at the end of the eighteenth century: as Champollion sought to understand "hieroglyphic inscriptions from a primeval era," so too the psychoanalyst tries to "decode written characters"; his "method of decipherment" (his *Chiffriermethode*, seeking the *Schriftzeichenentzifferung* of *hieroglyphischer Inschriften aus einer Urzeit*) now has as its text "the vast secrets of the developmental history of species" (ibid.) Not only Novalis and his apprentices at Saïs, however, but also Freud himself sanctions such hermeneutic decipherment. Indeed, Freud on many occasions dares to speculate on phylogenetic matters—how could it be otherwise? In the majority of Freud's many uses of the word *phylogenetisch*, however, what he intends is the early *human-specific* experience. Ferenczi, by contrast, uses the word to reach farther back into evolutionary history, and even into inorganic history— what Hegel would call *sidereal* history.

The point of departure for Ferenczi's own venture into bioanalysis is the symbol of the fish. Years of dream analysis and of therapeutic exchanges with his patients have shown him that the fish often appears to symbolize variously (1) the *act* of sexual intercourse, (2) the male *member,* and (3) the *situation of the fetus* in the maternal body. Ferenczi confesses that the "fantastic idea" struck him that the fish may not merely symbolize the male member in the vagina and the child in the womb but may also be "a fragment of phylogenetic knowledge concerning our provenance from aquatic vertebrates" (2:358/45). Not a mere fantasy, then, but an "insight" or an element of "knowledge" (*Erkenntnis*), albeit of a covert sort. As evidence of the fish in phylogenetic transition he points to *Amphyoxus lanceolatus,* a primitive fish (in the family of *Branchiostomidae*) that is generally taken to be the ancestor of all mammalian vertebrates and that has served as a model organism for vertebrate biology. Once that thought occurs to him, the leap to a very grand speculation seems all but unavoidable—and the italics in the following passage express nothing other than Ferenczi's excitement and wonder:

> For we then thought, how would it be if [*Wie denn, dachten wir uns, wenn*] *the entire existence in the womb that is typical of the higher mammals were merely the repetition of the form of existence during the age of fishes, and birth nothing other than the individual recapitulation of the great catastrophe that forced so many animals, and most certainly our own animal ancestors, to adapt to life on land once the sea had dried up, and, above all, to relinquish their breathing through gills and to equip themselves with organs that could take in air.*
>
> Ibid.

The personification of these ancestral fishes, "relinquishing" their gills and "equipping themselves" with lungs, of course makes us smile, inasmuch as such personification requires a fantastic leap from fish to Pirandello characters in search of a lung. Ferenczi readily confesses his Lamarckism, which is shared by Freud, and also his embrace of Ernst Haeckel's recapitulation theory, both of which would earn him the scorn of research biologists today, with the possible exception of the epigeneticists.[2] Yet Ferenczi departs from Haeckel (1834–1919) and supports the speculations of the Schellingian naturalist Lorenz Oken (1779–1851) and the late-Romantic popularizer Wilhelm Bölsche (1861–1939) when he declares his primary interest to be the evolution of "protective measures" for the embryo, namely, the *coenogenesis* of the amniotic sac and its fluid.[3]

Perhaps it is more accurate to say that the amnion is one of Ferenczi's two primary interests. For he is equally interested in the history of the penis, the "Melusinean member" as Bölsche calls it, precisely because sexuality in both women and men incorporates the

---

[2] Epigenetics studies the possible ways in which the inheritance of acquired characteristics may occur, not directly by altering DNA replication, but by affecting the *expression* of the inherited genes. Alterations of environment and even the behavior of a parent can, through "soft inheritance," as it were, affect the phenotype of succeeding generations. Epigeneticists thus call for a (highly controversial) reconsideration of Lamarck's theory of the inheritance of acquired characteristics.

[3] On the today not well known Wilhelm Bölsche, a popularizer of science and "the Darwin of German Poetry," see Safia Azzouni, "The Popular Science Book: A New Genre Between Literature and Science in the Late Nineteenth and Early Twentieth Centuries," published by The Max Planck Institute for the History of Science, at https://www.mpiwg-berlin.mpg.de/en/research/projects/deptiii-safiaazzouni_popularsciencebook[.] Thanks to the help of Alexander Bilda of Freiburg University, I have been able to examine two of Bölsche's works that are important for Ferenczi: *Das Liebesleben in der Natur: Eine Entwicklungsgeschichte der Liebe*, cited in what follows as BL with volume and page number; and *Entwicklungsgeschichte der Natur*, cited as BE with volume and page number. The first is an often whimsical and ostentatiously enlightened account of lovelife from rainworms to humans, the second a massively detailed and relatively sober history of evolutionary theory in the nineteenth century. In what follows I cite the former work of Bölsche, at BL 2:265–6.

sea. Allow me to cite Bölsche at greater length than Ferenczi does. By way of clarification, note that the German word *Nix* in what follows means both merman and mermaid, depending on the masculine or feminine particle; even though Melusine, the figure of a fourteenth-century Old French epic, is surely a maid, her lower half being a serpent rather than a fish, however, there is something about her story that encourages later poets—including Goethe—to see her (or him, or it) as symbolic of sexual life as a whole:

> Certainly, a past lies in this [male] member. It is a Melusinean member. Here the human being makes its way back to the fish, from which he has come, albeit back in days now lost in purple haze. The eternal merman [*Der ewige Nix*] stretches all the way forward to that member. But there is even more to it than that. Here we find the path that stretches all the way to the very crown of humanity.... A path of enlightenment, but also of doubt, errancy, and curse. On the day when the fig leaf falls away, a new path of illumination will open.... One day the grand transformation *must* come, that will enable us to drop the blinders from our eyes when it comes to matters of sex. Certain petty sorts of self-protection will fall away of themselves, and suddenly we will have a truth where once we had a public secret: that Melusine is not an animal-human mix but a demigod.
>
> BL 2:265–6

But to regain composure now and return to Ferenczi, who nevertheless clearly identifies himself with Bölsche's zealous enlightenment project. Ferenczi concedes that his phylogenetic parallel involving both the womb and the amniotic sac has to be qualified, insofar as earth, "Mother Earth," is as much the nurturer and rescuer of life as the sea is. If human beings begin as endoparasites, they soon become ectoparasites, first at the breast of their nurse and later at the dinner table. In spite of the Demetrian qualification, however, Ferenczi takes the primordial symbol—more archaic, more primitive than earth—to be that of life and nurture in the sea. When Sophocles, in his famous second choral song in *Antigone*, wants to say why the human being is monstrously uncanny, the very first thing he mentions is the ships that ply the waters "across the night / Of the sea" (ll. 351–2; CHV 2:331). If Michel Tournier's Crusoe makes love to the earth, which after all has saved him from drowning after his shipwreck, his *Melusinenglied* nonetheless fears desiccation and longs for the moist element. When Zeus moves the genitals of the bifurcated creatures around to the front, so that they can mate with one another and not, like the cicadas, with the dusty earth, it is surely a boon for all three gendered pairs, the solar, the terrestrial, and the lunatic— from which you and I are descended.

The first great danger to life, says Ferenczi, was not drowning but dehydration. The emergence of Mount Ararat from the flood, providing a legendary resting place for Noah's Ark, was actually "the original catastrophe" (2:360/49). Of course, the Ark itself is a symbol of the womb, at least for those animals that were rescued; but then again, not all mammals were represented on the passenger list of Noah's Ark. Moby-Dick, for example, had no need of the Ark, unless to butt it. For he is the antediluvian as such, and as such a kind of demigod. On the other hand, must we not indeed "fear death by drowning"? Is not mythology full of sea rescues? Does not Leukothea, the shining goddess, rescue Odysseus from the wrath of Poseidon by lending him the purple sash of Samothracian initiation?

We see this *ambivalence* with regard to sea water—which both spawns and drowns—once again in Otto Rank's work on birth trauma. Amniotic fluid rescues the fetus from desiccation, yet birth rescues the infant from death by drowning or asphyxiation. Our birth may be but a sleep and a forgetting, but we do not get our start without it. As Ferenczi confronts this ambivalence of sea water, two words collide or

8 *Volcanic rock at Balos Bay.*

collude in his text, namely, the words *pleasure, anxiety,* and once again, *pleasure*: the processes or "symbolic deeds" he is discussing involve the individual's (1) pleasure (*Lust*) derived from his or her existence while floating in the maternal body, (2) the anxiety of birth, and (3) the pleasure derived from the newborn's having *withstood* the dangers of birth (2:361/49). Yet ambivalence can also tip the scales in the direction of *Angst*: insofar as the individual identifies himself (there is no "him or her" at this moment in Ferenczi's text) with his member as it enters the vagina or with his sperm as it enters Dido's cave (*die Leibeshöhle des Weibes*), he also confronts symbolically the danger of demise, the menace faced by his predecessors "in the geological catastrophe of the drying up of the sea," *die grosse Eintrocknungskatastrophe* (ibid.).

Ferenczi's fantasy may be extravagant, he admits, but he is able to muster two arguments from embryology and comparative morphology that make him and us stop and think. The first is that a protective organ filled with amniotic fluid for the fetus develops only with the arrival of land-dwelling animals; the second is that animals whose embryos develop without the aid of an amnion do not reproduce sexually. In other words, the evolution of land-dwelling eutherians (that is, those "proper wild animals" that are placental mammals) goes hand-in-hand with the evolution of the dimorphic or bimorphic sexuality that expresses itself in intercourse. Sexual reproduction, at least of a provisional sort, begins with the amphibians, although mating proper comes on the scene only with reptiles: "The possession of organs for sexual reproduction, development in the maternal womb, and survival of the great danger of desiccation therefore constitute an indissoluble biological unity; this must also be the ultimate cause of the symbolic identity of the womb with the sea and the earth on the one hand, and the male member with the child and the fish, on the other" (2:361–2/50).

If this is a fantasy, then it is an old one, some aspects of which have been entertained by distinguished thinkers. Kant too, in his consideration of teleological judgment in *The Critique of Judgment* (section 80), focuses on the mysterious transition from "aquatic animals" to "swamp animals," and thence to "land animals." He does so in a remarkable footnote to the "Doctrine of Method" in teleological judgment (KU B370n.). That focus is required because of the need to posit something more than a merely mechanical causality in organized nature. The "archaeologists of nature," that is, the biologists who inquire into the history and development of species, go in search of "the large families of creatures," families based on the blood relation of family members to one another, that is, their relation through sexual reproduction, *Erzeugung* (KU B369). The "archaeologists" of biology trace these families back to the first awkward productions of the Earth's womb, *der Mutterschoß der Erde*, productions of organic creatures out of inorganic matter, creatures that possess a less than adequate purposive form (*Geschöpfe von minder-zweckmäßiger Form*), until those productions, after generations of sexual reproduction, become better adapted to their situation. Kant then imagines the Earth's womb drying up and rigidifying, so that the great families of plants and animals now multiply in the family way, much as they do in Kant's own day. A hiatus appears at this point in Kant's text. Kant notes that the archaeologist of nature must make an addendum to his or her conception: one must posit a purposive organization (*zweckmäßig gestellte Organisation*) that would explain the purposive form (*Zweckform*) that the self-reproducing plants and animals themselves manifest. Now comes the footnote. Such a hypothesis may seem a bold escapade of reason (*ein gewagtes Abenteuer der Vernunft*), but when organically organized creatures reproduce in such a way that *specific differences* arise, such variation and development of differences must be explained. "For example, when certain aquatic animals gradually developed into swamp animals [*wenn gewisse Wassertiere sich nach und nach zu Sumpftieren . . . ausbildeten*], and the latter, after several reproductions, into land animals" (KU B370n.).

Now, a priori, such a development involves no contradiction for mere reason. Yet no one has ever *witnessed* such a transition. Not even, one might add, when standing on the receding shoreline of the Aral Sea, which today is almost dry. Everything we see in nature is the result of *generatio homonyma*; we are not privy to *generatio heteronyma*. With that, Kant broaches the problem that will fascinate Hegel as well—the problem of the *monstrous*, that is, of the creation of malformations and monsters. For even if the monster "annihilates the purpose that constitutes the concept of the object" (KU B89), there would be no transition from one species to the next without initial monstrosities, that is, creatures without a family, misshapen orphans. And this would take us to the theme of sublimity in nature, nature as raw power and even violence, *Gewalt*, for example in "the boundless ocean stirred to anger" (KU B104). Or, we might add, the boundless ocean drying up. True, the tiny frog seems neither monstrous nor sublime. Yet were the mother lungfish to discover a frog in her cradle she would doubtless find it so. But to return to Ferenczi's fancy.

Another aspect of the possible extravagance of Ferenczi's hypothesis, one mentioned briefly earlier, is his unabashed support of Jean-Baptiste Lamarck and Ernst Haeckel over Charles Darwin. Whereas the latter explains the survival of species by the indifferent mechanism of natural selection through *accidental* variation, Lamarck is disposed to think of the *effort* of increasingly complex creatures (exerted by *le pouvoir de la vie*) to adapt to challenging environments, an effort that allows useful acquired characteristics to be passed on to future generations. Like Freud, Ferenczi is inclined to think the *drives* as working their effects not only in individuals but also in entire phyla. As we will see, Ferenczi tries to modify Freud's theory of drives—the "exquisite dualism" of the erotic and the destruction-and-death drives—by contrasting the forward-looking, propulsive, constructive, and unifying *drive* to the regressive and ultimately deadly *backward pull* of the sea. We might think of such a pull as a draw, draft, or "tug," trying to render in English the multivalent German word *Zug*; perhaps the most fruitful translation would be *undertow*, especially when contemplating the *thalassic* regressive tendency, the *Zug* that transports us back to the sea—or at least to dreams and hallucinations of the sea.

Chapter 7 of Ferenczi's essay on genital theory offers "Material Toward 'The Thalassic Regressive Tendency.'" *Tendency* is of course too weak a word; *der Zug*, to repeat, is more like a pull or tug having the power of a locomotive, an irresistible undertow. Ferenczi begins by admitting that his audacious idea of a universal "striving toward an existence in the sea that has been lost in primeval time," a striving that continues to work its effects on human genitality and sexuality, has sailed off far too swiftly, that it is time to be more patient and to argue more carefully and in greater detail. Such greater care begins with Ferenczi's suggestion that the striving in question might be better described as a "tugging force," *Zugkraft*, rather than a "driving force," *Triebkraft*. Whereas drives push us forward, the sea tugs us back. He adds the following note:

> The word *drive* [*"Trieb"*] would emphasize more the moment of adaptation, thus the purposive [*das Zweckmäßige*] in the activation of the organ; the expression *Zug* emphasizes more the regressive aspect. Yet I am obviously in agreement with Freud's view that what apparently impels us "forward" ultimately draws its energy from the tugging force of the past [*aus der Zugkraft der Vergangenheit seine Energie bezieht*].
>
> 2:363/52

The suggestion is that if there is a "beyond" to the pleasure principle, that "beyond" lies behind us. Freud, in the *Three Treatises Toward a*

Theory of Sexuality (GW 5:142), defines *regression* in terms of his general description of neurosis: "All moments that damage sexual development express their effects in such a way that they evoke a regression, a return to an earlier phase of development." By the time of *Beyond the Pleasure Principle*, however, regression refers to the restoration of a prior state—for the organic it means reversion to the anorganic or inorganic state. Likewise, if there is something like purposiveness at work in nature, that purposiveness too is perpetually behind rather than ahead. In a sense, the "beyond" is always in arrears. We are caught in the draft or pull of the inorganic state that precedes life; we are caught in the undertow that means our return to that earlier lifeless condition. Whether this concession poses an implicit challenge to Freud's "exquisite dualism" of drives is a question that will have to remain open.

In good Lamarckian style, Ferenczi argues that as one ascends the ladder of complexity in the evolution of species, true genitality begins only with the "more complicated destiny" of amphibians and reptiles, indeed with the "developmental catastrophe" they are destined to confront. Whereas frogs have the luxury of fertilizing their eggs either in water or in the female cloaca, reptiles, birds, and mammals do not have a choice. Yet the lack of choice does not simplify their life. Whereas the male frog develops calluses on its front extremities so that it can grip and penetrate the female (Ferenczi also speaks of a "drill," *ein Bohrwerkzeug*, that emerges from the male cloaca), one must wait for lizards and crocodiles for what one can call genuine erectility. Yet even newts and salamanders begin to develop a urethral tube that can also serve to ejaculate sperm. That development does not become complete until one reaches the level of primitive mammals, marsupials such as the kangaroo. Yet Ferenczi sees the same development occurring in each human individual, at least in children of the male sex: he notes the child's fumbling efforts to reenter the mother, his striving to reverse the catastrophe of his birth. Naturally, the same could be said of every young girl, even if Ferenczi does not say it.

What could have motivated the amphibians and reptiles to equip themselves with a penis (*sich einen Penis zuzulegen*)? Nothing other than "the striving to restore their lost form of life in a moist milieu that also contains nourishment, that is, *the restoration of their marine existence in the moist and richly nourishing interior of the mother's body*" (2:364/54). By a kind of "inversion of the symbolism," the mother becomes "*a symbol or partial replacement of the sea, and not the other way around*" (ibid.). Such inversion is reminiscent of Aspasia's words in Plato's *Menexenus*, where we read: "For a woman proves her motherhood by giving milk to her young ones—and she who has no fountain of milk is no mother. . . . And these [wheat and barley corn] are truer proofs of motherhood in a country than in a woman, for the woman in her conception and generation is but the imitation of the earth, and not the earth of the woman" (237e–238a). One only has to assert the priority of the sea, as Ferenczi does, to make Aspasia's symbolism Ferenczi's own. Wheat and barley belong to Demeter, but sweet milk belongs to Leukothea, the nurse of Dionysos, she of the wine-dark sea.

Yet what of the amnion itself, which no mere "drill" could have fashioned? Should not Ferenczi's question have been: What could have motivated the amphibians and reptiles to equip themselves with egg-producing organs and eutherians with an amnion and amniotic fluid? As for that fluid, it is not brine, even if, as we know, body fluids generally are saline. Estimates differ, some claiming that amniotic fluid has only nine parts of salt per thousand of water, whereas the seas range from twenty-six to thirty-five parts, a threefold increase in salinity, others that amniotic fluid has 2 percent salinity, the oceans 3–3.5 percent. In any case, the amount of sodium and chlorine atoms diminishes during the second half of a human pregnancy. Furthermore, that "cheesy" covering of the newborn, the *vernix caseosa*, which we may mistake as a kind of petroleum jelly smeared over a swimmer who is daring to cross the English Channel, is intended not so much to protect the fetus's skin from brine but to conserve body heat and to ease passage through the birth canal. Then again, it is not merely a question of salt: both the amniotic fluid and the sea are rich in trace elements and mineral salts of all sorts. In any case, the "parallel" between amniotic fluid and sea water is not an identity. And, above all else, what one has to object to is Ferenczi's apparent supposition that a "drill" could fashion the moist and nurturing milieu that *both* creatures desire and need.

Ferenczi now offers a highly complex analysis of the fetus's oxygen supply, not by the development of gill slits but by osmosis from the placenta by way of the villi of the chorion. In evolutionary history, the development of lungs and gills is every bit as complex as genital development: early fishes, we know, had lungs before they had gills. Ferenczi is fascinated by a number of rare species that have to be located somewhere *between* fish and amphibians, species still extant today, which may have been distant ancestors of ours: *Dipneusta* such as *Protopterus annectens* and *Lepidoseren paradoxa*, the African and Amazonian lungfish, which spend the arid portion of the year in a moist subterranean cocoon that has access to the earth's surface and hence to air. (Readers will not believe me, but the best illustration of the Amazonian lungfish one could hope for comes in an early scene of *The Creature from the Black Lagoon*, as Richard Carlson lectures his fellow scientists on this transitional creature, part fish, part amphibian. It seems that a Universal-International Studios filmmaker has been dipping into Sándor Ferenczi for inspiration.) Ferenczi concludes his detailed discussion of these two species of lungfish with perhaps the most explicit statement of his general hypothesis:

We need only accept that in the *higher vertebrates* (reptiles, birds, mammals) the placental breathing by osmosis[4] is limited to the *embryonic period* in order to have a continuous sequence of development from fish, by way of amphibians, to human beings, a sequence in which the striving toward existence in the sea is never wholly surrendered, even if in the case of human beings that striving is reduced to the period of development in the womb. We only have to add that this thalassic regressive undertow does not come to rest even after birth, and that it announces itself both in erotic expressions (especially sexual intercourse) and, as we may note by way of supplement and as we will later demonstrate in further detail, in states of sleep.

2:366/55–6

In another striking note, Ferenczi observes that the remarkable changes in breathing due to heightened excitement and emotion during intercourse mirror the *dyspnoe* of the infant at birth, both of these in turn mirroring the archaic struggle for oxygen as the seas, lagoons, and rivers go dry.

Ferenczi at this point reasserts his predilection for Lamarck over Darwin by insisting that no merely *accidental* variation could have produced the moist milieu—the womb and the amnion—that a fish gasping on the strand would have needed and strived to attain. He goes so far as to suggest that *"the amniotic fluid in the mother's body represents, as it were, an 'introjected' sea"* (2:366/56). One suspects that

---

[4] Ferenczi writes "die *plazentale Kiemenatmung*," but he has only now demonstrated at some length that the fetus derives its oxygen not from the use of gills (*Kiemen*) or gill slits but through osmosis—via the penetration by the chorional villi into the placenta. I have therefore translated *Kiemenatmung* in terms of such osmosis, even though the reference to fetal gills or gill slits would be stronger—if misleading—evidence for the phylogenetic parallel.

Freud, who was generous in his praise of Ferenczi's daring book, would have balked at this use (or abuse) of "introjection," but we, and perhaps he too, will let that pass. What one has to observe once again is that no drilling operation can explain such (un)canny "introjection" by the female. When Augustine chides the child at the shore for trying to empty the entire sea into his sandcastle's moat, the angel-child replies that he will sooner succeed at that impossible task than Augustine will at comprehending his heavenly father. Yet how are we to comprehend the amniotica of the earthly mother, who, emptying the sea into her own body, makes the impossible possible? In Ferenczi's theory of genitality on the basis of the thalassic regressive undertow, this "introjection" of the sea remains the arcane and archaic mystery, one that Ferenczi's fancy cannot comprehend. His fancy is not up to what one might call, in onto-theo-mytho-logical terms, the mystery of Zeus's thigh—the thigh in which a fragmented Dionysos completes his gestation.

Like the sea, the amnion is in perpetual motion. Remarkable even in the embryonic development of the chick in the egg is the fact that the amnion is set in motion by a series of contractions; the chick is gently rocked back and forth in the egg, as though in a cradle. "Let ourselves be cradled" would be the cry of all incipient vertebrate life, whether oviparous or viviparous. "It would not surprise me," writes Ferenczi, "were this provision for a rhythmic cradling to be compared by one or other naturalist in poetic terms to the swelling of the sea, but in the end it is more than a simile!" (2:367/57). We recall young Redburn's reference to this heaving and sinking of the sea, which reminded him of his infant brother in the cradle. The philosopher Schelling, himself a poetic naturalist, in his *Treatise on Human Freedom*, invokes *ein wogend wallend Meer*, "a swelling, seething sea," precisely at the point where he is contemplating the gestation and the birth of the human being:

All birth is birth from darkness into light; the kernel of seed must be planted in the earth, dying in gloom, in order that the more beautiful configuration of light [*Lichtgestalt*] arise and unfold along the beams of the sun. The human being is formed in the womb; and from the darkness of what is without understanding (from feeling, languor, the magnificent mother of knowledge) first burgeon buoyant thoughts. Thus we must represent to ourselves the original languor [*die ursprüngliche Sehnsucht*], which indeed orients itself toward the understanding that it does not yet grasp, just as in longing we yearn for some unknown and nameless good; and, moving on an intimation, languor bestirs itself as does a swelling, seething sea, like Platonic matter, according to an obscure and uncertain law, unable to form for itself something lasting.

I/7:360

One recalls, thinking of poetic naturalists, that Walt Whitman's "Out of the Cradle Endlessly Rocking" is a poem of the sea. And what the sea whispers to the young poet is "that low and delicious word *death*," repeated, as I recall, five times, as though it were whispered by waves lapping on the shore and "laving" the poet (ll. 172–3). For Schelling too the original languor, the primal longing (*Sehnsucht*), is mysteriously bound up with languishing (*Schmachten*), birth with "dying in gloom."

About that introjected sea, however. Almost as an afterthought, as though "moving on an intuition," and making no reference to Freud's dream of "Irma's Injection" (from *The Interpretation of Dreams*), Ferenczi now footnotes an aspect of genital theory that might well have arisen much earlier in his discourse, were it not so indelicate and so controversial. "Incidentally," he writes, "*Nur nebenbei*,"

I might refer to the remarkable happenstance that the genital secretion of the female in higher mammals and in human beings—a secretion which, as we have said, may owe its erotically stimulating effect to our infantile reminiscences [i.e., of our birth]—according to the description of all physiologists has a distinctive odor of fish (or of the brine in which herring have been laid); this vaginal odor stems from the identical material (trimethylamine) that is formed when fish decompose.

Ultimately those may prove right who assert that the twenty-eight day periodicity of female menstruation may be traced back to the influence of the phases of the moon (and thus in a direct way to the influence of the ebb and flood tides on our sea-dwelling ancestors).[5]

The footnote ends with a reference to seals, sea lions, and whales, which are remarkable for their having returned to the sea after having become mammals. These animals—except of course for the whales, an exception Ferenczi neglects to specify—mate and nurse their young on land rather than in the sea. They are therefore dominated by what would have to be called a *geotropic regressive tug*, one that forces

---

[5] 2:367n. 3/57n. 1. One searches in vain for straightforward corroboration of Freud's and Ferenczi's claim concerning trimethylamine in genital secretions, whether such corroboration is lacking because the physiological chemistry is too well known or because the chemists are too diffident—or, indeed, whether the psychoanalysts' chemistry is simply false. The preferred name of the chemical designated by Freud and Ferenczi is N, N-Dimethylmethanamine, its formula C_3H_9N or $N(CH_3)_3$. It is said to have a "fishy" odor in low concentrations and an ammoniac odor in high concentrations and to result from the decomposition of plants and animals generally. In humans it is synthesized out of dietary nutrients such as choline and carnitine by microbes in the intestine. It may be a cause of vaginal odor due to bacterial *vaginosis*, the pathologists concede, but nothing is said about its pertaining to vaginal secretions as such and in general. The pathology of *trimethylaminuria*, a rare metabolic disorder in both men and women, has to do with an enzyme that is missing from the digestive tract, causing the "fishy odor" to arise in a person's perspiration, urine, and breath, but this does not lend anything to Freud's and Ferenczi's thesis. Since Freud's account of the "Irma's Injection" dream in the *Traumdeutung*, trimethylamine has played a significant role in psychoanalysis, but more as a signifier—for God, for death, and for the symbolic as such—than as a chemical. I therefore set it gently aside. A bit later both Freud and Hegel will cause us to take up this theme again. But back to Ferenczi's note.

them to recapitulate for their young the catastrophic situation they themselves have overcome. All of which would leave the antediluvian whale in an apparently unique situation, tugged by neither land nor sea, giving birth to and nursing its young in the womb and on the breast of the sea itself, as it were.

Ferenczi's chapter on the thalassic regressive undertow does not conclude with this capacious footnote, however; it adds yet another daring hypothesis to the growing list. Ferenczi speculates that at the ontogenetic level, males and females alike strive "to penetrate the body of their partner" (2:368/58). Thus commences the battle of the sexes, a struggle that in phylogeny "ended with the victory of the male and the creation of a compensatory provision for the female" (ibid.). In the history of phylogeny, he claims, what we see are increasingly complex provisions for the male's domination of the female, a domination that requires "tools for both fascinating and overpowering," *Faszinierungs- und Bemächtigungswerkzeuge*, by which the male can make the female "submissive" or "docile," *gefügig*. Again the "drill," *Bohrwerkzeug*, is cited as the crucial tool in transforming the Hobbesian war "of all against all" into a war of the sexes. The smaller and weaker proto-amphibians succumb to domination and become females, the larger and stronger ones dominate and become the males. As Jacques Derrida points out in his seminar on the death penalty, Ferenczi is here recapitulating and affirming Freud's account in "The Taboo of Virginity" (1917–18), the third of his essays on lovelife, in which a principal theme is the undying resentment in the female felt toward her "deflowerer." If he has used a drill, one may say, such resentment becomes all the more comprehensible. In his seminar on capital punishment Derrida's overarching interest is the bloodletting and cruelty (the latter word derived from *cruor*, "I bleed") that characterize—up until quite recently—the long history of the death penalty. Indeed, Derrida's argument is that even if the blood flow has in large part been stanched, the cruelty goes on. At all events, Freud emphasizes the blood flow of deflowering in his "Taboo of Virginity" essay, but also the malevolence or *Grausamkeit* that is impacted in the word *Bemächtigung*, which Ferenczi has only now employed.[6] The original war of all against all, transmogrified into the war of the sexes, is in Ferenczi's view "properly a struggle for water, for moisture" (2:368/58). The threatening nature of the paternal phallus, concludes Ferenczi, which for ontogeny represents nothing more menacing than the passive child in the womb, is a relic of the phylogenetic period of struggle—the age of the "drill," so to speak. Yet what about the "compensation" for womankind? It is again reduced to a footnote, one that ends the chapter. And readers of every possible gender, I believe, will find the compensation paltry and therefore unconvincing.

When the male compels the female to *coitus per cloacam*, the "originally equally phallic eroticism of the female is replaced by a cloacal eroticism of the hollow," *von einer kloakalen Höhlenerotik* (369n. 4). This *Höhle* is difficult to translate and impossible to comprehend: a cave or cavern, a hollow, a void—doubtless a vagina and uterus to come, but characterless here, "a hollow, indeed," as Melville will say concerning the hand of God. Or, as Bunker translates the hollow of *Höhlenerotik*, a "cavity-erotism" (59n. 1). Even if one wishes to sustain the dental imagery, however, one must admit that a

---

[6] With regard to those (male) *Bemächtigungswerkzeuge*, Ferenczi employs the word *Bemächtigung* (and the verb *sich bemächtigen*) also elsewhere in his *Attempt*, namely, at 2:338/24, where Bunker translates it simply as "possession," and, at 2:382/7, "to secure." Jacques Derrida's two-volume seminar, *La peine de mort*, along with his July 2000 address to the Estates General of Psychoanalysis in Paris, *States of the Soul*, centers on the problem of the power (*Macht*) at the center of such empowering or overpowering. For *States of the Soul* see especially EA 238–80. For further discussion of *Bemächtigung*, see chapters 5, 8, and 10 of Krell, *The Cudgel and the Caress: Reflections on Cruelty and Tenderness*, forthcoming from the State University of New York Press.

drill can only drill a hole; it cannot "equip" that hollow with the astonishingly complex genitality and reproductive organs of the female, and a theory of genitality would surely have to notice the fact. However, to repeat, Ferenczi's fancy does not take him that far. He is content to aver that in the female the role of the penis is now assumed by feces and child, *Kot und Kind*, feces in the hollow of the colon and the child in the hollow of the womb. Whenever coitus is finally over for the struggling amphibians, the female is free to release her stool and is thus liberated from her "anal emergency"; to this extent, the sudden cessation of coitus "may have called up sensations of pleasure" (ibid.). I once asked my brother why he loved to jog, for this was and remains a mystery to me. "Because it feels so good when I stop," he replied.

It is fair to say that Ferenczian compensation can hardly have satisfied Ferenczi himself. Yet nowhere does he seem so unequal to the problems he poses as here. He is unable to explain how those aquatic creatures that are confronted with the catastrophe of desiccated seas are able to "introject" an ersatz sea and thus to rescue and transform the species. Indeed, periodically in *Thalassa* we have to raise the complaint—and we hear Ferenczi himself raising it—that the coenogenetic parallel is all too focused on the male, leaving the story of womankind and the female, considered both ontogenetically and phylogenetically, untold. And yet she is and has the inland sea. The war is a struggle for water, for moisture, but what will ensure *her* adaptation and survival, without which there is no moisture and no survival for anyone? Is hers the story of mere submission to the drill? Or must she not rather dominate the theater of dominion? Put in onto-theo-mytho-logical terms, is not the mystery of Zeus's thigh hopelessly overtaxed?

I recall that Darwin somewhere speculates that the male is the original gender, the female an offshoot of it—as Genesis suggests. As reluctant as I am to disagree with the august Darwin, to say nothing of Genesis, I am more convinced by Schelling's repeated insistence that the female is primary and primal throughout nature, the male a latecomer. In the 1811 version (the earliest draft) of his *Ages of the World*, Schelling writes: "The gently suffering and receptive [*das sanft Leidende und Empfangende*] everywhere comes to appear before the efficacious and active. For many reasons I do not doubt that in organic nature the female sex comes before the male, and that the ostensible sexlessness of the lowest plants and animals rests on this fact" (WA 47; cf. 24). If Hegel imagines that the clitoris is a penis that did not make it, Schelling replies that the penis is a clitoris that has grown too full of itself.

Yet all these discussants would have to concede that the origin of sexual bimorphism is, as Bölsche would say, lost in the "purple haze" of remote ages. Let me therefore trace the periodic concessions or confessions by Ferenczi that resist his own story of "compensation." Here I will have to turn to the first part of Ferenczi's book, which deals with ontogeny.

Ferenczi opens his *Attempt* by espousing a theory of erotic *amphimixis*—that is, the combined pleasures of retention and release, contraction and expansion, Goethe's *Zusammenziehung* and *Ausdehnung*, Schelling's force (*Kraft*) and inhibition (*Hemmung*)—in the "ejaculatory act" (2:321/5). *Amphimixis* is a term borrowed from the research of August Weismann, who describes the beneficial effects for one-celled animals of their "copulation" and exchange of substances, a temporary fusion that Freud describes as a prototype for the sexual union to come much later in the development of species (GW 13:51). One may assume (but why?) that the ejaculation Ferenczi has in mind for the "ejaculatory act" is that of semen. His analysis of various neuroses has convinced him that the retention and elimination of stool and urine have profound implications for the erotic life, with retention identified more readily with stool and release with urethral innervation. In any case, to paraphrase and slightly alter Augustine, *Inter urinas et faeces . . . amamus.* And if the speech disorders of stuttering and stammering result from what one must call a *genitofugal displacement,* disturbances in ejaculation can be called "a genital stutter" (2:324/8; cf. 2:66). The penis itself, argues Ferenczi, originates in and as a urogenito-cloacal protruberance, and that intestinal or peritoneal origin determines its fate. Origin will remain destination.

Are we therewith on the way to an account of *female* amphimixis? Not really—although we really have to be. Only at the end of the chapter does Ferenczi refer to "woman," *die Frau,* invoking Freud's account of the transfer of clitoral eroticism to the vagina. That, along with the transfer of erectility to the nipples of the breast and the nares of the nose, not to forget the general tendency to blushing "(erection of the entire head)," which is due to the "genital excitation of the virgin who represses" (2:329/14), is as far as Ferenczi goes—at least in his initial chapter. That the flaring of the nostrils should be typical of womankind seems strange. Perhaps it should seem equally strange that blushing be restricted to the woman. Male theorists and therapists too have multiple occasions for blushing.

The following chapter raises our expectations when it speaks of "the identification of those who are mating" and of all the "bridge building" between mates that foreplay achieves (2:331–2/17). Such identification is threefold: "identification of the entire organism with the genital, identification with the partner, identification with the genital secretion" (2:332/18). A footnote immediately adds the following: "In order to counter an obvious objection, I emphasize that these analyses have to do exclusively with the simpler relations of the male partner. I must postpone until a later opportunity a demonstration of the applicability of these notions to the more complicated relations of the female sex" (332n. 1/18n. 1). Like diamonds, however, postponements are forever. Concerning the male it can be straightforwardly argued that sexuality is "the ego's attempt to return to the womb" (2:333/19). The return is regressive and it has three aspects, aspects that seem to lie at the origin of, or at least contribute significantly to, Lacan's tripartite structure: (1) the *hallucinatory*, as in sleep; (2) the *symbolic*, as in the penis's penetration of the vagina; and (3) the *real*, as in the ejaculation of the genital secretion, "which alone has the prerogative, representing as it does the ego and the ego's narcissistic Doppelgänger, the genital" (ibid.). Thus what Freud calls the Oedipus Complex has its origin in "a much more general biological tendency, which lures the living creature into a return to the repose that it enjoyed before birth" (ibid.). Ferenczi does not venture to say anything of the woman's sleep, of her symbolic sea, or of her *real* genitality.

The most detailed response to the challenge of the "more complicated" sexuality of the female occurs in chapter 3, "Developmental Stages of the Erotic Sense of Reality." It is clear to Ferenczi that the oral and anal phases hypothesized by Freud must apply to both male and female infants, whatever differences may accrue. When it comes to the oral phase, there seems to be no evidence that male infants are more likely to bite the nipple, to slip more readily into the "cannibalistic" or even "sadistic" phase, than females. Ferenczi stresses that teeth are "the tools with which the child would like to drill its way into the mother's body [or womb: *Mutterleib*]" (2:336/21), but he does not differentiate between boys and girls when it comes to these strangely "drilling" teeth. When it comes to teeth, infant girls too have and know the drill. Likewise, Ferenczi suggests that during the early phase of masturbation "infant bisexuality" enables the child to play a double role, such that "every human being, whether male or female, can and does play the double role of both child and mother with its own body" (2:337–8/23). No elaboration. Ferenczi admits once again, however, that for the most part his account of the "erotic sense of reality" is geared toward the male. He attempts now to balance the account. The erotic sense of reality, he argues, is "suddenly interrupted" for girls and women during the final, "genital" phase, during which erogeneity is transposed "from the clitoris (the female penis) to the hollow space of the vagina" (2:338–9/24).

The standard psychoanalytic tale of the sad destiny of the clitoris has been so often and so thoroughly countered that I need not comment on it here. All I might add is that in this respect psychoanalysis takes none other than Hegel as its mentor, so that it cannot surprise us that it collapses back into the most traditional of philosophemes and prejudices.[7] A short version of that tale would run as follows. The genitality (or erogeneity) of the woman's ersatz penis (the clitoris) withdraws in such a way as to occupy a woman's entire body and her ego, so that the woman becomes the victim of "a secondary narcissism"; she becomes herself like a child, craving more to be loved than to love; when she herself becomes the child, if only phantasmatically, the "fiction" of "existence in the womb" appears to be preserved *in toto* (ibid.). The woman's predilection for conversion hysteria (neuroses that convert psychological troubles into physical disorders such as tic, paralysis of the limbs, and so on) stems from this "secondary genitalizing of the female body" (ibid.). Ferenczi concedes that after the woman's initial experiences of intercourse as violation, in which even blood is spilled, she may come to accept coitus passively or she may "even," *gar*, take pleasure in it (2:340/26). Yet in general female sexuality demonstrates for Ferenczi the truth of his thesis that women are fated to relive the "phase of struggle" in the phylogenetic

---

[7] See my *Contagion: Sexuality, Disease, and Death in German Idealism and Romanticism* (Bloomington: Indiana University Press, 1998, chapter 11, on Hegel's "dialectic of genitality." See also chapter 4 of *The Cudgel and the Caress*.

development of bimorphic sexuality. In that struggle the female "drew the shorter straw," writes Ferenczi, in either an inspired metaphor or a Freudian slip, so that she had to leave it to the males "really to force their way into the womb," finding her best consolation in identifying herself phantasmatically with the fetus that may come to reside there. It may be (Georg Groddeck thinks so) that she will even derive some hard-won pleasure from her birth contractions.

Ferenczi continues to insist that "the central tendency" of sexual life is "the return to the womb," and that such return "dominates both sexes" (2:344/30). Yet his own demonstrations clearly accept Freud's dictum that all libido is "masculine." For what he fails to mention throughout is something that Luce Irigaray has spent a lifetime trying to show, namely, that a woman can also identify with the "introjected" sea itself, taking pleasure and pride in the moisture of the mucous, which is her own. And who can deny that this pleasure and pride in the sea is what has been inspiring Ferenczi's *Attempt* from the outset?

The final chapter of Ferenczi's "Phylogenetic" section, "Sexual Intercourse and Fertilization," delves into the most profound mystery of the thalassic regressive undertow, namely, the mystery of a possible parallel between sexual behavior in the higher mammals and the behavior of the germ cells that are contained in or as sperm and egg. Can one extend the coeno-phylo-genetic parallel to germ cells? If the sea is the archetype of all motherhood, *das Vorbild aller Mütterlichkeit*, is it also the model for one-celled animals and for germ plasm? Are the forces of cell fusion and cellular amphimixis *marine* forces? Or, more accurately, are they too responses to the catastrophe of the seas' desiccation?

It is high time we asked about this putative "catastrophe." Surely what Ferenczi means is not the drying up of all the seas and oceans,

9 *The lighthouse, "Pharos," at the southwestern tip of the island.*

but a more local sort of event. He mentions the legendary emergence of Mount Ararat, which enables Noah to disembark but which also wreaks havoc among the animals for which the flood is home. In our own time, to repeat, the Aral Sea has dried up, much of its marine life dying of excessive salinity and eventual desiccation; and during the late Messinian age of the Miocene epoch, about six million years ago, when the Straits of Gibralter closed, the entire Mediterranean and Aegean became a desert. This sort of event is what Ferenczi has in mind. To be sure, what even the most devoted Lamarckian fails to see on the arid bed of the Aral Sea is fish equipping themselves with lungs in order to survive. Catastrophe is certainly not missing from Darwin's account of natural selection through accidental variation; when he observes the lilies of the field he sees them struggling for the available space and for adequate exposure to sunlight. Yet such catastrophe seems to be always at work, steadily at work over generations, and not an intermittent geological drama. The Lamarckian is more attuned to the struggle that occurs on a newly set stage designed by geological cataclysm, and especially to the *exertions* made by older life forms to confront the catastrophe of a deteriorating environment. Toward the end of Ferenczi's eighth chapter, as we will see, the bioanalyst offers his readers a Table of Catastrophes, five of them, all running in parallel for ontogeny and phylogeny alike. For him, and not only for him, stories of the sea are fundamentally catastrophic. Life founders.

The chapter begins by recollecting a particularly disconcerting aspect of human sexuality, namely, the hypothesis that for each individual sexual activity is ultimately about the release of "irritating tension" (2:370/60). Earlier on in his work, Ferenczi has defined the genital phase in terms of the descent of such tensions from other parts of the body to the genitals; the genital secretion, however narcissistically one's ego may identify with it, is a solute of every unpleasure one craves to expel. If sexuality is sublime, that is because, as Kant knows, it is characterized by *Unlust*, displeasure or unpleasure—even if regression to the womb and to the sea has its attendant phantasmatic pleasures. True, every excretion is considered a loss, as though it were something precious, something to be harbored, but the loss is a gain in equanimity. The flesh is willing but the spirit is weak.

Nature has united intercourse with possible fertilization, however, and the unifying process that involves germ plasm is much "older" than intercourse itself. Ferenczi goes in search of the archaic mystery of this union. For, to paraphrase *Menexenus*, germ cells do not imitate creatures who mate, but lovers imitate the germ cells they carry within themselves, and it is the germ cells that institute the process. If the existence of the individual begins *in utero*, then "*so also must the process of fertilization and even the development of germ cells (the genesis of spermatozoa and egg) correspond to something in phylogenesis*" (2:371/61). That "something" can be nothing other than a "primeval catastrophe," a disturbance in the life of one-celled animals that forces them to unite (ibid.). Ferenczi cites Freud's account in *Beyond the Pleasure Principle*, and he will alter that account in only one way, namely, in his version of the very first catastrophe. In general, he affirms Freud's speculation, and especially Freud's embrace of Aristophanes' tale concerning the three kinds of early human beings (GW 13:62–3). Freud writes:

> I mean of course the theory that Plato has Aristophanes develop in *Symposium* [189e–191d], a theory that treats not only the origins of the sex drive but also the most important variations with regard to the love object.
>
> "For our body was not formed at first as it is now; it was quite different. Initially there were three sexes, not as now merely the male and female, for there was a third, one that unified the two . . . , the androgynous." Everything about these humans was double, so

that they had four hands and four feet, two faces, double genitals, and so on. Then Zeus was moved to divide every human being into two parts, "as one halves quinces in order to make preserves of them. ... But because the whole creature was cut in two, longing drove the two halves together: they embraced one another with their hands, they wrapped themselves around one another *in their yearning to grow back together*. ..." [Freud's emphasis.]

Shall we dare to suppose, following the hint of the poet-philosopher, that the living substance, when it first came to life, was torn into tiny particles that ever since have been striving to reunite? And that these drives in which the chemical affinity of nonliving matter continues to work its effects throughout the kingdom of the protozoa, gradually overcoming the difficulties that an environment riddled with hazardous stimuli set in opposition to their striving, stimuli that compelled them to form a protective outer layer [*einen schützenden Rindenschicht*]? And that these scattered particles of living substance in this way reached a multicellular stage and ultimately transmitted to germ cells the drive to reunification in the most concentrated form? I believe this is the place to stop.

Ibid.

If I am right, Ferenczi—who will not stop—leaves out of his account Freud's hypothesis concerning the development of the cells' protective outer wall of (inorganic) cellulose. And there is one other major difference in their accounts. Whereas Freud describes Zeus's halving of the primal genders as a splitting "of the living substance," Ferenczi prefers to speak of a splitting of "matter," even if this shatters the frame of Aristophanes' tale. Ferenczi concedes that *Materie* refers to the mother, *mater*, yet he argues that the first catastrophe—which is life itself—is something that strikes "inorganic matter" (2:371/62). A second catastrophe, likewise in the form of desiccation, then causes these sundered bits of inorganic matter, which somehow become transitional elements leading to one-celled life—"somehow," because Ferenczi does not claim to solve the riddle of the origins of life—to engage in a frenzy of unification, a "conjugal epidemic" (ibid.). What is odd about Ferenczi's hypothesis concerning inorganic matter is that it does not seem to jibe with the notion of desiccation. Are we to believe that nonliving matter is struck by the catastrophe of desiccation? What would be the role of the sea during this pristine inorganic phase? Or have the seas even arrived yet, created as they were four billion years ago, as we now suppose, from the condensation of water vapor in the primeval atmosphere, aided by the collision of gigantic water-bearing meteors? Or is Ferenczi thinking of the more recent and more local rise of Ararat, caused by colliding tectonic plates, as the initial catastrophe? In any event, all of this is lost, as Bölsche would again say, in purple haze.

Ferenczi focuses on those initial cellular fusions by which cells appear to mate with or to ingest one another. Their symbiosis, over time, and by a process Ferenczi is at a loss to explain, produces germ cells that break apart. And thus begins "the eternal ringdance of germ cell unification (fertilization) and germ cell excretion (spermatogenesis and ovogenesis)" (2:372/61). The most important consequence of the ringdance is that every individual inherits the effects of "*all the earlier catastrophes since the beginning of life*," so that "in the feeling of orgasm we find represented not only *repose in the womb*, that is, peaceful existence in a friendlier milieu, but also *repose that is prior to the origination of life*, which is to say, *the repose of death in inorganic existence*" (ibid./63). The repose of death, in turn, is bound up with autotomy. The "law of autotomy," as Ferenczi calls it, requires that irritating tensions be released, even if, or precisely because, life is but a bowl of irritating tensions (2:373/63). This law or "tendency toward autotomy" is described in an earlier chapter in this way: "Now, we have said at the outset that all qualities and quantities of unpleasure that are shunted aside in the useful functioning of every organ gather together in the genital, there to be eliminated" (2:343/29). The very erection of the penis is an incomplete and therefore unsuccessful striving for autotomy, masturbation an attempt to rid oneself of the offending organ, which, as every puritan preacher has always warned us, forces the wretched sinner to scratch the itch of lust until the scratch becomes an excision. Even as a lover "builds bridges" of kisses and caresses with his or her partner, we are forced to speak of a tendency to unpleasure (*Unlusttendenz*) that is doubtless related to *anxiety*: "The tension that keeps the partners in a state of 'bated breath' is in itself unpleasurable, and only the hope for and expectation of a sudden release makes it also pleasurable" (2:347/34).[8]

The section on phylogenesis now picks up the same dire thread, spun by the Parcae: the reason that the genital secretion exits from the identical port of the body that urine does, and the reason that both of these substances exit in close proximity to the anus, is that the secretion has in some way stored up not only the individual's erotic tensions and discomfitures but also all the "*secular material of unpleasure*" in the human body (2:373). "Secular"? The word seems to refer to the *saecula saeculorum* of Gregorian chant. Bunker translates it as "*the age-old material of unpleasure*" (64). Ferenczi's argument is that the genital secretion is the anxiety-ridden solute of all the catastrophes that have occurred in the history of life, and perhaps in

---

[8] The self-mutilation or self-laceration of auto-tomy (from the Greek αὐτός and τέμνω) reminds us of today's growing tendency toward apotemnophilia, the condition by which one craves to have one or more limbs amputated, this placing the surgeon in the parlous position of either having to agree to an unnecessary surgery or causing the patient to go to unscrupulous persons who will perform the amputation. One has to wonder whether the epidemic of tattooing and piercing in our time is related to Ferenczi's law. And, due to recent political events in the United States, one must wonder whether an entire society is susceptible to the craving for self-punishment and self-laceration, a sort of national political autotomy.

the history of planet Earth. The inevitable result is that genitality and sexuality, symbolic as they are of the originally cloacal sanctuary that provides rescue from catastrophe, appear themselves to be catastrophic. The only way ahead is full steam backwards. In onto-theo-mytho-logical terms, one might call this the mystery of vicarious suffering passed on from father to son (Zeus's thigh) and from father to daughter (Zeus's head).

The sea's repose begins to look more and more like the deadly calms that Melville so chillingly evokes, or like the terrifying image depicted by Marguerite Duras near the conclusion of *L'amant de la Chine du Nord,* that of the motionless body of a drowned youth— *suspendu dans les eaux lourdes des zones profondes de la mer.*[9] As my doggedly cheerful Uncle Chuck said one day as he was getting older and more fragile, "Life is just one damned thing after another."

Yet one risks being unfair to Ferenczi by insisting on the puritanical heritage that appears to lie behind these dire accounts of sexual tension and displeasure. Our objections or our resistance may well result from our own tendency to romanticize sexual life down to the zygotes. Ferenczi notes that the tendency toward unification, visible in all forms of life, from germ cells to the individuals that carry them, "not only helps to mitigate unresolved traumatic shockwaves but also celebrates festivals of rescue from great calamity," *Feste der Errettung aus grosser Not* (2:376–7/68). Indeed, Ferenczi has spoken of festivals earlier in his work. He alludes to the way in which even childplay, which helps the child to abreact traumatic effects such as those caused by the mother's absence, may be counted among such celebrations.

---

[9] Marguerite Duras, *L'amant de la Chine du Nord* (Paris: Gallimard, 1991), 229.

Concerning sexual pleasure he writes, agreeing at least in part with Freud,

> We too view coitus as such a partial release of the effects of shock—the legacy of the birth trauma—that have not yet been alleviated. At the same time, coitus appears to us to be play, or better, a commemorative festival [*ein Erinnerungsfest*] by which the fortunate liberation from calamity is celebrated. Ultimately, however, it also represents the negative, hallucinatory denial of the trauma.
>
> In response to the question posed by Freud as to whether repetition, when it comes to the sex drive, is a compulsion or a pleasure, that is, as to whether repetition lies on this side of or beyond the pleasure principle, we cannot offer a unified reply. We believe that it is a compulsion to the extent that it gradually balances the shock effects, that is, that it is an adaptive reaction compelled by an extrinsic disturbance; on the other hand, whether the disturbance is negatively denied by way of hallucination or the memory of its overcoming is celebrated, in both cases we have to do with sheer mechanisms of pleasure.
>
> 2:352–3/40; cf. 2:171

Such memorious celebrations, carried out on this admittedly catastrophic Earth, at least *seem* to be about pleasure: "Thus the sex act reminds us of that sort of 'stage play' in which, no matter how many storm clouds gather, as they do in a genuine tragedy, one always has the sense that there is going to be a 'happy end'" (2:354/42). Not opera, but operetta; not tragedy, but melodrama. And yet. Much later in his book, treating of those very "memory traces" that he hopes will grant festivals of peace, Ferenczi's reflections remind us instead of the House of Atreus: "What we call *heredity* [Vererbung] is thus perhaps merely *the transmission of the largest part of those efforts to rid oneself of unpleasure to one's posterity*, so that the germ cell, as the mass of inheritance, is the sum of all the traumatic impressions our individual ancestors repulsed and passed on to us" (2:375/66; cf. 2:171). Are sexual embraces then festivals of pleasure and grateful remembrances? Or are they commemorations of our ingrate forefathers?

In any case, setting aside the knotty question of repetition as compulsive behavior *and* the celebration of pleasure, we can safely say that the geological history of planet Earth has not been about pleasure. Here is Ferenczi's synoptic Table of Catastrophes (2:378/69):

	Phylogenesis	**Ontogenesis**
Catastrophe I	Emergence of organic life	Maturing of the sex cells
Catastrophe II	Emergence of individual, one-celled creatures	"Birth" of the mature germ cells from the sex glands
Catastrophe III	Sexual reproduction begins ——	Fertilization ——
	Development of species in the sea	Embryonal development in the womb
Catastrophe IV	Drying up of the sea; adaptation to life on land ——	Birth ——
	Development of animals with sex organs	Development of the primacy of the genital zone
Catastrophe V	Ice Ages; the coming of man	Period of latency

Ferenczi's own *Attempt* has begun with Catastrophe IV, of course, the drying up of the sea, the amphibian struggle, and the birth of mammals such as humans. As for the earlier catastrophes, one must wonder whether the origin of life has ever before been characterized as essentially catastrophic. Even the most dismal ascetic priest would have shied from condemning as catastrophic the birth of life from his living God, although he would have adamantly refused to accept that there is no other God than natural life; even the most crotchety misanthrope, living in his hovel the woods, would hesitate to condemn the animals of the forest. Both would have had their troubles with the ontogenetic "maturing of the sex cells," but surely they would have made room for anastrophe, if only as an ongoing challenge, and most likely as a "happy end." Perhaps Schopenhauer in his most dour moments comes closest to a sense of life as catastrophe. Nietzsche would say that all classical or passive nihilism, as opposed to the "ecstatic" nihilism for which he pleads, stems from the ascetic idealism that prefers death—whether in the form of "spirit" or "will"—to burgeoning lifedeath.

Ferenczi himself notes that his separating the first from the second catastrophe distinguishes his view from Freud's, but his elaboration of that separation is unconvincing. He writes of a hypothetical *Belebung der Materie vorausgesetzten kosmischen Katastrophe*, "a cosmic catastrophe that the animation of matter presupposes" (2:378/70). We might think of a second Big Bang, or at least of a considerable number of bangs that occurred when gigantic meteors brought additional water—and thus the seas—to Earth billions of years ago. Marine matter would in some undisclosed way have been granted an "organizational plan" that made it receptive to life. One recalls Hegel's lucubrations on *crystallization*, which he postulates as being on the verge of life, and Ferenczi too refers to the crystals that seem to mimic the emergence of land from the sea by suddenly emerging from the "mother solute" (ibid.). Yet the "organizational plan" appears to have been imperfect, or to have undergone unfortunate alterations. In chapter 3 we will hear about Rousseau's astounding fantasy of the finger of God *tilting* the axis of the Earth, so that everything terrestrial would be off-kilter, a touch askew, never fully rounded off and perfected, as though from that point on everything we humans do in order to win a few points in the game of life shakes the pinball machine a bit too hard. *Tilt.* Be that as it may, Ferenczi is forced to concede that *matter* is *mater*, as Schelling long before him had argued, so that it becomes difficult to see whether Ferenczi has refined Freud's model or merely, as Schelling once said, "pushed the problem one point farther down the line" without resolving it (I/7:355). Ferenczi admits that he must return to Freud's model, reaffirming that life in any case, at least for the individual, begins with a sundering or rending, *in einer Zerreissung des Stoffes* (2:378/70). Crystals too seem to grow as fractals, repetitions of smaller structures rather than grand unifications.

The other aspect of the Table that needs comment, writes Ferenczi, is the designation of the Ice Age (or Ages) as decisive in human evolution. Already back in 1913, in an article entitled "Stages in the Development of the Sense of Reality," Ferenczi speculates that parallels might be found in phylogenesis for the ontogenetic events of birth, latency, and puberty—and all such parallels for the development of the sense of reality would involve the "cruel" forced march of the individual (and the species) from one challenging situation to the next (1:162). Whatever sense of "erotic reality" the hominids (*Homo habilis*, perhaps) may have developed by the time of the Pleistocene, it is clear that the periodic advancing of the ice sheets compel them to alter everything about their life. Glaciation furthers in the cruelest possible way the development of the "higher" human faculties, including increased socialization or, as Ferenczi writes, enhanced "moral" capacities. Since we ourselves live in an interglacial period, the Holocene, with the ice caps and ice sheets that formed early in the Pliocene some two and a half million years still with us, albeit in a state of severe deterioration, one can fairly say that the need for the "higher" faculties has not diminished. The development begins, according to Ferenczi, with the curvature of the brain in amniotic vertebrates and the development of the corpus callosum (which enables the two brain hemispheres to communicate) in eutherians or placental animals. Finally, Ferenczi argues that the development of culture and of what we would call "social skills" during the long period of human latency, from birth through adolescence and early adulthood, mirrors in a modified way the "intense imbrication of the genital drive and intellectuality," which is truly archaic (2:379/70–1). By way of closing, Ferenczi refers to the well-known fact that so-called "higher order" functions in the human brain were once devoted to the sense of smell. He notes the diminution of the sense of smell and the augmentation of vision in our species, themes that Freud elaborates in the long footnotes that open and close the fourth chapter of his *Civilization and Its Discontents*. The sense of smell is therefore properly speaking *"the biological model of thought"* (2:380/71). As today's dogs and cats imbibe by the nose the gaseous particles of what is before them as potential food or mate, friend or enemy, so, at least according to Freud's 1895 *Entwurf*, does the mind probe reality by absorbing minimal quantities of energy. "The organ of thought and the sense of smell: both are in service to the reality function, indeed that of both the egoistic and the erotic" (ibid./72). One might have expected Ferenczi to reintroduce the theme of trimethylamine, this time as a category of *thought*, of thought about the *sea*—but he does not.

The final chapter of Ferenczi's work, "Bioanalytical Consequences," also under the rubric "Prospects," will give us the chance to summarize the book's findings and regroup our own thoughts, which are indeed like scents wafting on the wind. The chapter that precedes "Bioanalytical Consequences," on "Sleep and Coitus," we may reduce to two long quotations, the first from Ferenczi, the second from a work of contemporary fiction. Sleep, Ferenczi says, approximates the state of the psyche in or after intercourse, and it is perhaps the closest approximation to our existence in the womb. Yet it also memorializes forms of existence that were left behind long ago, even before life began:

According to an old Latin proverb, sleep is the brother of death. When we wake up, however, and experience our daily rebirth, those traumatic forces that "awakened" matter to life are still at work. Every further development is a being forceably roused out of relative repose. "*Le végétal est un animal qui dort*," says Buffon. Yet embryogenesis too is like a sleep that is disturbed only by a palingenetic repetition of the history of the species, as by a biographical dream.

The main difference between sleep and coitus, however, may be this: sleep is but our fortunate existence in the womb, whereas coitus represents the struggles that followed one upon the other after our "expulsion from Paradise," to wit, cosmic catastrophes, birth, and the struggles surrounding our weaning and the need to accommodate ourselves [*Entwöhnungs- und Angewöhnungskämpfe*].

2:387/80

As if that were not bioanalytical consequence enough, and if only in furtherance of the "biographical dream," I present the following passage on sleep from Michel Tournier's *Les météores*. It is Alexandre who speaks:

I've always thought that each man, each woman, when evening falls, feels a vast weariness of existing . . . , of being born, and that to console themselves for all those hours of noise and ill winds they might undertake to be born in reverse, to be *unborn*. But how reintegrate oneself into mama's belly, abandoned so long ago? By having always at home a false mama, a pseudo-mama in the form of a bed (an analogue to those rubber dolls that sailors at sea kiss in order to deceive their enforced chastity). To seek silence and the dark, to slip between the sheets, to adopt the proper position, to huddle quite nude in the warmth and humidity, to make like a fetus. I haven't been born after all! That is why it is logical to sleep in a closed room, in a confined atmosphere. An open window—

that's good for daytime, for the morning, for the efforts of muscles engaged in energetic activity. At night these engagements should be curtailed as far as possible. Because the fetus doesn't breathe, the sleeper too should breathe as little as possible. A thick maternal atmosphere, the atmosphere of a stable in winter, works best.[10]

Let us turn now to Ferenczi's final chapter—which will require a chapter of its own. One cannot say that a thick maternal atmosphere pervades Ferenczi's conclusion. Indeed, the bioanalyst seems to have paused atop a sand dune at the sea's edge, remembering thinking knowing. Something like pleasure emerges in his thoughts, if only as a fleeting memory. Let ourselves be cradled by such memories, he seems to say. For what do we see when we look fore and aft in our own lives and in the entire history of life if not—catastrophe?

---

[10] Michel Tournier, *Les météores* (Paris: Gallimard Folio, 1975), 247–8.

10 *Near "White Beach" on the southwestern coast.*

3

Forwards and Backwards— Catastrophe?

Sea—the purest and most polluted water: for fish, potable and life-sustaining; for humans, undrinkable and lethal.

HERACLITUS OF EPHESUS (DK B61)

[T]he high sea is accustomed to toss asunder transoms, ribs, yards, prow, masts, and oars . . . seen floating around all the shores, a warning to mortals that they avoid the treacherous deep, with her snares, her violence, and her fraud, and never trust her at any time, even when the calm sea shows her false alluring smile.

LUCRETIUS, *DE RERUM NATURA* (2:553–9)

Ferenczi's effort to unite biological science and psychoanalysis, his *bioanalysis*, focuses on human genital and sexual life. In that context Ferenczi develops his theories of the phylogenetic catastrophe that initiated genitally bimorphic life-forms and the thalassic regressive undertow that tugs all life back to a sea that can no longer sustain it.

Allow me to reduce some of his most astonishing and problematic ideas to five thesis statements:

1 Viewed ontogenetically, human sexuality is ultimately about the release of "irritating tension." The genital phase of erotic life involves the descent of such tension from other parts of the body to the genitals; the genital secretions themselves are solutes of unpleasure.

2 Viewed phylogenetically, genitality is a response to the periodic crisis of the desiccation of the seas. Every individual inherits the effects of "*all the earlier catastrophes since the beginning of life*," so that "in the feeling of orgasm we find represented not only *repose in the womb*, that is, peaceful existence in a friendlier milieu, but also *repose that is prior to the origination of life*, which is to say, *the repose of death in inorganic existence.*"

3 The repose of death, in turn, is the covert goal of autotomy, which is to say, a particular form of self-mutilation. The "law of autotomy," as Ferenczi calls it, requires that irritating tensions be expelled and the organs associated with them excised.

4 Germ cells, both spermatic and ovoid, have in some way stored up not only the individual's erotic tensions and discomfitures but also all the "*secular material of unpleasure*" from the long history of the human body. "What we call *heredity* is thus perhaps merely *the transmission of the largest part of those efforts to rid oneself of unpleasure* [by passing it on] *to one's posterity.*" Sperm and egg alike inherit the effects of all the catastrophes that have occurred in the history of life, perhaps even the history of planet Earth. The inevitable result is that genitality and sexuality, while symbolic

of the cloacal sanctuary that provides rescue from the catastrophe of desiccation, appear themselves to be catastrophic.

5   The arcane mystery of this catastrophic scenario, which in mythopoeic terms one might call the mystery of Zeus's thigh, is how the female gender can have "introjected" the sea that rescues life from desiccation—at least for a time.

The question now—or for the rest of our lives—is this: are sexual embraces festivals of pleasure and grateful remembrances, or are they commemorations of callous forefathers and narcissistic mothers who passed the bulk of their repulsions on to us? Viewed ontogenetically, genital life can be interpreted either as a festival of memory, that is, as a pleasureful celebration of our earlier life in the sea or the womb, or as the hallucinatory effort to quell the anxieties of the near-suffocation and desiccation impacted in our birth. Viewed phylogenetically, a bimorphic genitality can be seen either as a successful strategy for overcoming desiccation or, especially when germ cell behavior is drawn into consideration, as the transmission of all painful tension—all unpleasure—from one generation to the next, turning biological inheritance into something like a catastrophic memorial, a monument not to life but to death. The house of love as the House of Atreus. To say nothing of the House of Usher.

Yet in all this we cannot evade a preliminary question, to wit: what *is* this *catastrophe* that Ferenczi sees multiplying itself across the eons of earth history? Why specifically the drying up of the seas or of freshwater ponds or of brackish swamps and lagoons? Ferenczi tells us nothing about where he has discovered such a theory of catastrophe, in which sort of literature in the history of science. Wilhelm Bölsche, a favorite source for Ferenczi, if not his most soberly scientific, gives us at least a place to begin searching. Bölsche, in his *Developmental History of Nature*, attributes the theory of "catastrophism" to the great eighteenth-century geologist Georges Cuvier.

In his *Discours sur les révolutions de la surface de la Globe*, Cuvier expands the results of his and other paleontological discoveries into a system of earth history as a whole. Impressed as he is by the discovery of sedimented strata in the earth's surface, for example in the work of the English engineer William Smith, Cuvier hypothesizes that the line of division between each stratum of the earth's crust indicates an entirely separate zone of vegetal and animal development; each period of earth and life histories, as manifested in the strata, ends in catastrophe, whether of a Neptunist or Vulcanist sort; a "period of storm," *eine "Sturmzeit,"* radically sunders each period from the periods before and after it (BE 1:187). "Monstrous catastrophes had devastated the earth's surface, totally annihilating every form of life," each new period, then, beginning as an entirely "new creation" (ibid.). Strangely, the drying up of seas does *not* appear to be one of Cuvier's catastrophes—at least, Bölsche makes no mention of it; rather, massive floods and the irruptive formation of new mountain chains seem to be on Cuvier's mind. In any case, to be sure, the eons encompassing the "new creation" between such tempestuous catastrophes are so vast that the arc of time readily simulates the continuous development of species.

The history of evolutionary theory in the nineteenth century, according to Bölsche, is one of the gradual subsidence of Cuvier's "catastrophism." Even Lamarck, who stresses the gradual complexification of life forms due to inherent alchemical forces and adaptation to environments, eschews the notion of repeated creations after devastating catastrophes (BE 1:194). The use and disuse of particular organs will affect the evolution of species, argues Lamarck, but that evolution occurs only after many successive, continuous generations. Even though his contemporaries mock the idea of the "inheritance of acquired characteristics," caricaturing it as the giraffe's instantly acquiring a longer neck in order to eat its way up the mimosa tree, Lamarck's system is more continuist than catastrophist. In spite of his emphasis on multiple catastrophes, Ferenczi is in this respect too a disciple of Lamarck.

Catastrophism, however, does not entirely disappear from the scene after Cuvier. Even the great empiricist Alexander von Humboldt, in his late work *Kosmos*, refers to "widespread revolutions" in earth history, each one fostering the development of new organisms while devastating the old; and from time to time biologists have been tempted to explain changes in flora or fauna in terms of "new coinages" resulting from "a sudden cataclysm," *einen jähen Ruck* (BE 1:198; 2:552). Cuvier's theory receives its hardest blow, however, from the geological science that initially spawned it. Charles Lyell's *Principles of Geology* (1830) stresses the *continuous* development of earth history and of the sundry species of life on the planet. Obviously, continental plates drift and collide, volcanoes erupt, seas expand and contract and dry up altogether, but the only catastrophe that counts is *time*, and the principles of geological change *over time* are the same ones we see in operation before our very eyes. As for Ferenczi's drying up of the seas as a repeated event in earth history, the closest one comes in Bölsche's *Developmental History of Nature* to such a catastrophe arises only quite late in the work. In a cautious footnote Bölsche cites the *Handbook of Paleontology* by Karl Zittel, who is enough of a Cuvierian to concede that "massive changes in the relief [of the earth's surface] caused by the distribution of water and changes in the climate" surely necessitate "new adaptations in the organic world" (BE 2:552n.). Yet that is only weak support for Ferenczi's catastrophe—and one must simply continue to search for the source of his obsession with the drying up of the seas in the history of the geological and biological sciences.[1]

Astonishing as it may seem, however, there *is* a tradition of the drying up of the seas, a tradition of catastrophism that takes us back well before Cuvier. The idea of the eventual desiccation of the seas is attributed to Diogenes of Apollonia (in the second half of the fifth century BCE) but also to Xenophanes of Colophon and Anaximander of Miletus (in the first half of the sixth century BCE). Indeed, Aristotle scolds Democritus for having had the same fear, which seems to be surprisingly widespread in antiquity. The fear seems to be justified for thinkers from cities on the Ionian coast, which, like many coastal areas in antiquity, experienced something like a recession of the sea or a build-up of the shoreline. Today's travelers to the ancient Cycladic city of Akrotiri, on Thira, may likewise be surprised by the distance of the sea from the ancient harbor. In his *Meteorology* (at 353b 6), Aristotle reports the following about that hoary tradition of

---

[1] A former student of mine at Brown University, William Shinevar, now a geophysicist at Woods Hole Oceanographic, tells me that anoxia—that is, a sharp decline in the oxygen content of the seas—is a more likely cause of the Devonian mass extinction than the recession or drying up of the seas. That extinction, best exemplified by the Kellwasser and Hangenberg events, happened around 375 to 360 million years ago, and scientists believe that amphibians started to evolve around 370 million years ago. The climate was generally warm in the Devonian, although some scientists claim that periods of glaciation might have led to a decline in sea levels. Yet the hypothesis currently put forward by most scientists is that mass extinctions and a severe reduction of biodiversity resulted from the oceans' becoming anoxic. Their becoming less habitable due to low oxygen content, followed by evolutionary mutations, led tetrapods (bony fish from which all reptiles, birds, and mammals have descended) to evolve during the mass extinction into amphibians. The anoxic hypothesis is supported by the fact that sedimentary rocks during this time period show deposition from an anoxic ocean. No doubt, to all this Ferenczi might well reply: "Very well, then, not desiccation but anoxia—parallel to the very *dyspnoea* we see in the gasps of every newborn and every lover. In any case, *catastrophe*."

desiccation: "For first of all they say that the whole area around the earth is moist, but, being dried by the sun, the part that is exhaled makes winds and turnings of the sun and moon, while that which is left is sea; therefore they think that the sea is actually becoming less through being dried up, and that some time it will end up by being entirely dry" (KRS 139). Democritus, otherwise the laughing philosopher, is said to have believed that the drying up of the seas would mean the end of the world. Aristotle counters that while in some areas the sea is receding in others it is expanding, so that one may have confidence in the cycle (ibid.). Diogenes, who explains the flooding of the Nile in terms of the drying up of the sea, would seem to have had some sense of this cyclical action of sea, evaporation, rainfall, and rivers (KRS 446).

Whether Xenophanes of Colophon, poet, thinker of the divine, and acerbic critic of Homer, believed that the seas were drying up seems doubtful. The evidence for Anaximander, the great Milesian thinker of the "unlimited" and the "ordinance of time," seems every bit as dubious (KRS 138). For both thinkers are aware of the "turnings" of sea, cloud, rain, and stream—and would not the catastrophe of total desiccation mean the outer limit of the "unlimited" and thus the collapse of the system by which, according to the ordinance of time, all beings reck the coming-to-be of the others' and their own perishing?

These Anaxamandrian–Xenophanean mysteries and Heraclitean marvels, along with those propounded by Thales, the thinker of water and gods, I reserve for the next chapter. For the moment, the ancient tradition of catastrophic desiccation, reported in many places, does not seem to survive intact—certainly not up to the time, eons later, when Ferenczi writes. Indeed the reverse seems to be the case: the perceived cycle of sea, evaporation, rainfall, and the return of sweet water to the sea seems to be older than the Greeks, and it surely endures through the ages. Hölderlin, in his novel *Hyperion*, has his hero write to his beloved Diotima that he wishes to be buried at sea: "I would be happy," he writes, "if my remains should sink to the bottom, where the sources of all the streams I loved are gathered and where the storm clouds rise to soak the mountains and the valleys I loved" (CHV 1:725). Yet before we abandon the idea of desiccation, let us make one more attempt to think the uncanny catastrophism implied in it.

Perhaps it may be no more than a parallel, but Cuvier's and Ferenczi's catastrophisms remind us of the role of catastrophe in Rousseau's thinking of *origins*, as interpreted by Jacques Derrida. The origins in question are those of both human language and human inequality. For in both the *Essay on the Origins of Language* and the *Discourse on Inequality* something like catastrophe alone can explain—or fail to explain—the way in which human beings in the state of nature are forced to become social, civilized, "polished," talking and writing beings. The paradox is that such a transition is both natural and forced; it is both a link in the chain of natural concatenation and the imposed manacles of a sudden, inexplicable, and unreasonable intervention.

The *necessity* of catastrophe cannot be part of Rousseau's system, but only a supplement to it; yet, whether with or without the supplement, the system does not hold. Derrida develops this account of catastrophe in Rousseau in the third chapter of the second part of *De la grammatologie*, "This 'Simple Movement of the Finger': Writing and the Prohibition of Incest" (G 361–78). His question is why, when it comes to Rousseau's accounts of origins, everything goes topsy-turvy, "in the form of reversal, return, revolution, progressive movement under the aspect of regression" (G 361). In the *Essay*, Rousseau describes the catastrophe as resulting from the touch of a finger that tilts the axis of the Earth. It cannot be the finger of

Providence, since such a touch is catastrophic and improvident; yet no one or nothing else than Omnipotence has the power to touch in this way. Rousseau's answer, ingenious in its side-stepping of all the onto-mytho-theo-logical pitfalls, is this: "The One [*Celui*] who willed that human beings become sociable touched with his finger the axis of the globe and bent it toward the axis of the universe" (G 362). This *chiquenaude*, or flick of the finger, comes from the outside, and so it is not a part of nature; yet nature is redefined by it, and, at least in retrospect, nothing could have been more natural, more *perversely* natural.

Derrida defines this flick of the finger as the play, *jeu*, of the world; yet it is not play in the ludic sense. Rather, if I am right, it is something like the play of a wagon wheel on its axle, the sort of play that, if it becomes excessive, wears down the axle. It would be the play in terms of which Gabriel García Márquez understands Nietzsche's eternal recurrence of the same, which cannot go on for all eternity *por el desgaste progressivo y irremediable del eje*, "because of the progressive and irremediable wearing away of the axle" (GM 334/402). It is this catastrophic sense of play, one that produces *monstrosities*, that Derrida wishes to emphasize: "The supplement to nature is in nature as its play. Who will ever say whether the lack in nature is *in* nature, whether the catastrophe by which nature *splits off from itself*, is still natural? A natural catastrophe conforms to laws only to upset the law" (G 364). And near the conclusion of "Structure, Sign, and Play in the Discourse of the Human Sciences," Derrida remarks, "Like Rousseau, one must always think the origin of a new structure on the model of catastrophe—the inversion of nature within nature, the natural interruption of the natural chain of events, nature's *own* split [*écart* de *la nature*]" (ED 426).

The flick of a finger seems a monstrous contingency, and contingency cannot be part of a system without disabling it. The origin of inequality among human beings, as among the sundry systems of humans signs, is therefore contrary to reason; it is an effect of *quelque funeste hasard*, "some disastrous accident" (G 366–7). One of the most untoward results of the accident is that the natural relations of brother and sister (though not of mother and son) come to be naturally prohibited—for the sake of the flourishing of the species, and indeed, to prevent the birth of monsters. Before the prohibition there is no such crime as incest; after the prohibition there is no incest by reason of the (putatively natural) law. Incest is therefore "the hinge between nature and culture" (G 375). Naturally, with the question of incest we arrive on a scene that is not foreign to psychoanalysis. Let us therefore return to the final pages of *Thalassa*.

For here too it will be a question of the continued effects of primeval catastrophe. And if for Rousseau the Golden Age of the state of nature, prior to the catastrophe, is one of continual *feast* and *festivity*, in which there is no gap "between the time of desire and the time of pleasure" (G 372), then for Ferenczi the ultimate question will be whether the pleasure principle must succumb to the destruction-and-death drives, the latter manifested in the thalassic regressive undertow, or whether, conversely, pleasure and the festivals of memory, celebrating our survival of the birth trauma, will prove to be the pure gold of our own age. Such is the closely kept secret of catastrophe itself: it will not surprise us if something like a logic of supplementarity invades Ferenczi's bioanalytic theory of genitality.

Ferenczi's "Bioanalytical Consequences" involve much more than a summary statement of his *Attempt at a Theory of Genitality*. They offer nothing short of what one might call an ontology of life. This final chapter is long and difficult. In what follows I will attempt to read it as closely as I can. I will also expand a bit on the sources Ferenczi cites—Nietzsche, along with Freud, being the most prominent of these.[2]

An initial surprise is that Ferenczi makes no reference to the key methodological theme of his preface, a theme that also appears in many other of his works, namely, *utraquism*. Derived from *utraque*, "taking from both sides," the term is a clear statement of Ferenczi's refusal to accept the putative opposition of the "hard" sciences, such as physics and chemistry, to the "softer" science of psychoanalysis. In the preface he writes, "The most succinct formulation of this insight is this: everything physical and physiological ultimately needs a 'meta'-physical (psychological) elucidation as well, and every psychology needs a meta-psychological (physical) elucidation" (2:319/3). Even if the meta-physical is here equated with psychology rather than philosophy, the philosopher is the one who has to remember where metaphysics has its start and to ponder where it might have its end. If Nietzsche is right when in *Beyond Good and Evil* (no. 23) he says that philosophy culminates in psychology, "the queen of the sciences" (KSW 5:39), then such psychology is not remote from ontology.

Utraquism is also a stark rejection (by way of anticipation) of C. P. Snow's classic depiction of the chasm dividing the "two cultures," the scientific and the humanistic. Ferenczi's resistance to the positivism that dominates his age, as well as to the unrivaled rule of technology that continues to dominate our own, will of course earn him the scorn

---

[2] The transcript of Derrida's 1975 seminar on "lifedeath" (*La vie la mort*) would no doubt touch on many of the themes to be discussed here. If I understand rightly, the French and English transcriptions of that seminar will appear in 2018 or 2019 at the earliest, the English translation by Pascale-Anne Brault and Michael Naas to appear with the University of Chicago Press. I mention Derrida's seminar inasmuch as Ferenczi's principal theme, in response to Freud's *Beyond the Pleasure Principle*, is the imbrication of the life and death drives, an imbrication so intense that one can apply the neologism *lifedeath* to Ferenczi's conclusions. Lifedeath—that is the catastrophe, forwards and backwards.

11 *The sea performing its own* utraquism, *"taking from both sides,"* at *Mavro Vouno.*

of "hard" scientists. Yet there are many signs that positivism and scientism are under gentle attack from the humanities. For example, the development of humanistic and phenomenological psychology is part of a far larger movement in the medical sciences that one might indeed call *utraquism*; even the most adamantly Western of medical practitioners will dip into homeopathy, if only, for example, in the treatment of tendonitis. True, no research scientist will refer to *utraquism* in his or her grant applications, for it will not bring in the cash. And university administrators (or corporate heads) today are not hesitating to transform their colleges of arts and sciences into colleges of "arts and *the social* sciences," sending off the "hard sciences" to join the faculties of technological "software" and "hardware," as though in obedience to what Heidegger fears in "The Question Concerning Technology." Philosophers are particularly stung by the move to relieve students majoring in science and technology of their humanities requirements or options, since they are losing young mathematicians, pre-med students, and others who need and most often want a philosophical education in addition to their technical training. Perhaps academic deans and provosts should be given a hefty injection of *utraquism*? That would bring them and us back to one of the oldest wisdoms of the academy, that of Plato. In his *Sophist*, at the point where the Eleatic Stranger tries to distinguish the true philosopher from the sophist, and where the crass alternative of "idealism" and "realism" or "intellectualism" and "materialism" is posed only to be rejected, what becomes clear is that the philosopher must become "like the child who desires and begs for both," no matter what the prevailing dichotomies may be (249d). No single *–ism* comprehends what *is*; that is why there are so many of them. Ferenczi, a physician and scientist, begs for the hard results of scientific experimentation and empirical demonstration; but as a psychoanalyst and a reader of myths, folklore, philosophy, and fairy tales, he craves the hermeneutician's skill in interpreting symbols and narratives. Perhaps the only reason he does not mention *utraquism* in his "Bioanalytical Consequences" is that he feels that by now his book has demonstrated the absolute need for such a method.

Still quite aware that much of what he has written will strike his more hard-pated colleagues as fantasy, Ferenczi declares at the end of his book the "heuristic value" of his *Attempt*: "Let us be satisfied here with the fact that this nexus of psychological and biological insights shows itself to be heuristically valuable for many difficult questions involving genitality and fertilization; it opens up perspectives of which the rigorous sciences have not an inkling" (2:388/81). He argues that the classic psychoanalytic concepts of displacement and compression, or deferral and condensation (*Verschiebung, Verdichtung*), also have use in discussions of the organism, and especially the organism's energy sources. The early history of conversion neuroses, in which *psychological* traumas trigger *physical* reactions, is evidence enough of that. The sciences of physiology and pathology have paid too little heed to the psychosomatic whole, feeling that they are permitted to ignore it because their approach to organs and to the organic as a whole is one of *use-function*. Psychoanalysis uncovers an entire range of pathologies that have an *affective* or *libidinal* etiology, however; not only use and disuse but also pleasure and unpleasure are phenomena relevant to health and disease. Hence the need for a supplemental biology of pleasure, *einer lustbiologischen Ergänzung* (2:389), even if, as Ferenczi concedes, it will more often be a matter of an *Unlustbiologie*. Catastrophe always calls for the supplement.

Yet the concession seems odd. At least early on in his book, Ferenczi seems optimistic about the pleasure principle: if unpleasure results most often from the culturally imposed need to renounce pleasure, renunciation itself can "learn" pleasure. In his account of anal-urethral amphimixis, Ferenczi writes of the child's "skillful combination of pleasure mechanisms," even during the fraught days of toilet training:

> The bladder learns how to hold back its urine only by acquiring another kind of pleasure, that of retention, and the bowel renounces the pleasure taken in constipation by borrowing something from the pleasure of urethral voiding. Perhaps if our analysis went deep enough we would learn that even the most successful sublimation, indeed an apparently total renunciation, could be broken down into its concealed elements of hedonistic satisfaction, without which, it seems, no living creature can be moved to alter its activity in any way.
>
> 2:327/12–13

Catastrophe here seems to be the stern instructress of unheard-of, hard-won pleasures. Other pleasures, however, seem to be skillful combinations of the destructive principle. It is important to remember how mysterious the pleasure principle is right from the start—for example in Freud's 1905 *Three Treatises Toward a Theory of Sex*. Is sex pleasurable at all? As in the case of hunger, says Freud, sexual intercourse and successful orgasm release the tension (*Spannung*) that can only be described as unpleasurable, so that pleasure (*Lust*) depends on a kind of pacification or "coming to peace," which is the more literal sense of "satisfaction," that is, of *Befriedigung* (GW 5:48–9). Where there is no war, there is no need for pacification. Sexual tension is thus inherently unpleasurable—the compulsive need to repeat the act demonstrates this, as does the sensation of the "itch," irritation, or general restiveness that occupies the genital zone (GW 5:85). Freud later describes that tension as possessing "a supremely compulsive character," one that is "entirely foreign" to what we normally call *pleasure* (GW 5:110). Yet if pleasure there must be, indeed as a matter of *principle*, then one must ask, as

Freud does, "How do this unpleasurable tension and this feeling of pleasure go together?" (ibid.). Freud wrestles with this question throughout his long career, but as far as I can see he never finds a satisfying answer.

Ferenczi's *autotomy* is part of his own answer to this question. The "tendency toward autotomy," the inclination to rid oneself of unpleasurable tensions *and* the organs that produce or suffer them, runs parallel to the psychoanalytic concept of repression, *Verdrängung* (2:327/12–13). Ferenczi and Freud alike would have been astonished to read another of those notes Nietzsche was writing at the sea's edge in Rapallo, at the Albergo della Posta, in preparation for *Thus Spoke Zarathustra*: "Lust and self-mutilation are neighboring drives" (KSW 10:194). Ferenczi, the bioanlyst, relates this autotomic tendency to Freud's notion of *organic* repression, which is developed in those two extraordinary notes that open and conclude the fourth chapter of *Civilization and Its Discontents*. Ferenczi assumes that his readers have Freud's two notes already well in mind, but we might take a moment to review them.

The initial point, developed at length in the first footnote (GW 14:458–9n. 1), is the gradual *regressive* development—that is to say, the deterioration—of the sense of smell and the resulting primacy of vision that comes with the erect posture of the hominids. The "taboo of menstruation" thus comes from the "organic repression" of an entire phase of phylogenetic development (periodic sexual excitation by way of the nose) that has been overcome. From this point on, sexual excitation will depend on *vision*, and it will be not periodic but *constant*. In an odd leap to a different level, Freud cites the way in which the gods of a civilization that has crumbled under the impact of a competing civilization become the devils of the latter: the *daimon* becomes a *demon*. Turning back to "organic repression," Freud notes the central importance of early man's erect posture: "At the beginning of the fateful process of civilization would thus stand the achievement of erect posture in humans" (ibid.). The cultural striving for cleanliness and the disgust felt toward excrement—at least that of others—have to do with that same achievement. "Anal eroticism is thus first defeated by 'organic repression,' which paves the way for civilization" (ibid.). The fact that the name of the human being's most faithful friend in the animal kingdom is hurled as an insult gives evidence of this.

Freud's second long footnote (GW 14:465–6n. 2) extends the discussion of organic repression to the presumed bisexuality of human beings and many other animals. "The individual comprises a melding of two symmetrical halves, of which, according to many researchers, one is purely masculine, the other feminine" (ibid.). The melding, *Verschmelzung*, does not stop here, however: it may be, as in a *mise-en-abyme*, that each of the two halves "was originally hermaphroditic" (ibid.). Freud continues:

Sexuality is a biological fact which, although of immense importance for psychic life, is difficult to grasp psychologically. We are accustomed to saying that every human being manifests the emergence of masculine as well as feminine drives, needs, and qualities; however, the character of the masculine and feminine, whereas it can be displayed by anatomy, cannot be shown by psychology. For psychology, the sexual opposition pales to the bloodless opposition of activity and passivity, whereby we mindlessly allow activity to fall to the masculine side, passivity to the feminine, a claim that among various animal species cannot be asserted without exception. The doctrine of bisexuality still lies very much in obscurity, and the fact that it has not yet been connected with the doctrine of drives has to be felt as a grave disturbance by psychoanalysis. . . .

Yet the most profound surmise, one that involves the matters
discussed in the footnote on page 66 [that is, GW 14:458–9n. 1],
is that with the erect posture of human beings and the
denigration of the sense of smell the entirety of sexuality, and
not merely anal eroticism, threatens to become a victim of
organic repression, so that from that point on the sexual function
has been accompanied by a further repugnance, one whose
cause cannot be ascertained but that hinders full satisfaction
and compels us away from the sexual goal in the direction of
sublimations and displacements of libido.... Every neurotic,
and not a few others besides, is repelled by the fact that *inter
urinas et faeces nascimur.* The genitals also produce strong
olfactory sensations, which many human beings find unbearable
and which spoil sexual intercourse for them. The result would be
that the deepest root of the repression of sex that continues to
advance with civilization is the organic defense of the new form of
life, the form achieved in the upright posture, against the earlier
animal existence.

                                                               Ibid.

Shades, or waftings, of trimethylamine. For Ferenczi, the primary
mark of organic repression is autotomy, the pull or tug that would
eliminate the genitals themselves, and not only their secretions and
their tensions. The erotic or libidinal drives, those in search of pleasure,
would thus be distinguished from useful drives, that is, those related
to the reality probe. The erotic drives themselves would yield to the
"regressive tendency" of drives as such, and the theme of regression
would take us to what Ferenczi calls "the *biological unconscious*"
(2:390/83). "It suffices if we refer here once again to the examples of
sleep and sexual intercourse: in both states, the entire psyche, but also,
at least in part, the organism as such, regresses to the prenatal phase

and probably also to a phylogenetically outmoded form of life"
(2:390/84). By adding a third dimension to the two-dimensional
world of utility and functionality in the biological sciences, to wit, the
dimension of (un)pleasure, Ferenczi feels that he can speak of a *depth
biology* (ibid./84).

Yet the third dimension never makes anything easier to understand.
In particular, the notion of *time* in depth biology is shaken to its
core. For while the emphasis is on history as development, albeit
development as progression *and* regression, depth biology confronts
precisely what Freud calls the "timelessness" of the unconscious.
Ferenczi writes:

> A remarkable fact, observed heretofore only in the psychical, is
> that the same element can be simultaneously inserted into a
> sequence that can be localized analytically as both *contemporaneous*
> and *memorious*. This is an expression of the "timelessness" of
> unconscious memory traces. When we applied these insights won
> from the psychical to biology as well, we could represent intercourse
> and sleep simultaneously as the expulsion of actual disturbance-
> stimuli and as expressions of the tendency to reproduce the
> situation—apparently long since overcome—of existence in the
> womb and in sea water. Indeed, in this we were able to surmise
> the recurrence of much more archaic and primitive tendencies of
> repose (the drive to the inorganic, the death drive). In a similar
> way, the bioanalytic investigation of all life processes would have to
> look beneath the manifest superficies and uncover the *biological
> unconscious*. It would reveal that all the futile questions concerning
> the meaning and the goal of development would be automatically
> transformed into questions of *motive forces*, and all of these would
> be rooted in the past.

2:391/84–5

If forwards we will not want to look, as though toward our impending death, the look back will not assuage us. For death is where we always already will have been, at least as far as our "development" is concerned. As we will see, Nietzsche has an inkling of this. And if, as some thinkers have averred, *being* has meaning only on the horizon of *time*, Ferenczi's asseverations concerning time have fundamental ontological import. Bioanalysis is all about the meaning of being, *der Sinn von Sein*.

Ferenczi now turns to one of the oddest of his examples, yet one of the most far-reaching. If we take the nourishment of the suckling infant as an instance for bioanalysis, we have to conclude that the infant's first source of nurture is the mother's body—or if that sounds too cannibalistic, then let us speak of the elements of tissue or the complex molecules that are suspended in mother's milk. Analogous to the parasitism of the genital and the embryonic, the neophyte human being's nourishment, "based on the mother's milk and on other animal products," is parasitic from beginning to end (ibid.). The human being thus ingests the bodies of its human and animal ancestors. Pursuing this line of thought, the bioanalyst will conclude that such ingestion of ancestors, or *Phylophagie*, characterizes everything that lives. Even the offspring of vegetarians and vegans imbibe elements of their mother's flesh. "In nurture by mother's milk, as the bioanalyst conceives of it, the entire species-history of nurture lies in some way concealed and yet at the same time portrayed in an almost unrecognizable form" (2:392). Likewise, the bioanalyst would see in the infant's or anyone's vomiting a reinstantiation of the *Urmund*, the "primal mouth" of the fetus or of some earlier animal form, where peristalsis and antiperistalsis are equal partners.

Similarly, the body's way of responding to infection—a theme to which Ferenczi returns several times in his book, repeating Schelling's fascination with the question of illness—represents the infected tissue's regression to something like an embryonic state, surrounding the irritant with fluid and, in some cases, with a cyst-like container. Both the disintegration of tissue and the healing process may therefore be viewed as "regressive tendencies" that have a progressive outcome (ibid.). Related to this is the fact that an organ's proper function, its utility, depends on the satisfaction of the libido of the entire organism. If such libido is lacking, the affected organ will take its own pleasure—to the detriment of its host. A perhaps more convincing instance of bioanalysis involves the sudden loss of consciousness. Whereas the physician describes a person's fainting and collapsing to the floor in terms of an anemia in the brain due to a sudden collapse in blood pressure, the bioanalyst will refer to the regression of blood pressure to the age when animals walked on four rather than two feet and thus were more intimate with the floor of the Earth.

In all this, the bioanalyst will take his or her clues from the symptoms of neurosis and psychosis, applying the symbols that arise in the analysis of those symptoms to phylogenetic history. For symbols are now a source of insight for the natural sciences, which no longer need to be guided exclusively by the thought of use-function. As helpful as the one-sided standpoint of utility has been, and it is the standpoint that has dominated all natural science, and especially disciplines (or practices) such as technology, which are based on the machine model of all utility, that standpoint has also greatly hindered access to the more profound insights of bioanalysis. For its part, bioanalysis is an extension of the general methodological move in psychoanalysis from a descriptive-economic standpoint (which Ferenczi also calls the *ontological*, confusing that word perhaps with *ontogenetic*) to a historico-phylogenetic account (2:351/38–9).

Ferenczi tries now to summarize the principal insights of bioanalysis. His research began with the idea that genital development could have ensued only with catastrophe or calamity, that is, with some dire force impinging from the outside and challenging the life of extant (marine) organisms. The pre-genital, pre-sexual organism would have had to alter its mode of life in a fundamental way. Such a catastrophe, the fourth in the Table but perhaps at the heart of all five, could only be desiccation, resulting from the drying up of a sea or pond or river—although the drying up of the sea Ferenczi at one point calls one of the more "recent" geological catastrophes (2:394/88). To repeat, not Noah's flood, nor the flood recounted in the epic of Gilgamesh, but the emergence of the land on which hominids will one day rise and walk is the calamity. If in the beginning only the stillness of the deep prevails, with spirits hovering over the waters, the emergence of land may be beneficial to what will later be called land animals, yet it means the demise of many forms of life, indeed, the original forms, which, as all agree, are aquatic. Yet the death of many, perhaps most, is also the challenge accepted by some forms of life to adapt, to improvise, to survive at all costs. These creatures did adapt, says Ferenczi, but he then adds an astonishing proviso: "but they did so with the ulterior motive [or hidden agenda or surreptitious intention, *mit dem Hintergedanken*] of restoring the opportunity to return once again, as soon as possible and as often as possible, to the old situation" (ibid.). Like every *émigré*, life pines for the Old Country.

The blatant animism and even prosopopoeia of this *Hintergedanke* is not lessened by the fact that the word is difficult to render in English. "Suppressed thought," one might say, even though such a "thought" is often as treacherous as the phrase "ulterior motives" would suggest. Are the amphibians disingenuous? Or is there some "thought" that one's destiny is written in the old books, the books kept on reserve in the archival grottoes of the sea? Ferenczi is sometimes apologetic for his tendency to personify, as he does here so shamelessly, but he would say that it is only a kind of *Nachträglichkeit* that guides his pen, the "deferred action" or the impact "after the fact" of bioanalytical thinking on every aspect of human life, including thought. We may smile at the proto-amphibian's secret desire to develop gills again and to return to the good life, but bioanalysis will cause our smile to blanch in the light of revelations concerning our own phylogenetic past, which make of the good life a search for the repose of death.

And yet. Ferenczi now introduces an important counterforce or inhibiting factor to phylogenetic regression. The desire to restore the repose of an older state may meet a *biological censorship*, one that resists the regressive tug toward the past by modifying the pleasure principle in the direction of ego interests, here the interest of bare survival, an interest expressed by what Freud calls the "reality probe" or even the "reality principle." Ferenczi's example here is the polar bear in hibernation: if the body temperature of the bear reaches a life-threatening low, the bear will not regress to the point where sleep induces death by hypothermia; the bear will stir, will awaken, making of the "bone marrow animal a brain animal once again" (2:395n. 6/ 89n. 2). The upshot is that the death drive does not prevail without resistance, without inhibition, without a censor. True, every external shock can augment the tendency to autotomy, and the elements of the organism, as Ferenczi wryly comments, "will not want to leave unused the opportunity to die that has been offered them" (2:395/89).

However, Ferenczi also recalls, without citing it, Freud's insistence that the destruction-and-death drives do not compel the organism to accept just any proffered death. It is as though Freud is thinking of the Heidegger he never read, for he emphasizes that one must die one's "own" death, the death that is "immanent" or in some way "inherent" in and "proper" to the individual's life. Freud appeals to the words *eigenen* and *immanenten* in order to state the paradox of a death drive that meets a certain—often very violent—resistance. What must be identified is "the organism's very own path to death," so that, as a corollary, "other possibilities of the return to the inorganic than the immanent one are to be held at a distance" (GW 13:41). In "The Decline of the Oedipus Complex," Freud suggests that the decline of this Complex, while rooted in the experience and the development of the individual, also has a phylogenetic or "inherited," "pre-programmed" component, and this component occasions the following very strange remark on death: "Even the entire individual is already at birth certain to die, and the disposition of his or her organs [*seine Organanlage*] perhaps already contains the clue as to whence this death will come. Yet it remains interesting to follow how this inherited program is carried out, and in what way the disposition will take advantage of accidental liabilities [*zufällige Schädlichkeiten ... ausnützen*]" (GW 13:396). In other words, the destruction-and-death drives work from within, accepting at least a modicum of Kant's "purposiveness," and they spurn the merely extrinsic accident. Accidental deaths cheat not only Eros but also Thanatos, which, like the sea, "will have its way."

In other words, the sea is not irresistible undertow alone. Sometimes its "way" is what we call *living on*. The inherited program of thalassic regression can be frustrated, at least for a time. Ferenczi refers to experiments with sea urchins in a very deteriorated state, near death; the urchins slough off necrotic tissue and, in some undisclosed manner, employ their own sloughings in order to regenerate. It turns out that when one looks forwards and backwards on the scene of life one sees not only catastrophe but also the successful averting of catastrophe—life on the upswing, if only for the time being. Ferenczi comments:

> The question of the philosophers as to how we are to represent to ourselves such regeneration and continued development can be answered without an appeal to mystical notions. It may be that the "altruism" expressed therein is but the skillful combination of rudimentary egoisms; but it is also quite possible that the degree

of complication that has already been reached has an impact on, or at least contributes to, the products of decay—in the sense of a regression. It may well be that the organisms are not in such a hurry to die, so that out of their own detritus they rebuild themselves, such that the *vis a tergo* [the force that comes from behind], which preserved them in their partial destruction, can be used for further development.

However that may be, the bioanalytical conception of developmental processes sees everywhere only *wishes* for *the restoration of earlier life—or death—states.*

2:395–6/90

Once again, the astonishing personification: the sea urchins, or the rudimentary elements at work within them, *wish* or *will* to postpone their demise, so that the products of the regressive tug will be employed successfully—or will be resisted by a life force that propels from behind instead of pulling the organism back—to adapt to the new catastrophic situation. And yet, once again, every wish, whether it "knows" it or not, tends to restore the earlier state, ultimately the inorganic or anorganic state. If Ferenczi's bioanalysis is a dialectic in Hegel's sense, then the new third object, beyond thesis and antithesis, the object that guarantees the *advance* of a synthesizing dialectic, is the one that lies *behind*; it is the object we have already passed through and negated. For every x, $x = x - 1$. Not so much one step back, two steps forward, as two steps back, one step back forward. It is difficult to say whether the strategy of lifedeath is revolutionary, evolutionary, or devolutionary. It is difficult to decide anything about the pre-programmed program of thalassic lifedeath, difficult to decide anything about the supplement.

That said, Ferenczi now advances toward his most radical claims on behalf of bioanalysis, claims that may not be meta-physical but are surely ontological. "Bioanalysis, the analytical science of life, will not be able to elude the task of taking a position with regard to the question of the beginning and the end of life" (2:398/93). Any attempt at a theory of genitality must push beyond the borders of life, seeking its basis in the chemical and physical forces of attraction and repulsion, attraction and unification—much in the way of Plato's Eros, to which Freud and Ferenczi both refer. Ferenczi is confident that he can say, in the name of modern physics, that the intense attraction among the ions in the outer shells of atoms can be called "lively," and not merely by way of metaphor. Absolute repose does not exist in inorganic nature, and Ferenczi is uncertain as to whether even the second law of thermodynamics will disperse the energies of the universe. Such a law is too much on the side of "accident," and no good Lamarckian, even a chastised one, can accept its consequences.

Ferenczi adds a footnote on some medical ideas that harken back to the theories of the Scotsman John Brown, ideas espoused by Novalis, Schelling, and many others at the end of the eighteenth century.[3] If one can accept that even in inorganic matter there is a prototype of "excitability," *Erregbarkeit*, then one can bridge the gap between the living and the nonliving. The bare minimum one can say is that the union of two elements of matter presents a smaller surface area to potentially hazardous forces from the outside world. Something similar could be said of the couple in sexual intercourse, *l'animal à deux dos*, and Ferenczi again cites Wilhelm Bölsche, who is ready to describe even the attraction of moon and sun in sexual terms. As a Lamarckian, Ferenczi emphasizes that a perfect isolation of or separation between "life" and "death," as between the life and death drives, is impossible, so that even in "dead" matter certain "seeds of life" will be found. Such *"Lebenskeime"* indicate "a regressive tendency

---

[3] See my treatment of John Brown in *Contagion*, especially at 48–9, but also throughout.

that pulls in the direction of those higher complications whose corruption produced the seeds" (2:399/94). This hopscotching forward and back or up and down must give us pause.

Astonishingly, the thalassic regressive tug is now being employed to drag moribund matter back into life, if only by way of "life germs." The sciences have long since demonstrated that there is no form of life that is unmixed with death, and Freud's *Beyond the Pleasure Principle* underscores this. True, in Freud's speculation death is powerful. It is powerful especially if life seeks the absolute minimum of energy exchange—that is to say, if Fechnerian constancy equals zero, as it certainly does on certain days of the week.[4] Ferenczi cites Freud's famous Monday morning pronouncement, "*'The goal of all life is death,'* for '*the lifeless was there before the living*'" (ibid., citing GW 13:40). Ferenczi's next sentence, however, begins with the words, *Wie denn aber wenn,* "But how would it be if. . . ." This is very close to the expression that opens Ferenczi's entire meditation on the fish and on life in the sea: *Wie denn, dachten wir uns, wenn.* . . . It is clear that the axis of Freud's doctrine of the destruction-and-death drives is about to be tilted, and it will take a powerful authority to justify such an improvident flick of the finger on a Friday afternoon. "But how would it be if 'dying' were not an absolute, if seeds of life and regressive tendencies lay hidden also in the inorganic, or if, furthermore, Nietzsche is right when he says, '*All inorganic matter originates from the organic; it is dead organic matter. Corpse and human being* [Leichnam und Mensch]'" (2:399/94).

Nietzsche's note, which has the Mette-number 23[34], comes from the winter of 1872–3 (KSW 7:554). During that winter Nietzsche is

---

[4] On Fechnerian constancy and the question as to whether it *must* equal zero excitation, see my discussion of Jean Laplanche's *Life and Death in Psychoanalysis* in note 11 of chapter 5 in Krell, *The Cudgel and the Caress,* forthcoming from SUNY Press.

12 *Layer upon layer of multi-colored ash on the west coast of Thira.*

writing *Philosophy in the Tragic Age of the Greeks*, a work he intends to be his next publication, the one to follow *The Birth of Tragedy from the Spirit of Music*. The note appears among other jottings under the general heading "Empedocles," indicating the Agrigentian philosopher whose grand "sphere" appears to be a *living whole* caught up in struggles of love and hate, struggles that have as their goal the reunification of the whole through love. The note is written four or five years after the period in which Nietzsche is considering pursuing a second doctorate, this time in philosophy, with a dissertation on "the concept of the organic since Kant" (KSB 2:269). A whole range of notes from this time, but also from later periods, ought to receive our attention here. But for the moment we need only observe how powerful this Nietzschean authority is for Ferenczi, who italicizes Nietzsche's note in his text. For would not the very thesis of Ferenczi's book—and the very thesis of Freud's *Beyond*—be made to stand on their heads if death may be said to *regress* to life? What would such an inversion imply concerning the sea, which both drowns and spawns? What would it mean for the very notion of coenogenesis, specifically, for the enigmatic development of the amnion and its fluid? And what would its consequences be for the thalassic regressive undertow, which now becomes more like the oncoming and eternally recurring wave of life? What happens to the very notion of "beginning and end" if, Eliot-like, my end is my beginning—if indeed, as Nietzsche also says, being is the eternal recurrence of the same?

Ferenczi writes, in response to his own "But how would it be if," the following revision of all teleological thinking: "Then we would finally have to drop the question concerning the beginning and the end of life, representing to ourselves the entirety of the inorganic and organic world as a constant to-and-fro tidal flow between the will to life and the will to death [*als ein stetes Hin- und Herwogen zwischen Leben- und Sterbenwollen*], a flow that never submits to a solitary rule, neither of life nor of death" (2:399/94–5). We may feel that Ferenczi himself is reduced here to a stutter and a stammer, if not of the genitofugal sort then certainly of the conceptual sort: it is as though the oppositional pairs that dominate his entire *Attempt* have become entirely problematic. For it seems that the thoroughgoing *amphimixis* of anal and urethral pleasures, of pleasure and unpleasure, of drive and tug, of expansion and contraction, of ontogeny and phylogeny, and even of Eros and Thanatos cannot but cause all the oppositional elements to tremble and perhaps even to crumble. These opposites now so mutually invade and contaminate one another that they suffer the original catastrophe of consonants that never find a vowel or vowels that never occlude in a consonant—Rousseau's nightmare of a language that remains mute. It is the ongoing nightmare of radical undecidability.[5]

This would have been the perfect place for Ferenczi to end the chapter and the book. Yet, perhaps fearful of the upward flight he has taken, with the death drive rising now on the afflatus of some sort of life drive, he remembers the gravity of his own life as a physician. He concludes his book with remarks on *agony*, the death struggle that yields to a peaceful death only in the rarest of cases. It seems as though "in reality life always has to end catastrophically" (ibid./90). The smile on the face of the fresh cadaver appears only when the struggle is over. And yet the catastrophe of death bends back to the catastrophe of birth, which is where death and life once again engage in their ringdance. The catastrophe of the corpse even reminds us that death

---

[5] It is fair to say that the trembling of the distinction between the organic and inorganic begins long before Nietzsche. Merleau-Ponty, in his lectures on nature at the Collège de France in the mid-to-late 1950s, realized that *Schelling*, following the insights of Leibniz, denied any *essential* distinction between the organic and the inorganic. See Merleau-Ponty, N 41. Such undecidability characterizes Schelling's thought in its entirety, from his treatises on nature in the 1790s, through his essay on human freedom in 1809 and his *Ages of the World* (1811–15), to his 1842 *Philosophy of Mythology*, this last to be discussed later in chapter 5.

is often associated with genital excitation, and not only in the hanged criminal. It may be, if the dying one accepts death in the final moments of life, that a kind of satisfaction and peace may be attained, as though after orgasm. It may be that the big death will coalesce with the last little death. And the regression may go even farther. In many cultures the corpse is buried in the fetal position, and sometimes it is placed in a giant protective urn, or *pithos*, which is an earthenware chorion. All that is missing for the fetus-like corpse, crouched in its protective stoneware container, is the amnion and its modified sea water that might restore and sustain the defunct. For a time.

It is not that, following Nietzsche, or rather Schopenhauer, the agonizing Ferenczi winds up with a pessimistic view of life and its chances. It is that, following Nietzsche as well as Freud, he winds up with what Nietzsche calls *tragic affirmation*. This would be not only the Nietzsche who reflects on the organic and the inorganic but also the Nietzsche who thinks life as will to power.

Yet are not the destruction-and-death drives, as thought by both Freud and Ferenczi, something like a will to powerlessness? Are they not a will to impotence, which is Nietzsche's definition of passive nihilism? If the prevailing force of life is regressive, a pulling back to the inorganic state that precedes life, can we think such a force as will to power? Is it not difficult to conceive of the earliest denizens of the sea in terms of will to power, if all of them—one-celled plants and animals, bacteria and archaea, chronista and kelp, phytoplankton, zooplankton, krill, and all the rest—are driven by the wish to resist every force but the regressive one, like the sleeper who resists the first light of morning and rolls deeper into his featherbed? Hegel's objection to fish, as we will soon hear, is that they eventually melt back into the element of the salt sea. Is such melting an instance of power? It would take a revolution in our thinking to be able to affirm it. Precisely that revolution is what Nietzsche means by tragic affirmation.

From the time of his study of Greek festivals on through the writing
of *Thus Spoke Zarathustra*, Nietzsche develops the thought that one
must not merely accept death grudgingly but learn to celebrate it. He
imagines that there could be festivals that celebrate human sexuality
and dying in other ways than sentimental kitsch and lugubrious
wake. "This should go so far that the supreme festivals for humankind
would be sexual reproduction and death!" (KSW 10:202; cf. 10:136).
His plans in the early 1870s for an Empedocles drama and in the
mid-1880s for a drama that would culminate in Zarathustra's death
and wake are among the most remarkable fragments in his literary
corpus.[6] One such plan, which makes clear the connection between
festivals and Nietzsche's principal thought, the eternal recurrence of
the same, begins this way: "**Decisive moment**: Zarathustra asks the
entire crowd at the festival, 'Would you have all this once again?'
Everyone shouts, '**Yes!**' *Hearing this, he dies from joy*" (KSW 10:599).
For Nietzsche, it is clear, such a festival would be empowering—it
would itself be the highest expression of will to power—even as it
celebrates both the little and the larger deaths. For *willing* the eternal
recurrence of the same is not the same as *believing* that it can prevail.

In the previous chapter we heard Ferenczi invoking such festivals
as *Erinnerungsfeste*, anniversaries or "festivals of memory." Sexual
intercourse was his prime example. Sexual acts would not be
memorials in the usual sense; they would not be solemn or lugubrious,
wreathed in crepe. Whether or not he has this thought from Nietzsche
I do not know, although he clearly is familiar with Nietzsche's work,
including the unpublished fragments. Perhaps he remembers that
"festival of peace" celebrated at the end of the Homunculus scene and
the entire *Klassische Walpürgisnacht* of Goethe's *Faust II*, a work

---

[6] Much of this material can be found, in German and in English, in Krell, *Postponements:
Woman, Sexuality, and Death in Nietzsche* (Bloomington and London: Indiana University
Press, 1986), passim.

Ferenczi knew and loved. Be that as it may, it is certain that the thought of festivals has importance for him not only theoretically but also therapeutically. In an article that aims to contribute to "therapeutic technique," written a year after his venture in bioanalysis, in the course of a discussion about whether sexual abstinence on the part of the analysand need be a part of therapy, Ferenczi writes: "The act of intercourse, after all, should be essentially neither an act of will nor a customary performance but rather a festival, as it were, in which energies that heretofore have been restrained can revel in their archaic form," *bei dem sich bisher zurückgehaltene Energien in archaischer Form austoben können* (2:161). As though such festivals were *Lebenskeime*, seeds of life.

Nietzsche too, as we have only now heard, dreams of festivals that some day may celebrate death as one celebrates a birth and a wedding. In his case such a hymeneal dream arises from his experiences as a careful reader of the Greeks—above all, the Greek philosophers of "the tragic age," to whom we will now turn.

At the end of our reading of Ferenczi's book a memory may suddenly blossom of Stanley Kubrick's astral fetus slowly turning toward us at the very end of his *Space Odyssey*, either to pose or to dispel the question of the origin and end of life. We see in the face of the star-fetus the features of Dave Bowman, the surviving astronaut, the character who has only now eaten his supper, drastically aged, taken to his bed, and died. The astronaut now becomes an amniaut. We are so mesmerized by those bulging, searching, scintillating fetal eyes that we fail to pay much attention to the surrounding amniotic fluid that will protect and nurture the fetus up to the happy catastrophe of its birth.

13 *"The first of fire's turnings." Three hundred meters above the sea near Mouzaki.*

4

Full of Gods

The first of fire's turnings is the sea.
HERACLITUS OF EPHESUS (DK B31)

At one time I became boy and girl both, and both
Bush and bird, and wayfarer fish leaping o'er the sea.
EMPEDOCLES OF ACRAGAS (DK B117)

The story always begins with Thales. Thales on water and gods—infinitely promising for an encounter with the sea. Aristotle, in his *Metaphysics*, tells us: "Most of the first philosophers thought that matter gave us the sole principles of all things. . . . Thales, the founder of this kind of philosophy, says that the material principle is water [ὕδωρ]" (A3, 983b6). In *On the Soul*, Aristotle says, "Thales also said that all things are full of gods [πάντα πλήρη θεῶν εἶναι]" (A5, 411a7). Yet Thales' water is not yet *sea* water. Surprisingly, the first Diels-Kranz listing for the word θάλασσα refers not to Thales but to Heraclitus of Ephesus, Heraclitus "the Obscure." Heraclitus is obscure perhaps because he always dives to depths where no light penetrates. After considering two fragments attributed to Heraclitus, I will turn, by way of Xenophanes of Colophon, to Thales and Anaximander, both of the coastal city of Miletus, and finally to the incomparable Empedocles of

Acragas. Empedocles, who swims like a fish, a sort of flying fish, leaps out of the western Sicilian sea into eternity.

Fragment B31 of Heraclitus, in rough translation, reads: "Fire's turnings: first of all, sea [πυρὸς τροπαὶ πρῶτον θάλασσα]; and of the sea half is earth, half squall [πρηστήρ]. . . . Earth disperses as sea, and the sea retains the same lay [τὸν αὐτὸν λόγον], the lay it had before it became earth." *Lay* here tries to translate the measure or proportion by which the *allotment* to beings occurs, the allotment granted by the *Logos* itself. The word πρηστήρ, here rendered as *squall*, means a storm at sea, a storm with much lightning—perhaps the very lightning bolt, as "ever-living fire," that "steers all things" (DK B30, B64). It is perhaps the fire that Melville describes in unforgettable fashion in "The Candles," chapter 119 of *Moby-Dick*. He explains that each mast of the *Pequod* is protected by a lightning-rod in trident form, upon which, during a storm at sea, a ball of fire sometimes appears—a "corpusant" (from *corpus sancti, corpo santo*) or "St. Elmo's fire":

> Towards evening of that day, the Pequod was torn of her canvas, and bare-poled was left to fight a Typhoon which had struck her directly ahead. When darkness came on, sky and sea roared and split with the thunder, and blazed with the lightning, that showed the disabled masts fluttering here and there with the rags which the first fury of the tempest had left for its after sport. . . .
>
> "Look aloft!" cried Starbuck. "The corpusants! the corpusants!"
>
> All the yard-arms were tipped with a pallid fire; and touched at each tri-pointed lightning-rod-end with three tapering white flames, each of the three tall masts was silently burning in that sulphurous air, like three gigantic wax tapers before an altar.
>
> MD 505

Whereas the crew remain rapt to the portent in awful silence, Ahab is defiant: "Oh, thou clear spirit, of thy fire thou madest me, and like a true child of fire, I breathe it back to thee" (MD 507). Sensing, however, that his own genealogy—especially on his mother's side—is in some way vulnerable, somehow wounded, he sees in the spirit of fire an "incommunicable riddle," some "unparticipated grief," and it is this grieving deity that Ahab worships: "I leap with thee; I burn with thee; would fain be welded with thee; defyingly I worship thee" (MD 508). But to return to the Ionian shore of Ephesus and a time long before the *Pequod* ever sailed.

All things are in exchange with fire; fire is their cosmic legal tender, as it were (DK B90). And yet the sea is the first of fire's tropisms. Why? Perhaps because the sea is fed by rain, not only directly by squalls and gales but also by all the streams that are fed by rainfall on the land, and rainfall comes from the sky, which is the "region" of lightning (KRS 199); in other words, because it is the sea that feeds the clouds that feed the rain that feeds the streams that flow to the sea, the sea is first among tropes. Sea, storm at sea, cloud, rainfall, and earth are engaged in an ever-changing yet ever-constant cyclical or periodic tropism fired by the sun, and the paradox of continuous change or an ever-altering continuity always seems to grip Heraclitus. He even seems to have thought that the exhalations of the sea make their way to the tipped bowls of aither that are the stars, there to burn like oil lamps— or candles, or corpusants—through the night (KRS 201). We leave Heraclitus now, reluctantly, and we leave him no doubt in the vicinity of the Artemision, where a very early form of the goddess Artemis is worshiped.

Xenophanes of Colophon had already indicated the importance of this cycle or exchange of sea, sky, and earth. Above all, we living beings and all things else are the progeny of the cycle: "All things that come to be and come to light [γίνοντ᾽ ἠδὲ φύονται] are earth and water," inasmuch as "we all came forth from [ἐκγενόμεσθα] earth and water" (DK B29, 33). Of the sea Xenophanes says, "Sea is the source of water, and the source of wind; for neither [would there be the force of wind blowing forth from] within clouds if there were no great expanse of brine [ἄνευ πόντου], nor flooding river nor rainshowers from the upper air: but the great salt expanse [again πόντος] is the begetter of clouds and winds and rivers" (DK B30; KRS 176). Already Homer had sung the sea as the source of clouds, rain, and rivers; and Anaximander too, as we shall see, clearly understood the vast circulation of the waters. Yet Xenophanes now speaks of the earth itself as having emerged from the sea. Hippolytus reports:

> [5] Xenophanes believes that earth and sea mix with one another, and that over time earth dissolves in the moist. He says that he has the following proofs: seashells are found inland and even in the mountains; he says that in the quarries of Syracuse impressions of fish and seaweed have been found, and that on Paros an impression of a bay leaf was located deep within a rock, and in Malta flat shapes of all sorts of marine life. [6] These, he says, were produced when long ago everything was covered with mud and the impressions dried there. All humankind is destroyed whenever the earth is swept down into the sea and becomes mud; then there is a new beginning of all that comes to be, and every new world begins by way of this reversal [καὶ ταύτην πᾶσι τοῖς κόσμοις γίνεσθαι μεταβολήν].
>
> DK A33:5–6; KRS 176–7

The catastrophe, for Xenophanes, alternates between desiccation and landslide into the sea; Ararat rising out of the sea, but also the sea's subversion of the mountain. Perhaps it is wrong to speak of catastrophe at all: his word is neither καταστροφή nor καταβολή but μεταβολή. The "inversion" of sea and land, the "reversal" of fortunes for sea creatures and land creatures such as ourselves, are part of an ongoing cycle. Thus it is not merely "the deduction based upon fossils" that is "a remarkable and impressive one" (KRS 177); one is also struck by the combination of astute observation, a sense of the antiquity of earth and sea, and imaginative speculation on the history of humankind as one of reversals and new beginnings. It is the same combination of thoughts that occurs to today's visitors to the Archaeological Museum of Thira, where the very first exhibit displays fossils (of olive leaves, palm branches, and insects) from some of the oldest strata of Santorini. Indeed, the interaction of earth and sea, and the fatality and promise of such interaction for life, is one of the oldest ideas, certainly as old as Thales.

Thales of Miletus, one of the traditional "seven sages," is said to have flourished early in the tragic age of the Greeks, as early as the beginning of the sixth century BCE. Tradition says that he was descended from the Cadmians of Boeotian Thebes and Lemnos, and that he was therefore of Phoenician ancestry. This may simply be a surmise based on his use of Babylonian star tables, but it could easily be that Thales was of mixed ancestry: in Ionian Greece intermarriage among Greeks and the sundry inhabitants of Anatolia was quite common, so that the early Greek thinkers—like Greek philosophy itself—remain indebted to the peoples and the wisdom of the Near East. Thales is said to have visited both Sardis and Naucratis, Egypt, the latter a Milesian colony, and to have mastered the astronomical and engineering skills of these places. Particularly notable for a meditation on the sea is Thales' discovery of the importance of Ursa minor for maritime navigation, as well as his learning how to estimate the distance from the shore of ships at sea (KRS 84–5). However, his purported authorship of books on the equinoxes and solstices, as well as of a *Nautical Star-Guide*, was disputed even in antiquity, and what we know about his teachings is but reported hearsay.

The most famous anecdote concerning him appears in Plato's *Theaetetus* (174a), which relates that while Thales was star-gazing he fell down a well; a young Thracian servant girl who was passing by remarked that whereas Thales endeavored to know all about the heavens "what was at his feet remained concealed to him." Plato notes that the young woman was both intelligent and beautiful, ἐμμελὴς καὶ χαρίεσσα, and for this reason male philosophers have never forgiven her. Heidegger, for example, remarks somewhere that girls always have to have someone to laugh at. Neither he nor anyone else bothers to note that the servant girl merely confirms what Socrates has been telling Theodorus midway through their dialogue with young Theaetetus, namely, that philosophers are famous for ignoring what everyone else "knows," ignoring it so thoroughly that they are as innocent of common know-how as they are of "the grains of sand on the seashore" (173d–e). And the biggest joke of all is that the philosopher "does not even know that he does not know" (ibid.), which is a joke only Socrates gets. Yet Socrates is able to teach the knowledge of one's own ignorance to young Theaetetus. For at the very end of the dialogue, which fails to give us knowledge about what knowledge is, Socrates confesses that he has been practicing his mother's midwifery on Theaetetus, hoping to help deliver a well-formed idea; the young man in turn confesses that he has produced only wind eggs, and that he is empty of ideas. What knowledge can be remains concealed from him. Socrates comforts him by saying that at least the young man does not think he knows what he does not know, so that he will be less burdensome to his companions, less likely to be an obnoxious mister know-it-all (210b–c). Socrates promises to meet up with Theaetetus—who, however, will soon be wounded in a battle and will contract diphtheria—so that they may try again on the following day. At the moment, however, Socrates has to go to court to answer the charges brought against him.

Now, Socrates and Plato have nothing against Thales, even at the bottom of a well, but only an admiring memory of the traditions and tales concerning him. I imagine that if one of Plato's pupils at the

Academy asked him why he had mocked the astronomer, Plato would have denied that he was mocking at all; he would have replied that he always leaves mockery to the citizens of Athens, who have mastered the art. Perhaps he would have wondered aloud whether that witty and charming girl offered to help old Thales out of the well. Surely, she must have. Surely, she was not only lovely and clever but also kind. But Thales would have demurred and said, "You know, from down here I can see the stars even during daylight—it doesn't really matter that my feet are wet—water is everything, you know." That would have been a happier end to the story than diphtheria and hemlock.[1]

But now to two passages in Aristotle's writings that refer to Thales. They are our most important testimonies. True, since Harold Cherniss wrote we have learned to doubt much of what they say, and much of what they say is what others have said, hearsay upon hearsay.[2] At all events, here is Aristotle on Thales:

> Others say that the earth rests on water [ἐφ᾽ ὕδατος]. For this is the most ancient account we have received, which they say was given

[1] I owe a special debt to John Sallis, whose *Being and Logos: The Way of Platonic Dialogue* (Pittsburgh: Duquesne University Press, 1975), along with the lecture courses that preceded the book, opened up for me (and for countless others) a way to take the Platonic dialogues both more seriously and more adventurously than they are usually taken. *Being and Logos* was published in a second edition by Humanities Press in 1986 and in a third (the current) edition by Indiana University Press in 1996. John Sallis also introduced me to the pre-Platonic thinkers, sponsoring a reading course for me on the occasion of my first trip to Greece in the summer of 1968. My little fantasy regarding Thales at the bottom of the well— and it is Schleiermacher who insists that it is a well, *ein Brunnen*, rather than a ditch—is therefore dedicated to him.

[2] Harold F. Cherniss, *Aristotle's Criticism of Presocratic Philosophy* (New York: Octagon Books, 1964 [originally published in 1935]). Cherniss writes: "He was 'nearer' to them than we are, . . . but nearer in time does not mean nearer in spirit, and it can be shown that Aristotle was so consumed with the ideology of Platonism and the new concepts he had himself discovered or developed that it was impossible for him to imagine a time when thinking men did not see the problems of philosophy in the same terms as did he" (x). He adds: "Aristotle's belief that all previous theories were stammering attempts to express his own aids him in interpreting those theories out of all resemblance to their original form" (xii).

by Thales the Milesian, and that the earth stays in place by floating like a log or some other such thing (for none of these rests by nature on air, but on water)—as though the same argument did not apply to the water supporting the earth as to the earth itself.

On the Heavens, B13, 294a28; KRS 88–9

Most of the first philosophers thought that matter gave us the sole principles of all things [τὰς ἐν ὕλης εἴδει μόνας ᾠήθησαν ἀρχὰς εἶναι πάντων]; for the original source of all existing things, that from which a thing first comes into being and into which it is finally destroyed, the substance persisting [οὐσίας ὑπομενούσης] but changing in its qualities, this they declare is the element and first principle of existing things [στοιχεῖον καὶ ταύτην ἀρχήν ... τῶν ὄντων], and for this reason they consider that there is no absolute coming to be or passing away, on the ground that such a nature is always preserved ... for there must be some nature [τινα φύσιν], either one or more than one, from which the other things come into being, while it is preserved. Over the number, however, and the form of this kind of principle they do not all agree; but Thales, the founder of this type of philosophy, says that it is water (and therefore he declared that the earth is on water), perhaps taking this supposition from seeing the nurture of all things to be moist [τὴν τροφὴν ὑγρὰν οὖσαν], and the warm itself coming to be from this and living by this (that from which they come to be being the principle of all things)—taking the supposition both from this and from the seeds [τὰ σπέρματα] of all things having a moist nature, water being the natural principle of moist things.

Metaphysics, A3, 983b6; KRS 88–9

Almost all the critical commentary that we have on these two passages, which are the most important passages for any interpretation of Thales, devotes its energies to stripping away from Aristotle's account all the Aristotelianisms and Scholasticisms—principle, material cause, original source, substance, substrate, element, nature— so that in the end only two words survive: the core of Thales' peeled onion consists of water and moisture. The usual debate surrounding water and the moist asks whether Thales means that earth is afloat on water—presumably the sea, although none of the words for sea have appeared here—or whether he intends to say that all things, whatever their appearances, originate from water and have water as their main ingredient. Things such as the human body, for example. We may take it that one of the seven sages of Greece did not think of the earth as a log adrift on the tide. Yet the relation of land and water is an ancient quandary. We catastrophists might think of the stories of the flood— not the fruitful flooding of the Nile but the destructive inundation of the earth as related in the eleventh tablet of the Sumerian epic of Gilgamesh.

Utnapishtim the Faraway tells Gilgamesh that Enlil, angered by the clamor arising from human beings, decides to destroy humankind by sending a flood. Utnapishtim is instructed by a friendly deity, a sort of Promethean helpmate to humanity, to build a ship in order to rescue himself and his kin, his servants, and every kind of animal and seed of plant he can find. While the sky gods send rain and the storm god storms, the underworld Anunnaki torch the earth, which "cracks like a cup" (EG 110). The gods themselves are terrified and flee to the heights, while Ishtar, the sweet-voiced Queen of Heaven, screams as though she were in labor: "Alas, the days of old are turned to dust because I commanded evil; why did I command this evil in the council of the gods? I commanded wars to destroy the people, but are they not my people, for I brought them forth? Now like the spawn of fish they float in the ocean" (ibid.). Utnapishtim's ark drifts for days, until finally it runs aground on the submerged tip of Mount Nissir (in today's Kurdistan). Utnapishtim releases a dove, which soon returns, unable to find a resting place. He then releases a swallow, which also returns. Finally, he releases a raven, which does not return, having found land and much to scavenge. Utnapishtim is thereupon welcomed into the assemblage of the gods.

Whether the mountain is called Ararat or Nissir, the land is clearly seen as the home and hope of humankind. The drying up of the seas after they have overflowed their bounds is therefore not a catastrophe but the anastrophe of a few surviving clans. Perhaps it is clear to Thales that water—in all its places and it all its transformations into liquidity and moisture—is of the essence even and precisely when it oversteps its bounds? Certainly this was clear to the Queen of Heaven. She sees the corpses of the drowned floating on the floodwaters like the spawn of fish, the fish that they, her people, once were, in her belly. Anaximander will soon say that the circulation of water and earth is all a matter of timing and of time itself.

There is another old story from Babylon about earth and water. The hero Marduk is said to have slain the monster Tiamat, whose two halves become sky and earth. (How and where Marduk gets a foothold so that he can wield his sword is of course a problem—it is what caused F. M. Cornford to postulate that every creation myth has to be told a second time, doubled and redoubled, in order to explain the action of the first telling.) In any case, sky and earth. Yet Tiamat is not so much earth as sea, salt water, while Apsu represents the sweet water of rain from the sky and all underground sources. "In the story of Eridu (seventh century BCE in its youngest extant version), in the beginning 'all land was sea'; then Marduk built a raft on the surface of the water, and on the raft a reed-hut which became the earth" (KRS 92). Kirk, Raven, and Schofield speculate that Tiamat may be the Old Testament Leviathan: in Psalms (136:6), "Yahweh stretched out the earth above the waters," "founded the land upon the seas and established it upon the floods" (24:2). As for the sea itself, the Old

Testament Tehom is "the deep that underlies" (Genesis 49:25), and "the deep that lies beneath" (Deuteronymy 33:12). To be sure, these are not old Greek tales, inasmuch as the landlocked Hyperborean Hellenes, we recall, had not so much as a word for sea. Yet Thales the Phoenician surely had as many words for sea as Eskimos have for snow, all of them native to the peoples of the south and east.

That the earth "floats" upon the deep seems a very strange notion; certainly Aristotle finds it incomprehensible. Yet anyone who has been caught in an earthquake, when the land shimmies and shakes as though its tectonic plates indeed rested on water, very furious water, will not find the idea so strange, especially if they have experienced what geologists call "earthquake or soil liquefaction." Aristotle— "solider" Aristotle, Yeats calls him—wants both earth and water well-rooted, not floating, and one can understand his desire. It is the desire for a substrate, for something to under-stand. Perhaps Thales is more realistic about the drift of what seems solid ground, even of entire continents?

The Near-Eastern idea of earth emerging "from an indefinite expanse of primeval water" may well have been an idea hovering in the background for all Milesians (KRS 12). Even though Homer's *Okeanos* is clearly held to be a fresh water river flowing about the disk of the earth, there may be something of this older idea in it. There are so many references in Ionian Greek poetry and myth to "the indefinite waste of water" (ibid.) that, even if the early Hellenes knew nothing of the sea, the emigrants who traveled to the south must have been struck above all by the untamable wildness of the sea, its bitterness and its terrors. The peoples of the Mediterranean, with whom the Hellenes mixed, were of course also struck by the differences between sweet and salt water. Whereas the fresh water that floods the banks of the Nile and the Tigris-Euphrates means fertility of crops, animals, and humans, the vast wastes of brine seem bootless—except for their netted fish. Some of the oldest stories, such as the Babylonian creation epic, from the second millennium BCE, dwell on the differentiation of the waters. The first six lines of the first tablet (KRS 12n. 1) read:

> When on high the heaven had not been named,
> Firm ground below had not been called by name,
> Naught but primordial Apsu, their begetter,
> And Mummu-Tiamat, she who bore them all,
> Their waters commingling as a single body;
> No reed-hut had been matted, no marshland had appeared.

Apsu and Tiamat, male and female, normally represent fresh and salt water respectively, even though here they are "commingled."[3] What is noteworthy is the fact that the commingled waters come "earlier" than any sort of land—no rafts, no reeds, no houses. Likewise, during the third millennium in ancient Egypt, a text tells of aboriginal waters and the emergence of "the primeval hillock": "O Atum-Kheprer, you dwelled on high, on the (primeval) hill," which was the first bit of land to thrust itself from the waters; various cult centers were dedicated to it throughout Egypt, and it was symbolized by the pyramid (ibid.). And this, from the *Book of the Dead*, second millennium: "I am Atum [the creator god worshiped at Heliopolis] when I was alone in Nun [the expanse of waters]; I am Re in his (first) appearances, when he

---

[3] KRS, in the second edition, has "fish and salt water," a rare typo surely, "fish" for "fresh," but an interesting one. It is high time I mentioned that this entire chapter is indebted to Kirk, Raven, and Schofield, even though their basic theme—the emergence of a truly scientific philosophy out the "primitive" and "naïve" worldviews of the Near East and early Greece—is so freighted with prejudices and "centrisms" of various kinds that I find myself resisting their argumentation at every moment. It seems impossible for us to encounter the Greeks without the prejudices of all the intervening systems of philosophy and science—I recall Heidegger saying to Eugen Fink and their Freiburg students that when they go to confront the Greeks what they are encountering is Hegel—but surely one may demand a bit more self-awareness and self-critique. Indeed, was this not precisely Cherniss's complaint concerning Aristotle?

began to rule that which he had made" (ibid.). Even if such ideas concerning the aboriginal waters had not been current in Miletus, Thales would have come across them during his travels to Egypt and Babylon.

We should revert to Aristotle's account, however, for one more particular. Aristotle speculates that Thales may have been induced to think of water as in some sense primary because of the moisture that is essential to life and necessary for its survival. The earth of flesh and bone would be nothing without the water of lymph and blood. To say nothing of sperm and egg and amniotic fluid. "Perhaps taking this supposition from seeing the nurture of all things to be moist," says Aristotle, who might have added that if our nourishment is too dry, the saliva in our mouths will moisten it. From the moisture of living beings—at least of mammals, if not of cold-blooded amphibians—comes the warmth that is essential to life. The corpse is cold and (eventually) dry, the living body warm and moist. And, "the seeds of all things having a moist nature, [and] water being the natural principle of moist things," it may be that Thales extrapolated and expanded on what he experienced locally, projecting it out into the cosmos at large. Even if the microcosm-macrocosm parallel belongs to a later age, the early Greek thinkers seem to have been aware of who they were and where they were.

Otto Rank, an avid reader of Nietzsche's *Philosophy in the Tragic Age of the Greeks*, remarks that philosophers do everything in their power to repress the question that is the only genuine philosophical question, namely, "Where do babies come from?" Very young philosophers, not yet schooled, often do pose this question, over and over again. Perhaps Thales, looking up from the bottom of the well to see a circle of stars—a cosmic diadem—crowning the face of that Thracian girl looking down at him, was an exception to the general rule of repression? It is worth citing Rank in full:

> As we know, Greek philosophy begins with the statement of Thales that *water* is the origin and the womb of all things. Before we pursue the further development of Greek thinking on the basis of this lapidary formulation, let us be clear about the fact that the formulation offers us the first cognitive conception of the origin of individual human beings as a universal law of nature. The mechanism of such an insight, which is doubtless correct in terms of biological occurrence, is that it distinguishes itself from the cosmological and mythical projection of celestial waters (the Milky Way) and underworld streams (the river of the dead) by making an actual dis-covery, that is, by actually drawing back the curtain, or, as we would say, relieving a repression that has heretofore obstructed our seeing in water the origin of all life, precisely because one had oneself at one time emerged from amniotic fluid [*Fruchtwasser*]. The presupposition of a discovery of truth is thus recognition by the unconscious of something in the outside world [*die Agnoszierung des Unbewußten in der Außenwelt*] by canceling an inner repression [*durch Aufhebung einer inneren Verdrängung*] that immediately proceeds—and this is what the development of philosophy clearly shows—from primal repression.
>
> OR 161

Thales, then, is above all else a psychologist, and philosophy, if it is psychologically intuitive, need not construct delusional systems, as Freud suspects it always does. With Thales, thinking for the first time thinks about *thinking*, along with the internal *obstacles* to thinking, and its first word is *water*. Yet by what resources does Thales overcome the obstructions arising from primal repression? Rank can offer no explanation. At the point where he asserts the biological truth of Thales' statement, he footnotes a reference to Sándor Ferenczi: "See now Ferenczi's phylogenetic parallel to individual development (*Versuch einer Genitaltheorie*, 1924)" (OR 161n. 3). If Thales' formulation is "lapidary," as concise and compact as stone, it is nonetheless not engraved on a monolith but writ in water—his words bathe in the water in which he spent his first nine months.

Nietzsche's *Philosophy in the Tragic Age of the Greeks* announces that it is interested only in the "personality" of the early Greek thinkers, not in their teachings. It is easy to underestimate what he means by *personality*, however, for he means by it what Emerson means by *character*. He also means by it a style of *thinking*, one that is not easy for us moderns to grasp. He finds this new kind of thinking in Thales—the very first philosopher of the tragic age. Nietzsche does not call it *meditative* thinking, to be sure, but he senses that Thales—the engineer and astronomer—is also capable of some other sort of thinking than the calculative. He tries to describe Thales' achievement, but his own effort is full of tensions and contradictions. Indeed, it may be that tensions and contradictions are what characterize the new kind of thinking. First of all, when Thales says that everything is water, presuming that this is what he says, then what he really means is Ἕν πάντα, "everything is one," or perhaps, and every bit as likely, although Nietzsche does not say so here, "the one wears many masks." For Nietzsche, Thales is already Heraclitus. His belief in the hidden unity of things, Nietzsche says in section 3 of his text, is both "a metaphysical principle of faith" and a "mystical intuition" (KSW 1:813). In order to discover and propound it, Thales has to be able "to leap over all the hedges of experience," his heels winged by "hope and intimation" (ibid.). Yet the talaria at his heels, the wings that distinguish him from those flat-footed persons who are only able to perform "a thinking that calculates and measures things," *dem rechnenden und abmessenden Denken*, flourish only in the soil of "a foreign, illogical power—*Phantasie*" (KSW 1:814).

Such *Phantasie* is difficult to translate. Perhaps "fancy," in Wordsworth and Coleridge's sense, or Coleridge's "esemplastic power," or Schelling's *Ineinsbildung* of *Einbildungskraft*. "Fantasy" does not seem adequate as a translation, and one fears the complexity of the word *imagination*, so that I am tempted simply to say that for Nietzsche *Phantasie* is what Aristotle means by φαντασία, a word that doubtless performs multiple tasks in the latter's work. At all events, Nietzsche tells us that by *Phantasie* he means the capacity "to leap from possibility to possibility" by virtue of "an ingenious premonition," *ein genialisches Vorgefühl*, the sort of feeling, Schiller says, that every serious composer has before he or she begins to write down the notes. Nietzsche describes it as a "lightning-quick grasp and an illumination of the similarities" in things (ibid.). Yet now comes one of those tensions or contradictions. "Fantasy" or "fancy" is not fanciful; it is not "imaginative" in the usual sense. Thales thinks "nonmythically and nonallegorically" (KSW 1:815); he is too much the engineer and astronomer for the fanciful. And here comes another tension. Thales thinks in a highly personal way, bringing the most abstract matters down to his own personal experience. Yet his principal insight is that not the *person* but *water* is "the reality of things" (ibid.). Thales, like Anaximander and Heraclitus after him, has nothing to do with the "biographical epidemic" that afflicts our own time (KSW 1:818). Nor, for all his *Phantasie*, is Thales interested in *phantastische Fabelei*, "the phantasmatic fairy tales" about nature that are prevalent in his time (KSW 1:816). What, then, is this new kind of thinking?

Nietzsche takes a clue from the word *wise*, since Thales is one of Greece's seven wise men or sages. The word σοφία, he says, is what gives us the Latin *sapio*, "I taste." *Savoir* is savor. *Homo sapiens sapiens* would presumably be the creature that, having taste, can also develop good taste and make good judgments about taste. What Thales cultivates a taste for is "the unusual the astonishing the difficult the divine," writes Nietzsche without the aid of punctuation, as though these, *des Ungewöhnlichen Erstaunlichen Schwierigen Göttlichen*, were one. And he now distinguishes between science in the usual sense, the sense that any competent engineer or astronomer today would have, from that special quality of Thales' *philosophical* thinking:

> Science seizes upon everything that is knowable, without the capacity to sort things out, without fine taste, attacking all things in its blind desire to know everything at any price; by contrast, philosophical thinking is always on the lookout for the things that are most worth knowing, knowledge that is grand and significant. Now, the concept "grand" is alterable, in both the moral and the aesthetic spheres: thus philosophy begins with its legislation concerning grandeur—its very name is bound up with that. "That is great," says philosophy, and in so doing it raises human beings above and beyond the blind and boundless craving of the drive to knowledge.
>
> Ibid.

The philosopher eschews the vulgar ditties of his time; he or she tries to hum along with the tune that expresses "the collective sound of the world" (KSW 1:817). Yet, as mad as he or she may be for the music of the spheres or the rhythm of the tides, the philosopher possesses a kind of *Besonnenheit*—a presence of mind, sobriety, or *meditativeness*. It is the same sort of quality the playwright and the actor possess, especially the actor who, even as he or she metamorphoses into another body and declaims from that body knows how to project the metamorphosis in measured verse. For the philosopher, that measured verse is *dialectic*. Yet sometimes dialectic is insufficient, and the philosopher grapples with ideas and then projects metaphors. Wanting to express the unity of all beings, "what he says is something about water!" (ibid.).

Is Thales, the psychologist and hydrologist, also a thinker of the divine? Is there not some talk of "gods" there? There are three more fragments that need to be considered, two from Aristotle and one from Diogenes Laertius. In his *On the Soul*, Aristotle refers to Thales twice. The first reference (A2, 405a19): "It seems that, according to what is remembered about him, Thales too supposes that the soul is something that moves things [κινητικόν τι τὴν ψυχὴν], if indeed he said that the [magnetic] stone possesses soul because it moves iron." Diogenes confirms that according to Aristotle Thales is said to have "given a share of soul even to soulless things [τοῖς ἀψύχοις μεταδιδόναι ψυχῆς], referring to the Magnesian stone and amber as indications." Aristotle's second reference (A5, 411a7) is the decisive one: "And some say that soul is intermingled in the whole of things [ἐν τῷ ὅλῳ δέ τινες αὐτὴν (τὴν ψυχὴν) μεμεῖχθαί], for which reason Thales also thought that all things are full of gods [πάντα πλήρη θεῶν εἶναι]."

When amber is rubbed, it produces static electricity, and magnetic stones had been important cult items at various mystery centers for centuries, above all in Samothrace, where iron rings were placed on the fingers of intiates in order to connect them with the force of the mysteries. Such things are relatively clear. What remains unclear is what Thales may have meant by "the whole of things" and "full of gods." Or even what he may have meant by "water." Much of the critical discussion surrounding Thales wants to defend the sage from charges of "primitive animism" and "hylozoism." His admirers do not want to see him stripped of his chiton, dressed in a loincloth, and given an uncut stone tool to work with. In a wonderful novel by William

Golding, *The Inheritors* (1955), the Neanderthal hero, Lok, is suddenly under attack from Cro-Magnons, who shoot arrows at him, arrows that stick in the tree near which Lok is standing. Lok is amazed to see that the tree is growing so many new branches so quickly, and that the branches are sprouting feathers at their tips. Critical discussion of Thales sometimes does seem to take the first philosopher for a Neanderthal. Yet he is said to have worked out some mathematical formulae and certain astronomical theorems that many Cro-Magnons would have a hard time reproducing or even understanding. Albin Lesky tells us how highly developed the Ionian cities and their citizens were at the time when their trade and colonization activities reached their peak in the late seventh and early sixth centuries BCE. It is impossible that the Milesian adventures in remote parts of the world did not have an impact on the culture and the learning of its citizens. No one can think it an accident, says Lesky, that precisely in Miletus questions were put to the entire world of things, "questions from which European science originated" (AL 190). Thales and Anaximander, above all, were the ones who formulated these questions.

Perhaps one needs to recall the architecture of these ancient cities. Think, for example, of the harbor city of Akrotiri on Thira, which was in its most flourishing phase when the nearby volcano erupted—exploded, really—and the city was buried in ash. This happened at about 1650 BCE, a millennium earlier than our Thales. When we walk through the city today, which has been only partly cleared of ash, we marvel at the three-story houses with indoor plumbing, the well-stocked cellars, and the beautifully designed city squares. Yet marveling is not enough when we study the wall-paintings that the ash so remarkably preserved. Some of these have been taken to the National Archaeological Museum at Athens; others are still present on the island of Santorini, the ancient Kallista, Strongyle, and Thira. As we study the paintings of the young girls and women gathering crocuses to offer the goddess, we have to wonder who these people were—people who were capable of building in this way, shipping and trading in this way, painting in this way, worshiping in this way. Sometimes one feels a little bit like Lok in the presence of these people.

A thousand years later we have Thales. How are things full of gods? Perhaps in the way Plato's Eryximachus believes that Eros is in all things, not simply in humans and other animals but also in the world of so-called inanimate things. This sense of the liveliness of things, of something "more deeply interfused," as Wordsworth says, surely need not die out altogether in a modern and even postmodern world. True, we have lost the word *soul*, but we have gained the word *psyche*. And how does it stand with *gods*? Already Hölderlin saw them in departure—he noticed the fact of their flight because no one was dancing in the temples anymore, no one was celebrating anything in festivals. Heidegger is not reluctant to preserve the word *gods* in his Quaternity of earth, sky, gods, and mortals (VA 159, 177, 199–201); yet we fear this recidivist religious talk, which seems to hide—unsuccessfully—the most pathetic sorts of oceanic delusions. Perhaps what can help here is the thought that Heidegger never speaks of the *immortals*, but only of gods as the departed ones. For what do gods do? They *pass*. Like herring, they get caught in the net of space-time, and, like herring, they pass. Their only hope is that in festivals of remembrance we remember them. Only in that way can things be full of gods.

According to Roberto Calasso, but also to Schelling and Nietzsche before him, the *passing* of the gods, rather than their *presence*, is what the ancient mystery religions were all about. Those who are ignorant of the mysteries, the uninitiated, believe that the mysteries are there for those deluded mortals who wish to save themselves, to make themselves undying. The initiates, however, understand that the mysteries are about remembering the passing of the gods—their vulnerability and their demise (RC 353/315–16). The mortals, in other words, are not alone. All things are full of gods? Samuel Beckett would say, "What an addition to company that would make."

It may be that for Thales the fullness of gods and daimons in things is writ in water. One need not be an "unscrupulous doxographer" (KRS 97) to want to think Thales' two thoughts together, the thought of water and the thought of gods. Cicero repeats a phrase of Aetius, perhaps repeating Theophrastus, that takes us in that direction. True, the appeal to Anaxagoras's νοῦς is anachronistic, and is perhaps Stoic in origin. Aetius writes (DK A23; 1:79), "Thales said that the mind of the cosmos is god [νοῦν τοῦ κόσμου τὸν θεόν], and that the totality of things is ensouled and is simultaneously full of daimons [τὸ δὲ πᾶν ἔμψυχον ἅμα καὶ δαιμόνων πλῆρες]; a divine force [δύναμιν θείαν] permeates the moist element and moves it [διήκειν ... διὰ τοῦ στοιχειώδους ὑγροῦ ... κινητικὴν αὐτοῦ]." Cicero's paraphrase is "that water is the beginning of things, and that god is the mind that fashions the totality out of water [*acquam dixit esse initium rerum, deum autem eam mentem, quae ex aqua cuncta fingeret*]" (*On the Nature of the Gods*, 1:10, 25; KRS 97).

Yet this "water" of Thales, whether fresh or salt, salubrious or unpotable, runs through our fingers when we try to grasp it. The liquid and the moist are as close to us as the saliva that pools in our mouth, and yet they remain somehow strange to us, even uncanny, as the gods are passing strange and uncanny. There is something "indefinite" about water, something "indeterminate," something "boundless," without external boundaries or intrinsic limits, somewhat ἄπειρον. For Thales that word—and it is his fellow citizen of Miletus Anaximander who says the word—perhaps means at least in part the vast expanse of the sea, which seems to spill over the horizon and into the sky, if not into the underworld. It spills over into all the divine regions, including that region where Thales spent his earliest months.

The extant fragment of Anaximander (DK B1), transmitted to us by Simplicius, following Theophrastus, reads, first in a traditional rendering and then in Heidegger's rethinking of its final phrase:

> The beginning and origin of beings is the unbounded [τὸ ἄπειρον]. Yet that from which all beings come to be is that into which they perish, according to necessity. For they pay one another penalty and recompense for their injustice according to the ordinance of time.
>
> [Heidegger begins with the phrase "according to necessity" and ends before the reference to time]: . . . along the lines of usage; for they [that is, beings] let order and thereby also reck [*Ruch, ruoche*, δίκη] belong to one another (in the surmounting of) disorder [ἀδικία].
>
> EGT 57

Whether the ordinance of time is conceived of juridically, as a judgment of justice and the paying of a suitable penalty, or as the jointure of order in response to a primordial disorder in things—for Heidegger, following Nietzsche, never doubts that the Anaximander fragment has to do with *tragedy*—it is clear that beings can *be* only for the time being. Every being must obey the imperious summons that says, "Go back where you came from." When an older sibling says this to the younger sibling, he is thinking of the deep blue sea as the proper destination of the interloper. Yet the younger sibling, understanding his or her privilege as the younger, and having perhaps at least an inkling of Anaximander, will reply to the older sibling, "Go jump in the ocean."

As we heard in the foregoing chapter, Aristotle attributes the idea of the drying up of the seas to Democritus, whereas Theophrastus adds that Anaximander and Diogenes of Apollonia have the same thought. "They think," says Aristotle, "that the sea is actually becoming less through being dried up, and that some time it will be entirely dry" (*Meteorology* B1, 353b6). Clearly, such an extreme situation would mean an outer limit to the "unlimited," a boundary-situation for the "unbounded," and it would mean that injustice or disjointure rules without contestation. Yet if such a catastrophe were not an outer limit but periodic, part of the cycle of moisture and aridity, then desiccation might be a part of Anaximander's and Xenophanes' view of the world. Nietzsche, in section 4 of his text, confirms this detail of Anaximander's teaching, placing the following words in the mouth of the heroic philosopher: "Behold how your world falters; the seas are dwindling and drying up; the seashells in the mountains show you how advanced the desiccation already is; fire is already destroying your world, and in the end that world will go up in smoke and vapor" (KSW 1:820). Yet we would expect Nietzsche, the future thinker of eternal return, to add to this dire forecast, "—at least for the time being."

To be sure, the drying up of the sea, and with it the evanescence of clouds and the disappearance of rainfall, would be equally catastrophic for fish and human beings. The two seemingly different creatures are fundamentally related in Anaximander's thinking—as also in Ferenczi's—as the following series of five fragments selected by Kirk, Raven, and Schofield (KRS 140–1) shows:

> Anaximander said that the first living beings [τὰ πρῶτα ζῷα] were born in moisture, enclosed in thorny bark; and that as their age increased they moved to a place that was more dry, and, when the bark had broken away, they lived a different kind of life for a short time [ἐπ' ὀλίγον χρόνον μεταβιῶναι].
>
> DK A30; 88:31–3

"For a short time." Is Anaximander intimating that every new development of the first living beings enables them to survive only

The Sea

14 *Tamarisk trees bordering the vineyards on the Loumarades hills of Thira.*

briefly—before they are caught in the undertow of time? And is that thorny bark something like the outer wall of a cell, dead to the world but protecting the moist life within? But let us move on, for Anaximander now seems to give us the first philosophical account of what much later will be called "the period of latency," namely, that long period of relative helplessness in human beings between infancy and maturity, or at least from birth until puberty.

> Further, he says that in the beginning the human being was born from creatures of a different kind, because whereas other creatures are soon self-supporting, the human being alone needs prolonged nursing. For this reason, the human being would not have survived if this had been its original form.
>
> DK A10; 83:37–40

> Anaximander of Miletus conceived that there arose from heated water and earth either fish or creatures very like fish; in these the human being grew in the form of embryos retained within until puberty; then at last the fish-like creatures burst and men and women who were already able to nourish themselves stepped forth.
>
> DK A30; 88:33–7

> Living beings came into being from moisture evaporated by the sun. The human being was originally similar to another creature—that is, to a fish.
>
> DK A11; 84:15–17

> Therefore [the Syrians] actually revere the fish as being of similar kind and nurture. In this they philosophize more suitably than Anaximander. For he declares, not that fish and humans came into being in the same parents, but that originally

human beings came into being inside fish, and that they have been nurtured there—like sharks—and having become adequate to look after themselves, they then came forth and took to the land.

DK A30; 89:2–6

These "brilliant conjectures" (KRS 141) on the origin of humankind from the sea and from the fish of the sea, although they sparked derision in haughtier times, now take our breath away. One must wonder whether Ferenczi, at some early stage of his education, encountered Anaximander—perhaps in the bookstore owned and managed by his father and mother, or perhaps in the learned salon they hosted? The vulnerability of the human being, its excruciatingly long period of latency following upon a lengthy gestation, make it plain that the species is indebted to earlier forms of life. It is as though the sea urchin with its quills or the stonefish with its poisonous spines is precisely what the fragile human being needs for its survival. And if no urchin or stonefish had been available, would not Anaximander have had to invent them? But how? There is no anecdote of a Thracian servant girl who might have helped Anaximander find a solution to the quandary of the origins of humankind. Is it too extravagant to suppose that the thorny bark is Leviathan, that is, the primitive "socialization" of the hominids, without which their life would have been nasty, brutish, and short? Is the thorny bark the mural crown on the head of the goddess Artemis who protects the city, her crown of thorny parapets signifying the walls of the πόλις itself? But, to repeat the question, why does the altered form of life—no longer in water but on the land—endure for only "a short time"? It does seem as though Anaximander is speculating on the difficulties of adaptation to catastrophic changes in the environment and perhaps also in the environs of the city. That "short time," whatever its explanation, would testify to the ordinance of time, which regulates the coming to be and passing away of beings.

Finally, then, to Empedocles of Acragas, the Sicilian magus. Why? Has he a theory of sea and fish? No, but he himself at one time *was* a fish, and so he deserves a sounding. We have inherited so much material from Empedocles, at least in comparison with the other pre-Platonic philosophers, that it is difficult to know what to select and how to order it. Perhaps an encounter with the sea will choose only those fragments having to do with liquidity and love, but begin with Empedocles' thoughts on meditation as such. For liquidity, and above all liquid blood, has everything to do with *thinking* as Empedocles understands and practices it. Thinking transpires not in the brain but in the heart, "which dwells in the sea of blood surging forth and back, / Where is especially what human beings call thought. / For the blood that flows about the human heart—this is thought [αἷμα γὰρ ἀνθρώποις περικάρδιόν ἐστι νόημα]" (DK B105). Such pericardial thinking has captured the imagination of commentators for centuries. Is it possible to give new life's blood to the vapid word *meditation* by virtue of it? Surely, this possibility is at least in part what excited both Hölderlin and Nietzsche about Empedocles.

What is it about blood that enables thought? Surely it is the saline solution, the extraordinary *mix* of elements in the blood, such that blood can go to encounter all its blood-relatives out there in the world. Certainly this is the case for young Redburn on his first ocean voyage—recall that "wild bubbling and bursting" at his heart, "as if a hidden spring had just gushed out there … like mountain brooks in spring freshets." The hematic mix has to do with Love, Φιλία, and Love has to do with Kypris Aphrodite. She, Aphrodite, had already played a central role in the conflicted system of Parmenides (DK B12–13). Yet

Love now mixes it up with (mixes itself up with?) Strife, Νεῖκος, in the one sphere that they share. Here are several fragments in which Empedocles instructs young Pausanias—not the later Athenian Pausanias, who is a hopeless case—concerning the sphere, its four "roots," of which water is one, and its forces of amity and enmity. His tale is "twofold," "duplex," and perhaps even "duplicitous," presumably because of the whirling confusion of Love and Strife in the sphere. Here are the four "roots" or "rhizomes," ῥιζώματα:

> Hear first the four roots of all things:
> Shining Zeus, life-bearing Hera, Aidoneus,
> Nestis, who with her tears waters mortal springs.

> DK B6

Zeus is the aither or upper air, the blazing sky; Hera, pregnant with life, φερέσβιος, is presumably (although all these attributions have been contested) both earth and the lower air of cloud and mist; in Aidoneus we recognize Hades, god of the underworld; and Nestis weeps tears that mortals eventually can drink. Our primary interest is of course this Nestis, presumably a local goddess who is identified with fresh water springs. And yet if she weeps salty tears, δακρύοις, she must have something to do with the sea and its exhalations. At all events, the four roots are subject to the forces that bring them together and pull them apart, as the double tale now tells us:

> A twofold tale I shall tell: at one time they grew to be one
> Out of many, at another time they became many out of one.
> Double is the birth of mortal things and double their collapse.
> For the one is brought to birth and destroyed by the coming
>   together
> Of all things, the other is nurtured and disperses as they separate

Again. And these things never cease their endless interchange,
Now through Love all coming together into one,
Now again each scattering by the hatred that is Strife.
Insofar as they have learned to grow one from many,
And again, as the one falls apart, to become many,
Thus far do they come into being and have no steadfast life.
Yet insofar as they never cease their continual ringdance
They exist forever changeless in the cycle.

The ultimate "duplicity" of the tale seems to be that whereas all things are changeless in the cycle that very changelessness is permanent instability. Empedocles puts a personal stamp on this paradox, perhaps making a little joke of it for Pausanias's entertainment: the stability of the "steadfast" is the root of his own name: ἔμπεδος. One can hardly avoid thinking centuries ahead to Nietzsche's eternal recurrence of the same, a recurrence that has nothing to do with either eternity or the same. If one may be allowed to push the paradox to an extreme, one may say that Love and Strife *strive* within the one sphere, so that even the universe of love is one of strife. Once again one can hardly avoid thinking centuries ahead, this time to Freud's *lovehate* and the ambivalence of all passions. No wonder Nestis weeps.

Now that Freud's *lovehate* or *Hassliebe* has been mentioned, it has to be admitted that Freud's theory of the dualism of drives reverts to an Empedoclean problem. For if love and hate themselves intermingle in the sphere of human emotion, the one with the other, then each of the two compromises its identity. As they *strive* within the sphere, the sphere remains one of Strife—even when Love prevails. Thus we are uncertain about these two principles in the one sphere, and neither *dualism* nor *monism* seem adequate terms, at least when our heart's blood is thinking. In a late essay, "On Finite and Infinite [or Limited and Unlimited] Analysis" (1937), Freud writes at great length about

Empedocles of Acragas. He chides the Sicilian magus for projecting human emotions onto the cosmos, yet in the end he concedes that the cosmos may prove to be precisely Empedoclean. And while he hopes that the philosopher may be an ally in his struggle to assert the *dualism* of drives, Freud may have an inkling of the fundamental undecidability that unsettles all dualisms and monisms. In any event, here is an abbreviated version of Freud's extended remarks in section 6 of his essay:

> Empedocles of Acragas, born circa 495 BCE, enters on the scene as one of the most magnificent and remarkable figures in the cultural history of Greece. His many-sided personality engaged in activities that went in the most varied directions; he was a researcher and thinker, a prophet and thaumaturge [*Magier*], a politician, philanthropist, and physician who was well-informed about nature; he is said to have freed the city of Selinunt of malaria, for which his contemporaries honored him as a god. His spirit seems to have united within itself the most acute oppositions; precise and sober in his physical and physiological investigations, he nevertheless did not shy from obscure mysticism; he constructed cosmic speculations of astonishingly phantasmatic boldness.... Yet our interest turns to that particular doctrine of Empedocles which comes so close to the psychoanalytic theory of drives that the two would be identical were it not for the difference that the theory of the Greek is a cosmic phantasm.... The philosopher teaches that there are two principles underlying all occurrences in cosmic as well as psychic life, two principles in eternal conflict with one another. He calls them φιλία—*love*—and νεῖκος—*strife*. One of these powers ... strives to compress the primordial particles of the four elements into a unity, the other, by contrast, tries to cancel all these intermixtures and to isolate the elements from one

another. He conceives of the cosmic process as a continuous, never-ending alternation of periods in which the one or the other of the two fundamental forces is victorious, so that at one time love, at another strife imposes its will and rules the world, at which point the other, defeated party rises up and wrestles its opponent to the ground.

The two fundamental principles of Empedocles—φιλία and νεῖκος—both in name and in function are the same as our two fundamental drives *Eros* and *destruction*. The one endeavors to bind everything at hand into ever-greater unities, the other to dissolve these unities and to annihilate the configurations they have brought into being. . . . We no longer think of the mixture and separation of material substances, but of the fusion and separation of drive components. We have also in a certain way provided biological support for the principle of "strife" by tracing our destructive drive back to the death drive, namely, the compulsion of living creatures to revert to lifelessness. Naturally, that does not mean to deny that an analogous drive existed already earlier on; it does not mean to assert that such a drive first came into being with the appearance of life. And no one can predict in what sort of guise the kernel of truth contained in the doctrine of Empedocles will show itself to later investigators.

GW 16:91–3

We may leave Freud to contemplate whether his dualism of drives will withstand the very duplicity emphasized in Empedocles' great poem, to which I now return. Yet not before speculating, not too disrespectfully, I hope, that with Empedocles Freud is experiencing the most jubilant and most turbulent countertransference of his life.

Empedocles repeats his warning, δίπλ' ἐρέω, and his twofold, duplicitous tale continues with some more details about Love:

I tell a twofold tale: at one time they became one out of many,

At another they separated and became many out of one,

Fire and water and earth and air up above;

Off to the side, Strife; the whole well harmonized,

And in the center, Love, equal in breadth and in height;

Look at her with your mind's eye, do not be abashed.

You know her, she surges in the limbs of mortals;

Thanks to her they think of love and do unifying deeds,

Crying out her name: O Delight! O Aphrodite!

As she spins there among the other elements, no

Mortal male can recognize her. But you must follow

The course of my words: they will not deceive you.

At this particular moment, Love is in the center of the sphere, Strife "off to the side." Strife is never banished from the sphere, but now the force of well-centered Love gathers the roots. Yet why does Empedocles stress, or seem to stress, that the mortal *male*, θνητὸς ἀνήρ, fails to see Love in the center? Does she not surge in the limbs of all mortals, this Aphrodite? Empedocles seems to be warning Pausanias that pericardial thinking may be difficult for him, that even some illiterate Thracian servant girl might be better at it than he is. Odd that the mentor insists that his words are "not deceitful," οὐκ ἀπατηλόν (DK B17, l. 26). "Let your mind not be deceived," οὕτω μή σ᾽ἀπάτη φρένα, he urges in a later passage (DK B23, l. 9). As we will hear in the following chapter, Ἀπάτη is the goddess or titaness Deceit, and she has to do with wiles and deceptions—Hesiod places her in the company of Love—which may befuddle young Pausanias and make him hard-hearted against Kypris. Many a tragedy tells us what happens to such truculent youths—Pentheus, Hippolytus—who fail to recognize what should always rule in the center of the sphere, the swollen belly of the sphere.

Sometimes it seems as though Empedocles, who like Heraclitus and Anaximander stresses the balance or give-and-take of all things in the cosmos, is especially sensitive to the Strife that haunts the perimeter. Perhaps that is the sense of the entire work we conjecture may have been called *Purifications*, Καθαρμοί. For in our time too, which is more or less the time of Empedocles, human beings prefer to shed blood—their own and that of other living beings—rather than to nurture pericardial thinking about the center. Even if Empedocles has been boy, girl, bush, bird, and leaping fish, he is now a "fugitive," as he says, a wanderer on the plains of Doom, Ἄτης ἂν λειμῶνα (DK B118). Indeed, his self-accusation is startling:

> There is an oracle of Necessity, ancient decree of the gods,
> Eternal and sealed with broad oaths:
> When anyone sins and pollutes his own limbs with bloodshed,
> One who by his deep flaw makes false the oath he swore
> By the daimons whose portion is long life,
> For thrice ten thousand years he wanders apart from the blessed,
> Being born throughout that time in all manner of mortal forms,
> Exchanging one harsh path of life for another.
> The force of aither chases him into the sea,
> The sea spews him onto the floor of the earth,
> The earth casts him into the rays of the blazing sun,
> And the sun chases him back to the aither.
> Each receives him from the other, but all abhor him.
> Of these I too am now one, exiled from the gods, a fugitive,
> Having put my trust in raving Strife.
>
> DK B115

If Empedocles embodies the evolution of flying fish to boy and girl, that evolution is perhaps devolution, his story the tragic tale of an

15 *"The limbs of the god began to quiver."*

exile who enjoys the hospitality of all the roots, but only briefly, since they all despise him and reject him. Storm-tossed, like Odysseus, is Empedocles. Nothing steadfast. Caught forever in the undertow. Indeed, the entire sphere suffers this same instability. To repeat, Strife is never altogether quelled in the circle, even if Love pursues it and tries to wrestle it to the ground (DK B35). When Love prevails and orders the sphere, all seems well, and harmony permeates the "rounded sphere celebrating its joyous solitude" (DK B27, ll. 22–3). Yet as Strife begins to gain supremacy in the sphere, Simplicius tells us, a more erratic motion arises on the periphery, "For one by one all the limbs of the god began to quiver [πελεμίζετο]" (DK B31, l. 15; KRS 295).

"The limbs of the god began to quiver." Hesiod uses the word πελεμίζω at least twice in his *Theogony* (ll. 458, 842), both times referring to the earth's trembling beneath Zeus's thunderbolts and his footfall. However, with Empedocles it is the god himself who quivers—as Hölderlin imagines it centuries later in the third version of his play, *The Death of Empedocles*. At first it is the philosopher himself who trembles:

> When brother fled from brother, when lovers passed
> Each other by in ignorance, when fathers failed
> To recognize their sons, when human words no more
> Were understood, nor human laws, that was when
> The meaning of it all assailed me and I trembled:
> It was my nation's parting god!
>
> ll. 421–6

Yet the philosopher's trembling may in fact be a response to the quaking and quivering of an apprehensive deity itself, as the ancient Egyptian priest Manes has already declared:

The lord of time, grown apprehensive of his rule,

Looms with glowering gaze above the consternation.

His day extinguished, lightning bolts still flash, yet

What flames on high is inflammation, nothing more;

What strives from down below is savage discord.

ll. 367–71[4]

Both Empedocles of Acragas and Hölderlin's eponymous hero begin to sound like much later, more modern thinkers, writers, and their characters—if one may put the matter so anachronistically: for example, the poet Neville in Virginia Woolf's *The Waves* (1931), who says, "Things quiver as if not yet in being" (100); or the philosopher Heidegger who writes in *Beiträge zur Philosophie* of the quivering, trembling, and shivering of the "last god." This *Zittern des letzten Gottes* is one of the most insistent themes of his text, and surely one of the most bizarre, inasmuch as it appears to be a relapse in Heidegger's thinking, the return to an onto-mytho-theo-logy he elsewhere spurns and wishes to leave behind. Indeed, most interpreters of Heidegger are happy to ignore the theme. Among the most striking phrases in this work of 1936–8, which is nothing short of apocalyptic, is *die Erzitterung des Seyns*, a phrase that appears over and over again throughout the work.[5] Such trembling, shivering, or quivering has to do with both the birthing (*Göttern*) and the passing-by (*Vorbeigang*)

---

[4] See Friedrich Hölderlin, *The Death of Empedocles: A Mourning-Play* (Albany: State University of New York Press, 2008), 184–5. For the German see CHV 1:897–9.

[5] The phrase first appears at 65:4 and 21, but it continues throughout the text, achieving its most significant force in what was meant to be the final section of the work, "The Last God." Such quivering or trembling of the last god is highly reminiscent of both Schelling and Nietzsche as well. For the sources, see Krell, *The Tragic Absolute: German Idealism and the Languishing of God* (Bloomington: Indiana University Press, 2005), 131n. 21. (I take this opportunity to correct an error in ll. 10–11 of the note, where the report on Schelling's *Philosophical Investigations into the Essence of Human Freedom* should read as follows: "What the 1809 *Philosophical Investigations* had called *die* ENDLICHE *gänzliche Scheidung* is therefore UTTERLY FINITE AND never total."

of the last god (65:8, 59, 120, 158, etc.). There are significant differences between Heidegger and the Sicilian thinker of old, to be sure. For one, Empedocles does not blame the resurgence of Strife on a particular people, and certainly not a Mediterranean or a Levantine people. For another, the *poetry* of Empedocles is memorable, unlike Heidegger's own stilted versifying.

It is odd that Heidegger has so little to say about Empedocles (he is not entirely silent about him, as my friend Will McNeill reminds me, but even so there is not a great deal of thought about Empedocles), and this is very strange. Not only because of Hölderlin's and Nietzsche's devotion to Empedocles, but because one can find a fragment of Empedocles that aptly summarizes the affirmative side of Heidegger's entire later thinking. Fragment B106 in the Diels-Kranz collection might be translated this way: "Fateful skill in human thinking grows as human beings encounter the presencing of what is present." The usual translation ("Men's wit grows according as they encounter what is present," [KRS 311]) needs only a bit of tweaking in order to bring it into intimate relation with Heidegger's thinking: μῆτις becomes not "wit" or "cleverness" but *Geschick* in thinking, that is, a thinking that is "skillful" precisely because it responds to what is "destined" or "sent" in the history of being; and, above all, παρεὸν becomes not merely "what is present," not merely beings-as-a-whole or this or that item that thrusts itself to the fore in our distracting world, but first and foremost the *presencing* and the accompanying *absencing* by which beings come into the open and withdraw into concealment. Perhaps this is the core of Empedocles' pericardial thinking—as it is of Heidegger's *Seinsdenken* when its polemic subsides, allowing tragic thinking to arise?

Empedocles is mentioned several times in Nietzsche's *Philosophy in the Tragic Age of the Greeks*, but there is no extended treatment of him there, as there is of Heraclitus and others. Instead, Nietzsche tries to write a *drama* about Empedocles, precisely as his much-admired predecessor Hölderlin attempted such a play. It is as though Nietzsche's thesis that the *personality* of the philosopher is what shines through the systems and the teachings finds its outstanding exemplar in Empedocles. Remarkably, those plans for a drama about Empedocles reemerge ten years later when Nietzsche sketches plans for a drama about Zarathustra.[6]

May one presume that Nietzsche's need to write a drama for his heroes of thought has to do with both *Verwandlung* and *Besonnenheit*, both transformation and meditativeness, which are the qualities exhibited by both Thales and the tragic actor? In his unpublished notes on Greek tragedy from this same period Nietzsche often describes the tragic actor as *ecstatic*—in the literal sense of being able to step out of himself and enter into the body and the character of a personage in the play. What Nietzsche emphasizes there too is that the ecstatic performer is nevertheless *besonnen*, capable of making the most discerning judgments and thinking the most measured thoughts. If philosophical thinking dares to legislate on what is worthy of thought, on what has "grandeur," it can do so only on the basis of this difficult mix of ecstasy and meditativeness. And these two qualities, to repeat, have to do with *tragic* drama above all.

The third of the six brief references to Empedocles in *Philosophy in the Tragic Age* occurs when Nietzsche is writing about Anaximander, who, he says, "raises his hand and sets his foot in place, as though our existence were a tragedy in which he, as the hero, is born to play his part" (KSW 1:821). In this respect, Anaximander is "the grand prototype of Empedocles" (ibid.). If there is unity in beings, and if that unity occurs as the "unbounded" or "indeterminate," τὸ ἄπειρον, such

---

[6] See Krell, *Postponements*, throughout; the German texts appear in an appendix.

unity is tragic. The tragic unity of existence is the very core of Nietzsche's "thought of thoughts," the eternal recurrence of the same, which here receives one of its earliest formulations. Anaximander believes that the totality of what comes to be must also perish, in accord with "the ordinance of time." But then a question occurs to him, one that Nietzsche formulates as follows:

> Why then has not everything that has come to be long since perished, inasmuch as an entire eternity of time has passed by? Whence the ever-renewed stream of becoming? He can rescue himself from this question only by way of mystical possibilities: eternal becoming can have its origin only in eternal being; the conditions for the collapse of such being and for its coming to be in injustice are always the same; the constellation of things is so ordered that no end can be foreseen, no end to that exit of individual beings from the womb of the "indeterminate." Here is where Anaximander stops. That is, he perdures in the deep shadows that lie like giant specters on the mountaintop of such a view of the world. The more one wanted to approach this problem as to how the determinate could have emerged at all from the indeterminate by way of perishing, the temporal from the eternal, injustice from justice, the more impenetrable grew the night.
>
> KSW 1:821–2

It is of course Heraclitus who espies the dawn—and yet it is also Heraclitus above all who affirms the tragedy of becoming. The rhythm of things, "the eternal pounding of the waves on the shore," is not unjust, but tragic.

However, to return to my question about meditative thinking as tragic affirmation: the thinking of Nietzsche's "thought of thoughts," eternal recurrence of the same, which is anticipated already in Nietzsche's earliest writings, is for me a preeminently *meditative* thinking. It is an experimental thinking; it has to do with the "what *if?*"; it leaps from possibility to possibility among the grandest of possibilities. Aspects of science and cosmology are not foreign to it, as the notebook M III 1 demonstrates so well.[7] And yet it remains the speculative or meditative thought that a daimon poses to us in our moments of loneliest loneliness. Nietzsche's formulation of the thought in *The Gay Science* (no. 341; KSW 3:570), is perhaps the principal communication of it in his oeuvre:

> *The greatest burden.*—How would it be if some day or night a daimon should steal upon you in your loneliest loneliness and say to you, "This life, as you are living it now and as you have lived it, you will have to live once again and countless times more; and there will be nothing new about it, but every pain and every pleasure and every thought and sigh and everything unspeakably petty and grand about your life will perforce return to you, and everything in the same order and sequence—and precisely this spider and this moonlight between the trees, and precisely this moment and I myself. The eternal hourglass of existence will be inverted again and again—and you with it, you, a speck of dust!" Would you not prostrate yourself and gnash your teeth and curse the daimon who spoke these words? Or have you once experienced a monstrous moment in which you would reply to him, "You are a god, and never have I heard anything more divine!" If that thought came to dominate you, you as you are now, it would transform you and perhaps mangle you; the question to all and sundry, "Will you have this once again and countless times more?" would weigh upon your every deed as the greatest burden. Or how good to yourself

---

[7] The 348 notes of this notebook are collected under the Mette-number 11; see KSW 9:441–575, and for a detailed discussion see Krell, *Infectious Nietzsche* (Bloomington and London: Indiana University Press, 1996), ch. 8.

and to your life you would have to be in order to *demand nothing more than* this ultimate eternal confirmation and seal?—

Meditation as that which transforms us? or mangles us? Perhaps Nietzsche demands too much of pericardial thinking. Or perhaps we have grown too pusillanimous for it.

As for the details of Empedocles' cosmology, we need not let them detain us. Once again the cycle of the evaporation of seawater and the development of raincloud is recognized here. An odd detail, but one that any photograph of the sea on a sunny day will show us, is the following: "The sun is not in its nature fire, but a reflection of fire like that which comes from water" (DK A30, ll. 29–30). Another odd metaphor raises Aristotle's ire: in his *Meteorology* Aristotle attributes to Empedocles the "ridiculous" assertion that "the sea is the sweat of the earth" (B3, 357a 24). As though the sweat of the earth, which labors so hard at its core, did not inspire love in the same way that the glow of a beloved does. In the development of living creatures, fire and water ("the glitter of Nestis") play crucial roles, each of them "harbored in Kypris Aphrodite" (DK B96, B98), even if the initial productions of life seem chaotic and monstrous. Aetius reports:

> Empedocles held that the first generations of animals and plants were not complete but consisted of separate limbs not joined together; the second, arising from the joining of these limbs, were like creatures in dreams; the third was the generation of whole-natured forms [τῶν ὁλοφῶν]; and the fourth arose no longer from the homogeneous substances such as earth or water, but by intermingling [δι' ἀλλήλων], in some cases as the result of the condensation of their nourishment, in others because the beauty of the female form [εὐμορφίας τῶν γυναικῶν] excited the

urge to implant seed [ἐπερεθισμὸν τοῦ σπερματικοῦ κινήματος ἐμποιησάσης]; and the various species of animals were distinguished by the quality of the mixture in them.

DK A72

Aristotle, in his *On the Heavens*, refers to the first phase of zoogony, apparently quoting directly from Empedocles' poem:

Here sprang up many faces without necks,
Arms wandered without shoulders, unattached,
Eyeballs strayed forlorn, in sore need of foreheads.

DK B57

It is surely the first stage, in which superfetated limbs and shards of humankind wander once again like Pirandello characters, that inspired Nietzsche, a devoted reader of Empedocles. In "On Redemption," in the second part of *Thus Spoke Zarathustra* (KSW 4:178), Zarathustra is astonished to see a gigantic ear crossing the bridge and advancing toward him. "It's an ear! an ear as big as a *Mensch!*" Beneath the ear Zarathustra eventually descries "a tiny, envious face." The people proclaim that the superfetated ear is a "genius," but Zarathustra is skeptical. "Truly, my friends, I drift among human beings as though among fragments and limbs of humanity!" There follows an account of the "It *was*" of time, of time's unbudgeable past, which is the boulder that no willful Sisyphus can budge. The tiny face of genius grimaces with the spirit of revenge—revenge against time and its simple past, its imperfect tense, its imperfection. It is redemption from the spirit of revenge that Zarathustra desires above all for humankind. And redemption will not come from our being all ears.

A passage from Alphonso Lingis's "The Rapture of the Deep," one not cited back in chapter 1, contemplates the various life forms of the deep as something very much like this first stage of Empedoclean zoogony. The diver, according to Lingis, encounters forms of life arrested at particular stages of evolution, stages that mammals, amphibians, and reptiles passed through millions of years ago (E 11). Such forms of life "are part-organs, gone no further than skin, ovaries, or a piece of intestine, or some muscles" (ibid.). The diver thus "drifts among dismembered partial attempts or rough drafts of evolution, gastrulas, sponges, sea slugs, plume worms, among dwarfish and monstrous forms, boxfish, giant squid"; the diver "drifts among them reduced to being part-organ oneself, eye without a look of one's own, touch apprehending, appropriating nothing" (ibid.). In retrospect, he writes, "The sea was full of the detached organs of some dismembered monster that never was" (E 12).

The second stage of Empedocles' zoogony gives rise to creatures that populate myth and legend for as long as Greece lasts—minotaurs and centaurs, dragons and giants, Cyclopes and Hydras and Chimeras. It also supplies Aristophanes (Plato's Aristophanes) with material for his comedy:

> Many creatures were born with faces and chests on both sides,
> Human-faced ox progeny, while others again sprang forth as
> Ox-faced human progeny, and others were compounded of male
> And female, and fitted out with shadowy parts.
>
> DK B61

Many stages of haphazard joining—perhaps Strife has as much to do with the confusions of duplicitous unification as Love does—and many phases of development must pass before a creature arises that is capable of pericardial thinking. Perhaps we are still not there. But in so saying we are back where we began, except for one further detail.

For it seems that in his *Purifications*, where Empedocles urges us to avoid bloodshed and cannibalism, the latter meaning the eating of animal flesh, he revises Hesiod's account of the origin of the gods, revising it in the direction of Love rather than Strife. For in the beginning,

> No war god Ares received worship, no battle cry,
> No Zeus the King, no Kronos and no Poseidon,
> But only Kypris the Queen.
> Her they propitiated with holy images,
> Portraits of living creatures, dappled and various,
> With perfumes of myrrh and sweet frankincense,
> Pouring to the earth libations of yellow honey.
> No bulls, horribly slaughtered, soiled their altars,
> For humans knew this to be the gravest defilement,
> To tear out the living soul and devour the limbs.

DK B128

It sounds as though Empedocles, at least until the last three lines, is here describing a wall-painting from ancient Thira—that of the crocus-gatherers who take their offerings of fragrant saffron to the goddess. But no Ouranos? no Kronos? no Zeus? no Thunderer? and no Poseidon? no Tamer of Horses? no Earth-shaker? no god of the sea? Only Aphrodite, the foam-born goddess, alone?

If I am not mistaken, Hemingway notes in *The Old Man and the Sea* that whereas in Spanish the sea is given the masculine pronoun, *el mar*, anyone who is familiar with the sea—as the old man certainly is—knows enough to call her *la mar*. Even so, we have to be astonished. Can Empedocles single-handedly alter Greek tradition? Can he replace Kronos with Kypris? If I am right, that is precisely what, centuries later, F. W. J. Schelling tries to do in his *Philosophy of Mythology*.

16 *"And that is why . . . the sea is called the tears of Kronos."*

5

The Tears of Kronos

The sea is the continuum, the perfection of the undifferentiated. Its emissary on earth is the snake. Where the snake is, there gushes water. Its eye is liquid. Beneath its coils flows the water of the underworld. Forever. Being sinuous, it has no need of joints. The same pattern covers its whole skin; its scales are uniform, its motion undulating and constantly self-renewing, like waves.

—ROBERTO CALASSO

In 1842, as professor of philosophy in Berlin, F. W. J. Schelling offers a course of twenty-nine lectures on *The Philosophy of Mythology.* The first six lectures, on the theme of "Monotheism," argue that the usual sense of monotheism derives from the happenstance that true believers fail to notice that there are many gods other than their own. Monotheism, especially when it is taken to be a refutation of polytheistic mythology, is therefore "purely illusory" (II/2:20).

One of the most telling demonstrations of the illusion is the failure of believers to take seriously Yahweh's exclamation after Eve and Adam have eaten the fruit of the tree of the knowledge of good and evil: "Adam has become like one of us," says the Lord in Genesis 3, 22. He ignores Eve, but never mind: millennia of misogyny, blaming Eve for whatever has happened to us, will compensate for this neglect.

However, to whom is Yahweh speaking? Who are "us"? Included in the "us," at all events, must be the serpent, inasmuch as the serpent has said to Eve, "Your eyes will be opened and you will be like God, knowing what good and evil are" (3:5). The serpent knows whereof he speaks, and Yahweh confirms the truth of the words of the serpent quite specifically, as though the serpent were indeed one of "us." The entire verse reads: "Adam has become like one of us, and he knows what good and evil are. Yet let him not partake of the tree of life and thus, eating the fruit, come to live eternally" (3:22). When later the Lord, dependably jealous, commands that his people abjure "false" gods, he once again confirms the truth of polytheism, inasmuch as the "false" are merely either the foreign or the ancient home gods—in any case, the others. Monotheism is a ruse of the priests, who dependably hate competition.

Lectures seven through twenty-nine, under the title "Mythology," therefore go in search of deities in the myths of China, India, Egypt, Assyria, Babylonia, the Arab lands, Persia, Phoenicia, and Greece. The grand narrative that Schelling relates cannot detain us here—it would take volumes to do it justice, if only because it is a narrative that in fact never comes to an end. Indeed, what is most fascinating about the lectures is that they very much want to conclude by announcing the end of mythology *at* and *as* the beginning of the Christian era; yet the complexity of the myths themselves, all of which contribute essential themes and patterns to Christianity, frustrates every attempt to come to a conclusion and to bring mythology to an end. An encounter with the sea, however, will set aside this enormous problematic and merely dip into Schelling's extraordinary lectures, focusing on only two figures, namely, Poseidon and Persephone. At the end, I will introduce a figure largely ignored by Schelling and by almost everyone else, namely, Ino Leukothea, "the radiant goddess" of the seas near the isle of Samothrace in the North Aegean.

Poseidon is hardly a central figure for Schelling. He surfaces only in the twenty-fifth lecture, in which Schelling discusses the three sons of Kronos, to wit, Hades, Poseidon, and Zeus. Hades is his father Kronos all over again: self-centered, simple contraction and pure centripetal force, inhering in and insisting on his own being. Whenever Kronos's consort Rhea gives birth to children Kronos swallows them. Or, in another version of the story, he so occupies Rhea with his sex that he prevents their birth until Rhea, conspiring with her oldest son, Zeus, has the future Olympian castrate and emasculate the father—precisely in the way that Kronos had castrated his father Ouranos. Hades, like his father, is entirely self-centered, even after he falls in love with Persephone. For the most part he remains invisible (τὸ ἄειδες means "the concealed"), and he is relentless in claiming the souls of mortals for the dark. Hades thus represents the most primitive form of deity, god in his first and weakest potency, characterized not by majesty and power but by bluster and moody brooding. When he does fall in love all he can do is abduct and rape. Insisting on being (*Seyn*) and on being the center of the circle, he can never move to the periphery in order to meet an Other; and that means that he can never truly *be*, since to be *able* to be (*das Seyn*können*de) is to develop possibilities by confronting differences, to travel to the edge, to live a bit.

To develop possibilities is what the divine "spirit" does, and the key to the life of spirit is that it "materialize." Mythology is the story of divine materializations, and the words *Materie* and *Mutter*, matter and mother, dominate Schelling's narrative throughout. For what the god invariably meets on the periphery of the circle is the woman for whom he does not yet know he languishes. And she will both show him the heavens and bring him down to earth.

One of the keys to the story of mythology, perhaps the most important one, is the one Schelling finds expressed in the earliest and most learned of the Church Fathers, Clement of Alexandria. Clement interprets the story of the Christian trinity in terms of "the becoming

woman of God," θηλύνεσθαι τῷ θεῷ, indicating the moment when the
self-centered Yahweh becomes the loving Christ. Clement adds, "And,
in loving, the father became womanly," καὶ δι᾽ ἀγάπην ἡμῖν ἐθελύνθη
(II/2:195). Schelling sees this feminization of divine power as essential
not only to Christianity but also to the great mythologies of India,
Egypt, Babylon, Persia, and Greece; the most remarkable turning-
points in his own narrative invariably involve mothers and woman
lovers—Urania, Mylitta, Mitra, Melakaeth haschamaim ("the Queen
of Heaven"), Demeter, Persephone, Kypris Aphrodite. And the central
figure of mythology, Dionysos, turns out to be the most ambiguously
androgynous of gods. Moreover, Dionysos is always "the *coming* god,"
the god of advent, who in his essence *remains* in the womb of Urania.
The Arabs will say that these two are one, Urania *with* Dionysos.
According to Otto Rank, every child of the deity and every lieutenant
of the deity on earth, every king or pope, is essentially an *infans* who
remains unborn (OR 126). Schelling, in his tenth lecture, explains the
importance of Urania as clearly as he can, and, as we will see, Urania
is important even for such an eminently masculine god as Poseidon:

> Hence, Urania is in mythology the first prostration [*Niederwerfung*]
> of the principle that at one time found itself in the vertical position
> [*im Zustand der Aufrichtung*]. I can best express it by calling it the
> first καταβολή [i.e., "descent," "downgoing"]. In mythology, it is the
> selfsame moment in nature that we have to think of as the proper
> inception of nature, the transition to her, when everything that was
> originally spirit gradually set about becoming material, releasing a
> matter that only then became accessible to the higher demiurgic
> potency; it is the moment when the ground of the world is laid,
> which is to say, when that which is first of all erected and enters
> into existence comes to be relatively nonexistent, comes to be
> ground. It becomes the ground of the world proper, if by *world* we

understand the collectivity of manifold things that differ from one another and are hierarchically ordered—in short, the world of articulated being [*des getheilten Seyns*]. For, prior to that, there was only undivided being.

II/2:201–2

Let me tiptoe on by the thousand necessary questions this passage raises and pose only one. What has the sea god (and all the goddesses of the sea) to do with this downgoing of undivided being into the ground of articulated being? Poseidon, like his brother Hades, is his father's son. When he is angry the seas are turbulent, and Odysseus knows how wrathful Poseidon can be. Yet Poseidon's element is fluidity, and the sea god can "materialize" in a way that is blocked to Hades. Poseidon "himself" has therefore "become material for the higher potency, has materialized in her direction" (II/2:580). That is to say, he has become the basis or ground of an entire world. True, his epithet is "broad-chested," and his brow is always furrowed. He is in fact Joyce's Citizen, a "broadshouldered deepchested stronglimbed … barekneed brawnyhanded hairylegged ruddyfaced sinewyarmed hero" (U 382). Yet he is *expansive*, and expansiveness is materialization. Poseidon *flows* as the sea. That quality he has from his mother's side, since Rhea means "to flow." From his father's side he has his anger and his willfulness—along with the inability to control his temper. But it is as though the Oceanides, the daughters of Okeanos, and Ino Leukothea herself can from time to time assuage his wrath and calm him. Schelling demonstrates the connection between Urania (or downgoing) and Poseidon much later in the course:

That he is represented as the god of the moist element derives from the fact that water in general is the first material expression of nature's voluptuosity, which she feels in becoming nature, when she emerges from the original tension, letting go of the stiffness that is in her, when her rigor softens. The very first καταβολή, designated by way of Urania, was accompanied by the appearance of water. In the religions of Syria that primal nature, the oldest of nature goddesses, was worshiped as a water or fish goddess. Every morning in Babylon the goddess Oannes emerged from the sea in order to teach civil order, law, and science.... Poseidon is in the material sense what Dionysos is in the formal or causative sense. But Dionysos is called the lord of moist nature.

II/2:581

We might pause to note that the first lines of this passage appear to be quoting anachronistically from Ferenczi: nature releases its tension (*Spannung*) and relaxes its rigor (*Strenge, Starrheit*) in the voluptuosity (*Wollust*) of water. Water is the primary materialization of divinity, as Thales will have insisted all along. By the end of the passage, Poseidon seems to be conflated with Dionysos, lord of the moist element, who is forever in the fluid state of coming. Yet Schelling turns now to the darker side of the expansive sea god:

Yet only one side of the god is explained this way. For Poseidon is not god of the moist element in general but god of the wild *sea*. What is moist and liquid in him comes from the higher potency, from Dionysos; but the wild, bitter, and salty in him comes from Kronos. For Poseidon is but the mollified Kronos, a Kronos grown liquid, as it were. The rage of Kronos, his bitterness over the feeling that he has been overcome, communicates itself to the sea. And that is why ... in certain mystery religions, as Plutarch tells us, the sea is called the tears of Kronos, Κρόνου δάκρυον.

Ibid.

Schelling attributes to Plutarch the phrase, "tears of Kronos," as a poetic etiology of the sea and its briny bitterness. Yet he could have found it also in Clement of Alexandria, who, as I noted, also gives

Schelling one of his principal themes, to wit, the higher potency of the feminine principle in deity. According to Porphyrius, Aristotle attributes the phrase "tears of Kronos" to the almost mythical figure of Pythagoras. In any case, Schelling must have suspected that the tears of the Titanic father are tears not only of bitterness but also of an incipient tenderness. For Poseidon is neither as sclerotic nor as bitter as his father. Sea storms sometimes do abate.

Schelling now reinforces one of his most "Romantic" tendencies: he insists that the science of physics focus not simply on numbers and quantities but also on sensibilities and qualities. This would be the "physics with wings," an early form of Ferenczi's *utraquism*, that Schelling and his friends, Hölderlin and Hegel, hoped for when they were young and foolish—or young and German Idealists—and drew up their manifesto-like "Oldest Program for a System in German Idealism." By the 1840s, however, everyone can see the direction that the "hard" sciences will take, their wings clipped forever. Another less well known "Romantic" tendency—indeed, a tendency that one might take to be quite *unromantic*—is to emphasize the dire forces and foreboding qualities of nature. Who can imagine, asks Schelling, that sulfur insults the nose as it does merely because of numbers? And the stench of methane gas escaping from the earth's surface or from metals in flux? Or, final example, the "inexplicable bitterness of the sea"? (II/2:582). Lucretius tries to explain that bitterness, which he calls *Neptuni corpus acerbum*, "Neptune's bitter body," altogether scientifically by noting that whereas atoms of sweet water are round and smooth the salt sea contains "spiky" atoms, atoms that stick in the throat, molest the sinus cavities, and attack all our tender tissues (2:461–72). Schelling's question to Lucretius would be, "Are not those substances manifestly the children of terror, anxiety, discouragement, despair?" (II/2:582).

Whose *Schrecken, Angst, Unmut,* and *Verzweiflung* are expressed in the bitterness and acrid taste and smell of the sea? As Schelling's

Weltalter-Fragmente (1811–15) make perfectly clear, these are the qualities of the primal potency of the deity—before he has confronted the higher potency of Urania. We are not mistaken in identifying this primal potency with what Schelling in *Die Weltalter* calls "the barbaric principle," an idea that greatly intrigued Merleau-Ponty (N 38). That principle is represented by the Titan Kronos, who weeps bitterly because he senses that his day is done, his race run. Which makes one wonder whether the Earth-shaker and Tamer of Horses, whom we often see in a rage, ever weeps a more tender and less barbaric tear. The Homeric Hymn to Poseidon calls his element the unharvested or barren sea, ἀτρυγέτοιο θαλάσσης, and it begs the god to be kind of heart "and help those who voyage in ships!" Yet Poseidon seldom takes that plea to heart, and the shipwrecked would do better to apply to the radiant goddess, Ino Leukothea. There must be *something* about the sea, however, that the word *bitterness* does not cover.

Now that we have mentioned the bitterness and the stench of the sea, it is time to introduce Hegel into the discussion. For *bitterness* and *stench* are the first words that fall when Hegel contemplates the sea. His earliest reflections on the philosophy of nature, in his Jena writings from the years 1803 to 1806, do not have much to say about the ocean as the source of life; yet in his mature system the sea plays an important—if ambiguous—role.[1] The sea is "the neutral Earth," that is,

---

[1] On the "stench" or "smells" of the sea, *Gerüche*, see JS 3:103; the most detailed early discussion of the sea occurs at JS 3:103–4. My primary text in what follows is addendum (b) to section 341 in the second volume of Hegel's *Enzyklopädie der philosophischen Wissenschaften im Grundrisse*, 3rd edn (1830), "Philosophy of Nature," which appears in vol. 9 of the Suhrkamp edition, cited in the body of my text by volume and page number. See also the introductory remarks to my three chapters on Hegel (9–11) in *Contagion*, especially 117–25 and 145–9.

"earth" as a *salt* in the chemical sense, neither acid nor base but neutral; it is also the ebb and flood tides, its motion responding to the positions of the sun, the moon, and the Earth itself. The moon is particularly significant in this regard: dry as dust and dim of wit, with only reflected light at its disposal, the moon is dying of thirst, and so it tries to suck up the seas (9:128). That is lunatic, of course, inasmuch as the last act of a castaway is to gulp seawater when no sweet water is there to drink. Delirium and death soon follow.

Nature sets limits to philosophy, says Hegel, not because of its power but because of its cognitive impotence. Because it is unable to avoid accident and contingency, botched births and monstrosities, nature cannot always be reduced to an intelligent concept (9:35). Hence, whereas some expressions of the life of nature seem sublime, others seem ludicrous and pathetic. In Hegel's view nothing is more absurd than the attempt of many natural philosophers to seek meaningful parallels, analogies, and symbolisms everywhere in nature. He is thinking above all of Schelling. As Merleau-Ponty remarks, "Schelling has a bad reputation, and he owes it to Hegel" (N 48). True, the land emerges from ocean waters like a crystal rising out of the mother solute; true also is the fact that sweet water has its source in the evaporation of the seas, and is merely "abstract neutrality," whereas the sea itself is "physical neutrality"; finally, it is true that abstract neutrality desires physical neutrality, so that the rivers that rush to the sea deserve to be called Naiads. Hegel, perhaps influenced by the "river hymns" of the other friend of his youth, Hölderlin, waxes eloquent about the great rivers: "I do not see mountains as mere collectors of the rainwater that penetrates them; rather, the true sources of such rivers as the Ganges, the Rhone, and the Rhine have an interior life, a striving, a drive, like Naiads; the Earth expels her abstract sweet water, which hurries in these outpourings of her concrete vitality to the sea" (9:363). The sea *is* the "higher vitality," however, higher than air and earth and sweet water—as elevated as fire. The sea is perhaps what Heraclitus says it is, namely, the first of fire's "turnings." Yet the sea is also, as Hegel says, "the subject of bitterness and neutrality and dissolution" (9:363). That is to say, brine contains *Bittersalz* or *Bittererde*, magnesium sulfate, is neutral chemically, and is a universal solute of all the life that eventually dissolves back into it.

The sea is "a living process that is always on the verge of irrupting into life"; yet no sooner does the irruption occur than "it falls back into the water," *aber immer wieder ins Wasser zurückfällt* (ibid.). "To fall into the water" is an idiom in German for failure and frustration. True, the combination of salts in ocean water means that such water is "organic," or at least that it "shows itself everywhere as being pregnant" with life, *das sich überall als gebärend zeigt* (9:364). The sea, like a woman or any other female mammal, although Hegel does not extend the parallel, *gebiert*, or "bears" life. This is perhaps the only allusion, itself indirect, to amniotic fluid. Indeed, whereas Hegel is fascinated by human genitality and sexuality generally, and also by the varieties of species, from aquatic animals, through amphibia, to the mammals, he has nothing to say about amniotica. Cetaceans—the whales, for example, although they would be the one example that does not serve the point to be made—who fall back into the sea, are a bit dull; the reptiles and amphibia, so ungainly on the land, are "wretched formations" (9:512: *jämmerliche Gebilde*), and indeed there is "something repulsive" (9:513: *etwas Widriges*) about them. As for mammals, Hegel notices that they have breasts (what's in a name?) so that they nurse and protect their young, thus possessing the rudiments of family life. But he is most interested in their extremities—their feet and hands, since the apes too have hands, he says—as *weapons* by means of which the mammals defend themselves (9:514–16).

Hegel does not notice that mammals, in Ferenczi's also quite Hegelian expression, "introject" something like the sea in which to harbor their young. Although the instant of fertilization or conception (*Empfängnis*) is important to him as the culmination of sexual reproduction (9:519), there is nothing in his lectures about fetal development, which at least seems to recapitulate the vitality of the odorous fish, the repulsive amphibia and reptilia, and the more highly individualized mammal. For a philosopher who is everywhere fascinated by process and development, and one who is nothing if not thorough, entering as he always does into chambers where the angelic philosophers fear to tread, the omission of fetal development in amniotic fluid is quite remarkable. It is perhaps the greatest single lacuna in Hegel's thinking of nature, even if others share that lacuna with him. But let us, like the whale, return to the sea—although, admittedly, the whale never leaves the sea of its own accord, not even to give birth.

Pregnant with life, the sea is simultaneously pregnant with death. "The sea has a peculiarly foul smell—a life, as it were, that is always dissolved in corruption" (9:364). Thus what sailors call the "blossoming" of the night sea, that is, the appearance of swarms of phosphorescent phytoplankton on the surface, popularly known as "Sea Sparkle" (*Noctiluca scintillans*), is actually a sign that the sea has become "impure, turbid, slimy" (ibid.). In a moment Hegel will compare this phosphorescence to fools' fire, *ignis fatui*, the will-o'-the-wisp: what the naïve enthusiast takes to be the firelight of forest fairies is an emanation of rotting wood in a swamp (9:365). True, the sea has its fantastic geometry of points, threads, and flat surfaces, all of it a living phantasmagoria; to repeat, ocean water *is* "the tendency to irrupt into vegetal life" (9:364). Yet that phosphorescent sparkle on the surface of the sea, "partly an endless shining, partly an immeasurable, unsurveyable sea of light," is precisely on the surface, hence superficial:

it is a light that never becomes subjectivity, never the inner light of reason and spirit; it is a deceptive glow that quickly degenerates to "*gelatinous slime*" (ibid.). The tiny plants and animals of the sea do develop into higher forms, become infusoria and transparent soft-shelled fish, and so they seem destined for "a longer life"; yet the bulk of sea life is but "a momentarily existent slime," and the millions of living creatures "quickly melt away into the element," *zerschwimmen schnell wieder in das Element* (ibid.). The verb *zerschwimmen* is noteworthy: *schwimmen*, as Nietzsche would doubtless confirm, is the energetic swimming that shows how vital these tiny creatures are; yet their swimming to excess or to exhaustion—for that is what the prefix *zer-* suggests—is their dissolution into the very sea water that spawns them. They are going nowhere.

At this point Hegel contrives out of Sea Sparkle his most extraordinary analogy, parallel, or symbol—most extraordinary and most remarkably ambiguous. "The sea in this way manifests an army of stars, thickly compressed into Milky Ways: they are as much as [*so gut als*] the stars in the heaven" (9:365). What more elevated and edifying symbol could one find? Certainly Kant could find no more sublime figure for the pursuit of critical knowledge than the starry heavens above him. Yet Hegel is not so edified. He says that the stars are no more edifying than an outbreak of pox on the human skin or a swarm of flies (9:81). He chides his students for being so shocked by his remark—apparently they have been talking about it all over town, causing a scandal. Hegel, not relenting, holds to his argument: irruption is irruption, and an *Ausschlag* can as readily be smallpox and a swarm of insects as the chunks of rock and fire that fill outer space. The phosphorescent sea is nothing but the reflection of a profusion that in and of itself has no dignity. True, as Leibniz supposed, every drop of sea water is "a living globe" (9:365) and contains an infinity of evanescent subjects. Yet "the neutrality of the sea snatches such neophyte subjectivity back into its indifferent womb" (ibid.). *Die Neutralität des Meers reißt diese beginnende Subjektivität in dessen gleichgültigen Schoß.* The womb of the sea may be teeming, but its profusions invariably melt back into it, and the sea is unsolicitous of them. That is what smells.

The sea's vitality trickles (*zerfließt*) into abstract generality. Even if philosophers since Thales have praised the sea as the very provenance of life, its *Hervorgehen*, life itself must repulse (*Abstoßen*) the sea, tearing itself away from her (*losreißend*). Certain animals are cast back into the sea even after they develop outside of it. The whales, again, are Hegel's example, but the cetaceans impress him only by their "undeveloped torpor," *unentwickelten Dumpfheit* (ibid.). Hegel therefore struggles onto the land now, as uninviting as it may be, with proper subjectivity and a luminous spirit in tow—or perhaps in a glass retort. He seems to believe that the sea can be left behind.

Let us return to Schelling's meditation on bitter, wrathful Poseidon in the *Philosophy of Mythology*. "The unpleasurable, discouraging aspect of Poseidon's essence, which he manifests continually throughout the *Iliad*, is, as it were, merely the aftertaste of that original discouragement that Kronos feels, sensing as he does that he has been overcome" (II/2:582). Whether Zeus, the oldest son of Kronos and the one who claims sovereignty over his two brothers, can truly be what Schelling hopes he will become, namely, the god of wisdom and intelligence, is a question we may set aside for the moment. True, Zeus has enough sense to fall in love with Μῆτις, "intelligent counsel," but was it sensible to swallow her whole after he impregnated her? The result, we recall, was severe migraine and the head-splitting birth of Athena, which is a mystery all its own. Even if we agree to leave the question open, it does seem that Zeus is incapable of loving wisely. He is just like people. He

17 *Aphrodite, the Roman Venus, is the goddess "born of sea spume."*

deceives countless mortal women and men, and he betrays his divine consort more often than she deceives him. In fact, all his life he seems to be deceiving only himself, running away from the inevitable. As matters turn out for Schelling's lectures, however, deception and deceit are of the essence when it comes to deity.

In the very opening lecture on "Mythology" proper, the seventh, the theme of deception and deceit looms large. For the self-centered god, unhappy in his perfect narcissism and masculine willfulness, is inevitably overcome by the desire for other possibilities. Possibility, however, *das Seynkönnende*, is the capacity to move beyond the center and to be outside oneself, *ausser sich seyn*, on the periphery, and this, in mythology universally, always and everywhere, is an attribute of "sheer womanliness," *der blossen Weiblichkeit* (II/2:141). Pure being-in-itself finds itself wanting. Wanting what? Something else. Something possible. Yet possibility-being involves a twofold, a δυάς, a duplex nature and even a duplicity. For if a possibility comes to *be*, it is an actuality, not a possibility; if a possibility *remains* a possibility, then matters can always be *otherwise*. But that means we can always be deceived about them.

The first three mythological figures of woman that enter on the scene in Schelling's lectures are Nemesis, Apatē, and Maja. Let us focus on the central figure, Ἀπάτη, Deceit. She is so important to the Greeks that they have a yearly festival devoted to her. The feast of the Apaturia (τὰ Ἀπατούρια) is widespread in Greece, from Attica to Ionia and even to the Caucasus and the Black Sea. We know very little about the festival, although its cult practices appear to involve rites of passage—the votive offerings are often children's toys, playthings now to be put aside. Many different gods are celebrated during the Apaturia, and they vary from place to place; in far-off Scythia, for example, Aphrodite is at the center of the cult. A constant is Ἀπάτη herself. She is the personification of deceit or duplicity, although the carnivalesque face of the twofold is sometimes less menacing than one might think. Ἀπάτη is, to be sure, a child of the Night, mentioned in Hesiod's *Theogony* (l. 224) alongside Fatality, Cares, and Death, Blame and Woe, Nemesis, Senescence, and Strife, Clotho, Lachesis, and Atropos. Yet lovely amiability, Φιλότητα, is also cited as closely accompanying Apatē. This last association may seem strange, until we notice that Deceit has already been introduced into Hesiod's poem, inasmuch as "smiles and deceits" unfailingly accompany Aphrodite. The foamborn goddess, beloved of the undeceitful Empedocles, has emerged from the severed genitals of Kronos that Zeus tossed into the sea. The Titan's μήδεα or "parts" are what grant Aphrodite the epithet φιλομμηδέα (l. 200), "lover of the male parts." The *Theogony* continues:

> And with Aphrodite went Eros, and comely Desire [Ἵμερος] followed her from the first after she was born and as she went into the assembly of the gods. This honor she has from the beginning, and this is the portion [μοῖραν] allotted to her among human beings and immortal gods—the whisperings of maidens and smiles and all that arises from deceits [ἐξαπάτας] that are sweet and delightful, and love and grace.
>
> *Theogony*, ll. 201–6

Whisperings, smiles, grace, and everything that flows from sweet Deceit, ἐξαπάτας. Thus we confront the two faces of Deceit, child of the Night: a sister to lovely amiability, she is nonetheless eminently capable of duplicity and betrayal. Indeed, she is herself double; she is the *dyás* in person. At her friendliest she is mascara, eye-shadow, a fragrance, and all the womanly wiles; at her worst she is trickery, treachery, guile, and fraud—all these are her epithets.

Hera too, in complicity with Aphrodite, embodies these epithets. The fourteenth book of the *Iliad* sings "the deception of Zeus" by Hera, Διὸς ἀπάτη. One might even speak of the "anaesthetization" of

Zeus, as the translator of the Tusculum edition does, *Die Betäubung des Zeus*. We could borrow a word from Heidegger and speak of Zeus's *Benommenheit*, his being "benumbed" or "stupefied." How it happens is as follows: the Trojans, supported by Zeus, have destroyed the wall that the Achaeans hoped would protect their ships, and even Agamemnon is losing heart. Hera determines to protect and inspire her Greeks by distracting Zeus. She bathes in ambrosia, on which the gods usually dine, dresses and bejewels herself, plaits her hair and dons a new veil that shines like the sun; she then borrows Aphrodite's girdle or sash, the ultimate weapon, into which are woven the threads of love, desire, whispered words, and flattery enough to rob the wisest god or mortal of his or her composure. The mere sight of her would be enough to stun Zeus. But, leaving nothing to chance, she takes a reluctant Hypnos (Sleep, the brother of Thanatos) with her to Zeus at his lookout on Mount Ida, and the two of them, Hera and Hypnos, she first, do their work. Hector is suddenly in the dust—not killed, but struck by a stone—and it seems the tide will now turn in favor of the Greeks. Until, of course, Zeus wakes up. At the beginning of the fifteenth song (15:31, 33), Zeus scolds his irresistible wife, using two forms of the word for deception, ἀπατάων and μ᾽ ἀπάτησας.

For Schelling, the twofold sense of glittering, blinding Apatē is what is most important about her. For the very meaning of *possibility*, as we have seen, includes the immitigable possibility of *deception*. As the Hindu philosophers realize, the veil of Maja, "the net of semblance," is cast over all possibility. For *Schein* is "the other *Seyn*" (II/2:149). Apatē is therefore not some contingent illusion or some accident that has befallen being, but *Ur-täuschung*, "primordial deception." For Schelling, as for Nietzsche, the words *Schein* and *schön* are essentially related; radiant beauty coalesces with blinding semblance. The capacity to be, *Seynkönnen*, for gods, heroes, and other splendid mortals, "is merely a semblant can-do," "a deceptive can-do," "a magic that betrays, an Ἀπάτη" (II/2:151). It is therefore no surprise that Schelling, hundreds of pages later, in the twenty-seventh of his lectures, reverts to Hesiod's great poem and to the theme of Deceit. For the possibility of deception is crucial to the becoming-woman of deity. Deception in multiple senses: one recalls Dionysos dressing young King Pentheus as a woman so that he might spy on the Maenads; by the time Pentheus is costumed and primped, he *is* the woman he wants merely to appear to be.

The entire philosophy of mythology, to repeat, is about this becoming-woman of the gods. Yet what does this have to do with the sea? For an answer, we have to dive below the seabed and enter the underworld.

In Schelling's *Philosophy of Mythology* the story of Persephone or Proserpina is one of the essential stories. For she herself is deceived twice, first by her father, Zeus, who in the form of a serpent takes her, and then by Zeus's brother, Hades, who abducts her to the underworld. Hers is what Schelling calls *das unvordenkliche Verhängnis*, "the fatality back behind which no one can think," the immemorial doom. Schelling cites a late representation of this fatality, one that has immense importance for the Romans—namely, the figure of *Fortuna primigenia*. That is the Τύχη, Fortune or Luck, who presides over the birth and early infancy of every mortal. And *Fortuna primigenia*, who survives in all the good and bad fairy godmothers of folklore, is often enough *Fortuna adversa*. For no act of will, no assertion of masculinity and no feminine resistance, can withstand her influence. She is fatality prior to all memory and all consciousness. She is, says Schelling, surprise, deception, the unexpected: *die Überraschung, die Täuschung, das Unerwartete* (II/2:153). And the unexpected often comes in the form of a severance or cut. The life of divinity is characterized by its being "cut off from its earlier state," *abgeschnitten*; indeed, this cut will return as the ever-present mytheme of castration. And the first form of this violent cut, as counter-intuitive as it may seem, is the ever-recurring theme of rape, as though sexual violence were essentially Ferenczian autotomy:

> In her emergence ... as she first comes to the fore (in an ideal figure) and as she shows herself in being, she [Persephone] is the unobserved, the unthought; already in this respect she is also *Fatum*, fatality, called Μόρος, "lot," and similarly *Fortuna* (all concepts that the ancient philosophers apply to the essence of Persephone). *Fortuna*, universally considered, is what is constantly in motion and never identical with itself, the inconstant in general. Yet as the *actually* emerging figure, Persephone is surely *Fortuna* **adversa**, misfortune, mischance; indeed, she is thought to be not merely accidentally unfortunate but the essential misfortune itself, the *first* misfortune, primordial accident.
>
> II/2:160

Fortune, *adverse* fortune, may toll at least two bells of memory in more recent times. First, the familiar opening (and closing) lament of Carl Orff's *Carmina burana*, the lament addressed to *Fortuna Imperatrix Mundi*, "Fortune, the Empress of the World": "*O Fortuna, / velut luna / statu variabilis ... / Sors immanis / et inanis, / rota tu volubilis.*" The constantly shifting fortunes of humankind, shifting always toward *adversity* as it seems, might then also remind us of one of Merleau-Ponty's most thought-provoking essays, "Human Being and Adversity," which contains passages like these: "When our initiatives get stuck in the paste of the body, of language, or of the immense world that we are given to complete, it is not that an evil genie opposes his will to ours: it is merely a matter of a kind of inertia, a passive resistance, a faltering of sense—an anonymous *adversity*" (S 304). Merleau-Ponty concludes his essay with a word about his own times, those difficult years immediately after the Second World War, but it is a word that points forward to our own madhatter present and back to time immemorial: "The discussions of our time are so convulsive merely because they resist a truth that is very close to us; and perhaps because our time is closer than any other to this truth, with no veil interposed, we recognize the menacings of adversity, the metamorphoses of Fortune" (S 308).

In short, Persephone is a mask, a tragic mask, of Urania. As such, she too is the initial καταβολή, the initial *downgoing* and *catastrophe*. Crucial to the mystery of her—she and her mother Demeter are the key figures of many mystery cults—is the fact that the catastrophe both *happens to her* and *is inflicted by her*. Persephone is *die leidige Dyás*, "the suffering [or the wretched] twofold" (II/2:163). Even if one does violence to Persephone, it is Persephone who eventually overcomes deity. To meet Persephone is to have already become history; it is to be *überwunden*, "overcome," as Schelling repeatedly says. It gradually becomes clear that the catastrophe has to do with the sea—not only as the always possible desiccation of the seas but also as the treacherous inconstancy of the sea. Zeus's rape of Persephone, his daughter, occurs when he assumes the figure of a snake—for the bull from the sea is also a snake on land, "the sea's emissary," as Calasso says (RC 236/207). Zeus had already assumed that serpentine figure in order to rape Persephone's mother, Demeter, the rape that produced Persephone herself.

Zeus, python-like, even swallows some of his victims, Metis, for example. Perhaps that makes him smart enough to realize what is at stake in these acts of violence: it is Zeus who has to find a way to mollify Demeter when her search for her abducted daughter fails, that failure causing the enraged mother to interrupt the circulation of the waters of sea, cloud, and rainfall. After the earth becomes an arid wasteland, at the very nadir of the catastrophe, Zeus is forced to work out that famous compromise by which Persephone will remain beneath the barren earth for an allotted time, emerging each spring in order to initiate the greening. As Calasso notes, even when the male acts violently against the female, it is the female alone who possesses the μῆτις, the good counsel and "the intelligence that preordains action in the silence of the mind" (RC 231/202). From the rape by Zeus of Persephone—of his daughter the snake, "the girl whose name cannot be uttered," as Euripides says—the result is Zagreus, the first and most fragile figure of Dionysos, god of moisture and of dissolution. That fragile, vulnerable, thoroughly androgynous figure is at the heart of the mysteries, and Schelling is wise to their essential teaching, which Calasso calls "the vertigo of the mysteries." We have heard it before, but it bears repeating: "For those not initiated in the mysteries, they seem to have to do with the immortality of human beings; for the initiates, the mysteries are a moment when the gods have to deal with death . . ." (RC 353/315–16).

The secret of Zeus, known only to the initiates, is that the Corybants in the Cretan cave where his mother hid him from Kronos in fact killed him (RC 340/304). Throughout the history of mythology, says Schelling, there is a sense of the "transience" of deity and hence the "vanity" of all cult; "the feeling of the finitude of these gods" dwells with the storytellers and the devotees. That is what is *tragic* about mythology, and it accounts for the "undertow of profound dejection," *der Zug tiefer Schwermuth*, that accompanies mythology from beginning to end (II/2:346). If indeed the ebb tide comes to an end. The vulnerability of the gods—as though they are wholly absorbed in the cycle of sea, evaporation, cloud, rainfall, and stream—is the enduring lesson of mythology, which culminates in the mysteries. The essential name of that lesson is Persephone:

Without Persephone's coming-out [*Herausgehen*], there would be no mythology, and without mythology, no Zeus. Her coming-out is therefore, when one looks to the end, in the interest of Zeus, so to speak, and accordingly the work of Zeus. Yet as long as Persephone— the potency of primal consciousness—remains in that pure apartness [*Abgeschiedenheit*] which does not know itself, nothing can subdue her; she is, as it were, in a place of safety, protected from all danger. Yet just as she knows herself to be the possibility that brings ill [*die unheilbringende Möglichkeit*], she is already the suffering *dyás*, already in danger of losing her purity. But as soon as she actually rises out of her virginal solitude, turning to the outside, because she is much more the god-positing one than the god-posited, she is inherently—not in an inauthentic sense but in an authentic sense—to remain the true *interiority* of deity [*das wahre Innere der Gottheit*]. As soon as she actually tends to the outside, she is from that point on subjected to an unavoidable process; she is consciousness that is now already properly dedicated to downgoing. . . . As the one dedicated to downgoing she has already fallen to the god of the underworld, Hades, who in what follows will indeed abduct her.

II/2:163

What Schelling wishes to emphasize, however, is that Persephone is less a victim than the fatality for deity. Mythological consciousness recognizes her as "what ought not to be [*das nicht seyn Sollende*], as the unjust, the sinister" (ibid.). Persephone as *sinister*, as the Queen of the Night, or as Kurosawa's Snow Queen, the Queen of Dead Souls, is precisely the *uncanny*. We have to remember that Freud has his very definition of *das Unheimliche*, which the Italian translates as *sinistra*, "left-handed," from Schelling, and precisely from the *Philosophy of Mythology*. The brilliant aither of Homer's Olympian panoply can come to shine, says Schelling long before the youthful Nietzsche says it, only after the darker insights of mythology have been preserved in the mysteries; those darker insights Schelling attributes to an "uncanny principle," to wit, "the dark and darkening force of that uncanny principle (one calls *unheimlich* everything that was supposed to remain in latency, in secret [*im Geheimnis*], in concealment, and yet has come to the fore) ..." (II/2:649). Nine pages later, Schelling, reflecting on the figures of the Aegina temple frieze, the temple of Aphaia on Aegina being arguably itself a monument to Persephone, observes that the ancient Greek sculptors were able to reveal *something* of the gods by way of human forms. Yet they always reveal the divine— whether deceptively or for the sake of some hidden truth—by introducing a "nonhuman" or "extra-human" trait into their figures, veiling them "in a certain *Unheimlichkeit*" (II/2:658). Perhaps when Thales says that all things are "full of gods" he is thinking of the uncanniness of limpid water; but he may also be thinking of the uncanny veil of spume that rises over sunken ships. Millennia after Thales and decades after Schelling, Rudolf Otto, cited by Otto Rank, will define such uncanniness as the essence of religious feeling as such and in general. Rudolf Otto calls that origin the "primal feeling of numinosity," the feeling that causes us not to bathe in oceanic feeling but "to shudder in the face of the uncanny" (OR 117).

The unrevealed revelations of mythology, which culminate in the mystery cults, have to do with the crisis every deity undergoes when it confronts, as it must, the feminizing principle that was present at its birth and throughout its life of longing and languishing. That crisis neither begins nor ends with the reign of Zeus. At the center of Schelling's attention is not Yahweh but the Queen of Heaven, Melakaeth haschamaim, who breaks the power of a god who knows only how to punish his people with floods, locusts, and hemorrhoids. Not Yahweh but the Queen of Heaven; not Mithras but Mitra and Zeruane Akherene, who as a figure of Fortune (Τύχη) reconciles the principles of good (Ormuzd) and evil (Ahriman); not the astronomer priests of Babylon but the temple prostitutes—that is, the wives of the citizens—who worship Mylitta and the coming god with whom Mylitta is pregnant (if the priests garner Schelling's attention at all it is by way of their cross-dressing and self-mutilation: II/2:249–50); not Herakles the strongman but Herakles disguised as a woman and protected by the women; not mighty Allah, but the mother of the child Allah, Alitta or Al-Ilat; not the *monos* of the solitary male god but the *dyás*, the duality of the female, or, at best, of the male *with* the female; not the face of the Angel of the Lord but the Janus head, one face male, the other female; not a single seat of power but Chaos, which is but two shorelines with an abyssal gap in between; not monotheism but a polytheism of *dii consentes et complices*, gods and goddesses who "can only originate together and die together" (II/2:605); not a single godhead but "the moiling mix of deities," *das Gewimmel von Göttern* (II/2:669); and in all this, the καταβολή or downgoing of the self-centered deity carried out in and by Urania, who is pregnant with Dionysos, the coming god, who if he ever emerges does so from the sea and in the arms of his nurse, Ino Leukothea. About whom more in a moment.

About that "fishy" odor, the odor of herring brine, and the chemical phantasmagoria of trimethylamine, discussed back in chapter 2, which may be the secret of Hegel's consistent misogyny. Roberto Calasso tells the offensive story of the women of Lemnos—an island not far from Samothrace visited by Jason and his Argonauts—who became famous for their fragrance. The story as recounted by Calasso is one of the most disconcerting in all of Greek mythology:

> After slaughtering their men, the women of Lemnos were struck by a kind of revenge the gods had never used before nor would again:

they began to smell. And in this revenge we glimpse the grievance that Greece nursed against womankind. Greek men thought of women as of a perfume that is too strong, a perfume that breaks down to become a suffocating stench, a sorcery, "sparkling with desire, laden with aromas, glorious," but stupefying, something that must be shaken off. It is an attitude betrayed by small gestures, like that passage in the pseudo-Lucian where we hear of a man climbing out of bed, "saturated with femininity," and immediately wanting to dive into cold water. When it comes to women, Greek sensibility brings together both fear and repugnance: on the one hand, there is the horror at the woman without her makeup who "gets up in the morning uglier than a monkey"; on the other, there is the suspicion that makeup is being used as a weapon of *apátè*, of irresistible deceit. Makeup and female smells combine to generate a softness that bewitches and exhausts. Better for men the sweat and dust of the gymnasium. "Boys' sweat has a finer smell than anything in a woman's makeup box" [Pseudo-Lucian].

RC 97/79

Calasso's story alters one important detail of the myth: he suggests that the gods punished the Lemnian women by making them smell *after* they had murdered their husbands, whereas other accounts say that the men of Lemnos had imported concubines from Thrace (ancestors, no doubt, of Thales' servant girl) because their own women were too strongly scented before the punishing gods ever intervened. In the context of Apatē, Deceit, one may expatiate a bit on the Greek grievance against women, because there is something else about women that is even more disturbing, even more deceptive. The story of Hera's blinding of Tiresias points toward this more irksome grievance, which involves "the very pleasure of the woman, the pleasure of passivity"; that very pleasure, speculates Calasso, "might conceal a mocking power that eludes male control" (RC 99/80). Love between women was not the scandal, not exactly. It was rather "the suspicion, which had taken root in their minds, that women might have their own indecipherable erotic self-sufficiency, and that those rites and mysteries they celebrated, and in which they refused to let men participate, might be a proof of this" (RC 98-9/80-1). It is as though the Greek women had been taking the texts of Luce Irigaray to heart millennia before they were written. Calasso adds, "And, behind it all, their most serious suspicion had to do with pleasure in coitus. Only Tiresias had been able to glimpse the truth, and that was precisely why he was blinded" (RC 99/81).

Here the ghost of Tiresias rises to confront Ferenczi: whereas the latter labors to eke out some paltry compensation (*Trost*) for those weakling frogs who lost the phylogenetic battle of the as yet nonexistent sexes and had to submit to the "drill," Tiresias reveals that it is the bull frog who needs our sympathy. Calasso's conclusion to the Lemnos story is all the richer for our having taken a detour through the Tiresias story: "One gets a sense, in these reactions to womankind, of something remote being revealed as though through nervous reflex. In the later, more private and idiosyncratic writers, we pick up echoes that take us back to a time long, long before, to the terror roused by the invasion of the Amazons, and to the loathsome crime of the women of Lemnos" (RC 97/79).

We are so accustomed to thinking of the Greek relationship to femininity and womankind as one of successful repression and oppression that we fail to remember that one of the friezes of the Parthenon depicted the battle of the Greeks against the Amazons. That frieze was no cartoon. We also fail to remember that almost every tragedy played out in the Theater of Dionysos on the south side of the Athenian acropolis tells a story about women who slip away from a desperate and desirous man's control. Always another catastrophe abides in those creatures of the sea such as Ino Leukothea—who *will* have their way.²

A certain mythical Lycurgus, made famous by a choral song of Sophocles' *Antigone*, insults Dionysos and blasphemes against him. The god then distracts his wits and Lycurgus is driven to suicide. He leaps into the sea. Similarly, Ino—before she becomes Leukothea, the shining goddess—is hardly a model citizen. Like Lycurgus, Ino at first insults the god Dionysos. Her sister Semele has become pregnant with this god, who is eternal advent; Semele tells her sisters that Zeus himself did the deed. Ino and her two sisters, Agaue and Autonoë, mock their sister. How many careless girls get themselves pregnant and then blame a god! Semele pays the ultimate price for her pregnancy: when, tricked by the jealous Hera, she begs Zeus to show himself to her in his full power, he does so. But he is lightning, and Semele is consumed by fire. After her death, Dionysos, remembering his abused mother, drives his blaspheming aunts mad. Euripides' *The Bacchae* tells the grim story of two of the sisters, especially the story of Agaue, but it leaves Ino out of the account.

The story of Ino Leukothea is every bit as shocking. In her case too it is Hera, jealous because of her husband's escapade with Semele, who drives Ino mad. Zeus has given Ino the infant Dionysos, after the god's second birth from the thigh of Zeus, with the request that she nurse

---

² The darkest aspect of Bachofen's *Mutterrecht* thesis is represented by the Lemnian women, who are clearly, in Bachofen's view, avatars of the murderous Amazons. See ch. 4, "Lemnos," of J. J. Bachofen, *Das Mutterrecht: Eine Untersuchung über die Gynaikokratie der alten Welt nach ihrer religösen und rechtlichen Natur*, ed. Hans-Jürgen Heinrichs (Frankfurt am Main: Suhrkamp, 1975 [1861]), esp. 232.

the god and hide him, and this Ino faithfully does. But one day, after Hera has done her vindictive work, Ino curses, seizes the infant Dionysos, and boils him in a cauldron of water. She then takes the boiled flesh of the god into her arms and leaps from a cliff into the sea. She drowns, and that is the end of her mortal life.

Yet in her case that lethal plunge into the sea turns out to be a lustral rite, a spiritual bath, as it were. The blasphemer and deicide is transformed into a goddess—why and how we do not know, since the mysteries remain mysteries, although a mortal woman with a god at her breast is a very special sort of woman. Her name becomes Leukothea, the shining or radiant goddess. As we know, Dionysos too is twiceborn, even thriceborn, and in a sense he remains—as the *coming* god, the god of perpetual *advent*—always and forever to be born again. An artist's or copyist's faded rendering of a statue of her in antiquity shows a lovely matron holding the infant Dionysos in her left arm; his left hand holds a jug, doubtless containing wine, while his right reaches up toward her face as though in tender supplication. Leukothea is surely one of the original Madonnas. And if her name is soon forgotten—even the omniscient Schelling neglects to mention her—many temples were dedicated to her in antiquity.[3]

Roberto Calasso tells the story of Ino Leukothea in the following way, responding to his own question as to why and how she was elevated to divine status. Nothing seems less likely, especially when we consider those parts of the myth that have to do with her marriage to King Athamas of Boeotia, her conspiracy to murder the infants of a

---

[3] Robert Graves, *The White Goddess: A Historical Grammar of Poetic Myth* (New York: Farrar, Straus and Giroux, 1966 [1948]), 63, has little to say about Ino Leukothea, even though the "shining" goddess may as readily be translated as the "white" goddess. He seems therefore to have passed on by the most telling figure of the goddess whom he clearly worships as the source of all poetry.

18 "*Statue of Leukothea with the young Bacchus on her left arm, from the Royal Museum of Naples.*" *W. Vollmer,* Wörterbuch der Mythologie *(1836), 2nd edition (1874) by W. Binder. Electronic edition, Berlin: Zweitausendeins (ISBN 978-3-86150-863-2), 2008.*

rival, and so on. Yet even if we remain with the story of her nursing the infant Dionysos at Zeus's behest, her accession to divinity is still mysterious. Calasso writes:

> She had shown kindness to the orphaned Dionysos; she had disguised him as a little girl in her palace; she had given him her white breast just as she did to her own son, Melicertes; she had hidden him in a

dark room wrapped in a purple veil while Mystis the serving maid gave him his first taste of the sound of the cymbals and tambourines and offered him his mystical objects as toys. But it wasn't only Dionysos who remembered Ino. Aphrodite remembered her too. "*Spuma fui*," "I was foam myself," the goddess [in Ovid's account] said to Poseidon, encouraging him to accept Ino among the divinities of the sea. That foam was the ribbon in Leucothea's hair; it was the veil around the hips of the initiates in Samothrace; it was the slow upward spreading of the light as the hidden is made plain in the dawn; it was the whiteness of appearance itself and the sovereign purple of blood; it was the only veil that is laid over the shipwreck.

RC 410/368

Ino's association with the foam of the sea, "the only veil that is laid over the shipwreck," hence with Aphrodite, is perhaps crucial to her accession. One of the shipwrecks in question is Odysseus's raft, shattered by Poseidon's waves. And the purple veil that saves Odysseus from drowning is the veil worn by all the initiates into the cult of the Great Gods on Samothrace. The scene of Odysseus's rescue is worth recalling in detail:

> But then Cadmus's daughter saw him, she of the shapely ankles, Ino
> Leukothea. She was once mortal and spoke with a mortal voice,
> Until she received godlike honors in the waves of the salt sea.
> She felt pity for Odysseus now, for he was wretchedly tossed about.
> She emerged from the depths, and, swooping like a gull,
> She alighted on his raft and spoke these words to him:
> "Miserable man! Why is Poseidon so angry with you?
> Why does the Earth-shaker send you one ill after another?
> And yet he will not destroy you, although he would like to.
> Strip off your clothes and let your raft fly to the winds
> Whichever way they blow; you have hands to swim...."

Take this immortal veil [κρήδεμνον ... ἄμβροτον] and tie it around
Your breast, so that you will never have to fear suffering and death.
Untie the veil as soon as your hands touch land beneath you,
Then toss it far behind you into the winedark sea,
For it dare not touch the land. And then go your way."

Odyssey, 5:333–50

This is the original Samothracian story, or certainly one of them, inasmuch as Jason too and all his Argonauts, including Heracles, become initiates at Samothrace. Yet it is safe to say that Odysseus, naked but for the goddess's purple sash about his body, is the most famous of the initiates into the Samothracian rites. Even though those rites are swathed in mystery, we know that they involved a combination of vegetation and fertility rites—as at Eleusis—along with the promise of sea rescue. The island itself, in the North Aegean, was and is difficult of access; choppy, foaming waves prevented (and still prevent) many a would-be initiate from landing there. As to how the infant Dionysos in Ino's arms fits into the story of sea rescue, W. K. C. Guthrie emphasizes the importance of the sea and ships in the stories surrounding Dionysos. There are multiple accounts of Dionysos having been locked in a chest soon after his birth, and the chest being thrown into the sea, so that his rebirth is an operation of the tides. One is thus constantly reminded of the story of Ino Leukothea. The "arrival" of Dionysos, who is the god of advent, is often by ship, the same sort of ship that his Tyrrhenian captors sailed (WG 162). Precisely in the case of Dionysos and his nurse, then, sea rescue and burgeoning vegetation are mystically united.[4]

---

[4] Guthrie refers to one of the most beautiful representations of the god, portrayed on the kylix by the sixth-century artist Exekias, "which depicts him reclining in a sailing-boat with dolphins playing around him and a vine growing out of the deck and overshadowing the sails" (WG 163). Albin Lesky, in *Thalatta*, discusses the kylix at 104–5 and offers an illustration of it (*Abbildung* 21) at AL 192.

19 *The arrival of Dionysos in the vineyards of Thira.*

As for the veil itself, Calasso expounds upon it as though it were the essential emblem of the mysteries, which are all about veilings and concealments. One is tempted to say that he grants the veil *ontological* significance, in the sense of Heidegger's notion of *Verborgenheit*, "concealment," and perhaps also in the sense of Schelling's "uncanniness," *Unheimlichkeit*:

> The veil, or something that encloses, that wraps around, or belts on, a ribbon, a sash, a band, is the last object we meet in Greece. Beyond the veil, there is no other thing. The veil is the other. It tells us that the existing world, alone, cannot hold, that at the very least it needs to be continually covered and discovered, appear and disappear. That which is accomplished, be it initiation, or marriage, or sacrifice, requires a veil, precisely because that which is accomplished is perfect, and the perfect stands for everything, and everything includes the veil, that surplus which is the fragrance of the thing.
>
> RC 410/368

However, to repeat, what is most astonishing about the story of Ino Leukothea is that the most grievous mockery, blasphemy, cruelty, and murder precede her accession to divinity. It is as though Hölderlin is right when he says that those who are docile and pious never even get close to the gods. Docility is too quick to oblige, and piety suffocates; they leave no space for the divine to appear. Indeed, Hölderlin says that the space for divinity opens only when something like blasphemy occurs, and he finds evidence for this counter-intuitive happenstance precisely in Sophocles. In his "Notes" on Sophocles' *Antigone*, Hölderlin calls Antigone *Antitheos*, and he describes the heroine's struggle with divine forces in terms of a consciousness that exceeds the normal range of consciousness: "When the soul labors secretly, it is of enormous help to it that at the point of supreme consciousness it eludes the grasp of consciousness. And before the present god can actually seize the soul, the soul goes to encounter the god with bold words, often the very words of blasphemy. And in this way it preserves the sacred, the living possibility of spirit" (CHV 2:371–2).

Translated into terms of early Christianity, one may suppose that Augustine's vigorous fornicating, especially if his lips snarl in curses against his nagging mother's God, is a timid recollection of this ancient insight. It becomes a hackneyed wisdom for later Christendom—"only a great sinner can become a great saint," runs the refrain—which at least would make the lives of the saints more interesting than they otherwise are. Perhaps such blasphemy has something to do with the theme of violence and the sacred, or with the proximity of the pummeled scapegoat to the untouchable holy man or woman. It is as though both pollution and cleansing, defilement and purification, belong to the holy. As Bloom observes, "Dirty cleans."[5]

In Ino's case, however, it is not about the mere cleansing of someone who has polluted herself. It is about elevation to a status beyond the heroic, an elevation to deity, achieved, it seems, by plummeting to the bottom of the sea. It is as though Herman Melville's Pip is a later instance of the same lesson, Pip, who sinks to the bottom of the Pacific and drifts among its coral reefs, "where strange shapes of the unwarped primal world glided to and fro before his passive eyes," eyes rapt to the motion of "God's foot upon the treadle of the loom" (MD 414). Ino

---

[5] For "Dirty cleans," see U 83. Zahra Birashk, of Freiburg University, made me aware of another instance of crime and salvation (not crime and punishment) in a quasi-Christian context—with Goethe it can only be *quasi*. The final scene of *Faust I* and also of the *Urfaust*, "*Kerker*," finds Gretchen imprisoned, apparently—but her madness makes everything here unclear—because she has murdered her (and Faust's) infant. Apparently, again, by drowning him in a forest pond. In the *Urfaust*, Mephistopheles declares, "She is judged," *Sie ist gerichtet*. In the later *Faust I*, a "voice from above" responds to Mephistopheles: "She is saved," *Sie ist gerettet*. In the famous final scene of *Faust II*, it is Gretchen's intercession—or quite simply her love—that saves Faust. No doubt one could find myriad crime and salvation stories of this type.

Leukothea, in the figure of the *Pequod*, eventually comes to the rescue, but she arrives too late and Pip never recovers his mortal wits. Whether or not he accedes to divinity would be a good question to put to Melville. Yet Melville, who ponders the mysteries, might respond by asking us if we are certain that such an accession would be a good thing for poor Pip. For the gods, whether Melville's or Schelling's, "are not forever glad." The tears of Kronos are evidence enough of that.

20 *The Caldera, some 400 meters deep, often swells like the open sea.*

6

These Drowning Men Do Drown

O sea of love, known only to those who are drowning, not to those who sail across it.

ROBERT MUSIL, *THE MAN WITHOUT QUALITIES*

Immediately after the hectic period in which *Moby-Dick* is written and rewritten—for it is never quite finished—and before the book's commercial failure becomes painfully evident to its author, Melville creates a second magnum opus. It is an inland tale, even though he describes it to a friend as a *Kraken*, a giant squid of a book. It is about a young writer, a "juvenile author," who is struggling against the odds to write a mature work, hence a failed writer. His name is *Pierre*, and the subtitle of the book is *the Ambiguities*. Perhaps only one aspect of *Pierre, or the Ambiguities* is unambiguous, and it has to do with drowning men and the limits of the power of consciousness:

From these random slips, it would seem, that Pierre is quite conscious of much that is so anomalously hard and bitter in his lot, of much that is so black and terrific in his soul. Yet that knowing his fatal condition does not one whit enable him to change or better his condition. Conclusive proof that he has no power over his condition. For in tremendous extremities human souls are like drowning men; well enough they know they are in peril; well enough they know the causes of that peril;—nevertheless, the sea is the sea, and these drowning men do drown.

P 303

To write about Melville and the sea is foolishness. Owls to Athens, coals to Newcastle, seas to Melville. It is as though I were yet a third Duyckinck brother, seeing in Melville nothing more than a sailor-naïf who dabbles in sea stories. Yet the present book is an encounter with the sea. Herewith I carry owls to Athens and the seas to Melville.

If I begin with his two earliest novels, *Typee: A Peep at Polynesian Life* (1844–6) and *Omoo: A Narrative of Adventures in the South Seas* (1846–7), I inevitably seem to be giving credit to the general view of the early critics, namely, that here we have two adventure romances. Yet in these early works the ocean at first appears to be a vast prison without walls, where all are "tossed on the billows of the wide-rolling Pacific—the sky above, the sea around, and nothing else!" (T 3). The reader then discovers that the sea is primarily an avenue of escape from Puritan America and all its hypocrisies and bigotries. The clergy recognize immediately the danger these works by Melville represent; the professed and professional Christians become Melville's lifelong enemies. Theirs is largely the "credit" of Melville's having had a wretched life as an author. Not that *Typee* and *Omoo* are unsuccessful, because they are indeed widely read—perhaps the scoldings of the pastors even help them sell. Arguably, it is Melville's conscious decision not to write sea romances, but to aim higher, that cost him his career as a popular writer. Unless, of course, "conscious decisions" cannot help writers like Pierre. In any case, Melville's consistent criticism of the missionaries and their colonizing partners make him some influential lifelong enemies.

In retrospect, it is difficult to countenance Melville's acquiescence in the face of the bowdlerization of the American edition of *Typee*, first published in England. The deletion of almost everything related to sex and love, including elimination of the word *Mother*, and especially the excision of Melville's scathing critique of American missionaries in the South Seas does great harm to the book—inasmuch as the peep at Polynesian life has as its foil a squint at the aggressive Puritanism of American and European "civilization." The unexpurgated *Typee*, by contrast, is a great work to read in tandem with Freud's *Civilization and Its Discontents*. A character in one of Melville's later novels will refer to "civilization" as "snivelization."

"Peep" is perhaps the correct word. For the novel—once the excisions are restored—reveals the erotic dimension of life in the Marquesas, a dimension that does not conflict with but permeates the social order. Perhaps the central theme of the novel is the beauty, grace, voluptuousness, and power of the Marquesan women:

> Their appearance perfectly amazed me; their extreme youth, the light clear brown of their complexions, their delicate features, and inexpressibly graceful figures, their softly moulded limbs, and free unstudied action, seemed as strange as beautiful. . . . These females are passionately fond of dancing, and in wild grace and spirit of their style excel everything that I have ever seen. The varied dances of the Marquesan girls are beautiful in the extreme, but there is an abandoned voluptuousness in their character which I dare not attempt to describe. . . . Unsophisticated and confiding, they are easily led into every vice, and humanity weeps over the ruin thus remorselessly inflicted upon them by their European civilizers. Thrice happy are they who, inhabiting some yet undiscovered

island in the midst of the ocean, have never been brought into contaminating contact with the white man.

T 15

Melville's fate as an American author is perhaps sealed by these words. Light brown voluptuousness meets white contamination: the dye is cast. The charge against white civilization is relentless throughout the novel:

> When the inhabitants of some sequestered island first descry the "big canoe" of the European rolling through the blue waters towards their shores, they rush down to the beach in crowds, and with open arms stand ready to embrace the strangers. Fatal embrace! They fold to their bosoms the vipers whose sting is destined to poison all their joys; and the instinctive feeling of love within their breasts is soon converted into the bitterest hate.... It may be asserted without fear of contradiction, that in all the cases of outrages committed by Polynesians, Europeans have at some time or other been the aggressors, and that the cruel and bloodthirsty disposition of some of the islanders is mainly to be ascribed to the influence of such examples.

T 26–7

However, if the sea first appears as an avenue of escape from Puritan America, as well as from joblessness and an unpromising future, it now shows a very different aspect: the sea, once Melville has experienced it, becomes the boulevard for the "big canoe" of the colonizers. Melville makes the same point in a public lecture he delivers ten years later in New York, New England, and the Midwest:

> Any one who treats the natives fairly is just as safe as if he were on the Nile or Danube. But I am sorry to say we whites have a sad reputation among many of the Polynesians. The natives of these

islands are naturally of a kindly and hospitable temper, but there has been implanted among them an almost instinctive hate of the white man. They esteem us, with rare exceptions, such as *some* of the missionaries, the most barbarous, treacherous, irreligious, and devilish creatures on the earth.

9:415–16

He ends the lecture in this way:

I shall close with the earnest wish that adventurers from our soil and from the lands of Europe will abstain from those brutal and cruel vices which disgust even savages with our manners, while they turn an earthly paradise into a pandemonium. I hope that these Edens of the South Seas, blessed with fertile soils and peopled with happy natives, many being yet uncontaminated by the contact of civilization will long remain unspoiled in their simplicity, beauty, and purity.

9:420

No doubt Melville's sympathy for the colonized inclines him to idealize the inhabitants of the Marquesas. As the hero of *Typee* explores the island, wavering between his admiration of the tribe that is sheltering and feeding him and his fear that he is a virtual captive of their hospitality, he is nonetheless certain about the relative benefits and disadvantages of "the tainted atmosphere of a feverish civilization" and the new life he is leading:

As I extended my wanderings in the valley and grew more familiar with the habits of its inmates, I was fain to confess that, despite the disadvantages of his condition, the Polynesian savage, surrounded by all the luxurious provisions of nature, enjoyed an infinitely happier, though certainly a less intellectual existence, than the self-complacent European. . . . In a primitive state of society, the enjoyments of life, though few and simple, are spread over a great extent, and are unalloyed; but Civilization, for every advantage she imparts, holds a hundred evils in reserve;—the heart burnings, the jealousies, the social rivalries, the family dissensions, and the thousand self-inflicted discomforts of the refined life, which make up in units the swelling aggregate of human misery, are unknown among these unsophisticated people.... The fiend-like skill we display in the invention of all manner of death-dealing engines, the vindictiveness with which we carry on our wars, and the misery and desolation that follow in their train, are enough of themselves to distinguish the white civilized man as the most ferocious animal on the face of the earth.

T 124–5

To repeat, in the history of the Occidental world the sea has been above all the boulevard by which the expansionist technologies of the West invade and exploit distant cultures. Today we experience the trash of our civilization as "plastic islands" covering hundreds if not thousands of square miles in the vortex areas of the Atlantic and the Pacific. Yet such trashing of the oceans and of the ocean peoples is as old as our civilization, and the seas have been the very thoroughfares of that aggressive civilization.

At moments, Melville's depiction of island life—rather, of what island life excludes—amounts to biography, the story of Melville's own life as the father of a family that must be fed and housed. *Typee* is both hilarious in its catalogue of familial and civil ills back home and sobering in the reality that lies behind the hilarity. For, on the islands, by contrast,

there were none of those thousand sources of irritation that the ingenuity of civilized man has created to mar his own felicity. There were no foreclosures of mortgages, no protested notes, no bills payable, no debts of honor in Typee; no unreasonable tailors and shoemakers, perversely bent on being paid; no duns of any description; no assault and battery attorneys, to foment discord, backing their clients up to a quarrel, and then knocking their heads together; no poor relations, everlastingly occupying the spare bed-chamber, and diminishing the elbow room at the family table; no destitute widows with their children starving on the cold charities of the world; no beggars; no debtors' prisons; no proud and hard-hearted nabobs in Typee; or to sum up all in one word—no Money! That "root of all evil" was not to found in the valley.

In this secluded abode of happiness there were no cross old women, no cruel step-dames, no withered spinsters, no love-sick maidens, no sour old bachelors, no inattentive husbands, no melancholy young men, no blubbering youngsters, and no squalling brats. All was mirth, fun, and high good humor. Blue devils, hypochondria, and doleful dumps, went and hid themselves among the nooks and crannies of the rocks.

T 126

Now, of course, no one can believe this encomium entirely, neither then nor now. Especially now as we sophisticates look askance at Gauguin's dreamy canvases and read D. H. Lawrence's novels and treatises with a jaundiced eye and a condescending nod. It is all a vacuous and fantastic Rousseauism, we are sure of that. Oddly, it is at this moment in the text that Melville himself mentions Rousseau. The context is physical health, and the narrator speculates that the "continual happiness" of the island had

> sprung principally from that all-pervading sensation which Rousseau has told us he at one time experienced, the mere buoyant sense of a healthful existence. And indeed in this particular the Typees had ample reason to felicitate themselves, for sickness was

almost unknown. During the whole period of my stay I saw but one invalid among them; and on their smooth clear skins you observed no blemish or mark of disease.

T 127

All this Rousseauism of the South Seas—without the improvident tilting of its axis—comes to a head in a chapter, the twenty-seventh, on "The social Condition and general Character of the Typees." The narrator is struck by the sheer fact of a social order that seems to do without law and law enforcement, an order that appears to reflect Rousseau's dream that there may be "precepts graven on every breast" (T 201). And if Nietzsche, in the ninth chapter of *Beyond Good and Evil*, asks the question, "What is noble?" the Typees seem to offer convincing models. Melville concludes:

Civilization does not engross all the virtues of humanity: she has not even her full share of them. They flourish in greater abundance and attain greater strength among many barbarous people. The hospitality of the wild Arab, the courage of the North American Indian, and the faithful friendships of some of the Polynesian nations, far surpass any thing of a similar kind among the polished communities of Europe.... I will frankly declare, that after passing a few weeks in this valley of the Marquesas, I formed a higher estimate of human nature than I had ever before entertained.

T 202–3

Melville's ardent advocacy of the natives and his bitter attack against the Christian missionaries and the exploiting powers might have done him little harm, however, were it not for his portrait of "the beauteous nymph Fayaway." His description of her agitates Melville's contemporaries and may be said to haunt even our own jaded twentieth and twenty-first centuries.

Her free pliant figure was the very perfection of female grace and beauty. Her complexion was a rich and mantling olive, and when watching the glow upon her cheeks I could almost swear that beneath the transparent medium there lurked the blushes of a faint vermilion. The face of this girl was a rounded oval, and each feature as perfectly formed as the heart or imagination of man could desire. Her full lips, when parted with a smile, disclosed teeth of a dazzling whiteness; and when her rosy mouth opened with a burst of merriment, they looked like the milk-white seeds of the "arta," a fruit of the valley, which when cleft in twain, shows them reposing in rows on either side, imbedded in the red and juicy pulp. Her hair of the deepest brown, parted irregularly in the middle, flowed in natural ringlets over her shoulders, and whenever she chanced to stoop, fell over and hid from view her lovely bosom.

T 85–6

The implication of Melville's portrait is that when Fayaway does not chance to bend forward her hair hides nothing from view. Moreover, her association with the stranger, Melville's narrator, appears to liberate her entirely from the already inadequate strictures of her society: she smokes the pipe (T 133: "Strange as it may seem, there is nothing in which a young and beautiful female appears to more advantage than in the act of smoking"), and she alone is allowed to ride in a canoe, which otherwise is taboo. But, oh, that canoe! Behold what power it possesses! Contemplate Fayaway's happy idea!

One day, after we had been paddling about for some time, I ... paddled the canoe to the windward side of the lake. As I turned the canoe, Fayaway, who was with me, seemed all at once to be struck with some happy idea. With a wild exclamation of delight, she disengaged from her person the ample robe of tappa which was knotted over her shoulder (for the purpose of shielding her from the sun), and spreading it out like a sail, stood erect with upraised arms in the head of the canoe. We American sailors pride ourselves upon our straight clean spars, but a prettier little mast than Fayaway made was never shipped a-board of any craft.

T 134

We are told that when Sophia Hawthorne—Nathaniel's wife, who gives us the most detailed and most remarkable physical and psychological descriptions of Melville that we possess—met him for the first time in 1850, "she saw Fayaway in his face" (HP 1:413). No man has ever received such a stunning compliment from a woman, and it is a tragedy that in all likelihood she was unable to say this to Melville himself.

And if the Calvinist reader of *Typee* is secretly dying to know whether the narrator is sleeping with the nymph—for the natives sleep a great deal, says the demure storyteller—then the narrator all but admits it without admitting it (T 149). That the narrator is smitten is of course evident. And that the nymph is willing is likewise evident. Yet the storyteller is coy:

The young girls very often danced by moonlight in front of their dwellings. There are a great variety of these dances, in which, however, I never saw the men take part. They all consist of active, romping, mischievous evolutions, in which every limb is brought into requisition. Indeed, the Marquesan girls dance all over, as it were; not only do their feet dance, but their arms, hands, fingers, ay, their very eyes, seem to dance in their heads. In good sooth, they so sway their floating forms, arch their necks, toss aloft their naked arms, and glide, and swim, and whirl, that it was almost too much for a quiet, sober-minded, modest young man like myself.

T 152

And the storyteller is sardonic:

> When I remembered that these islanders derived no advantage from dress, but appeared in all the naked simplicity of nature, I could not avoid comparing them with the fine gentlemen and dandies who promenade such unexceptionable figures in our frequented thoroughfares. Stripped of the cunning artifices of the tailor, and standing forth in the garb of Eden,—what a sorry set of round-shouldered, spindle-shanked, crane-necked varlets would civilized men appear! Stuffed calves, padded breasts, and scientifically cut pantaloons would then avail them nothing, and the effect would be truly deplorable.

> T 180–1

When the coyness and the sarcasm abate, however, the narrator is most dangerous. He is never more dangerous than when he concedes that the beautiful women—the dancers, the pipe-smokers, the laughing women—are powerful, and that they know themselves to be powerful. Nowhere else than in the Marquesas are women "more sensible of their power" (T 204). And that power both mirrors and shapes a remarkable society.[1]

---

[1] Melville scholars who pay close attention to the socio-cultural background as reflected in popular and reformist literature during the first half of the nineteenth century would object that I am oversimplifying. Surely Melville is playing both sides of the moral-reform debates, titillating his readers with the very details he pretends to be deploring. This is particularly the case with alcoholism and sexual license. Methinks Melville protests too much in both cases, one might say, and some contemporary reviewers of Melville's early novels do say so. Yet Melville's observations concerning the power of the Marquesan women, a power both erotic and political, are surely meant to be taken seriously. In any case, Melville's strategy certainly pays off: *Typee* and *Omoo* both sell quite well, whatever the missionaries might wish. See David S. Reynolds, *Beneath the American Renaissance: The Subversive Imagination in the Age of Emerson and Melville* (New York: Alfred A. Knopf, 1988), 4–7 and especially 138–41. My thanks to Helm Breinig for this reference and for his critique of my own account here. But let me return to Melville's Fayaway—by way of a slight detour through Hölderlin.

Hölderlin dreams of a political realm modeled on what he calls, without defining it more precisely, "the more tender relationships" (CHV 2:51–7). By the words *zart* and *zärtlich* he means perhaps family relationships, or the relations between friends and lovers. He is dreaming of a *politics* of *Zärtlichkeit*. Thanks to the political theories and the political practices of the Western world, we know, or think we know, that the desire to extend such familial or erotic intimacy to the community at large is delusional. Melville's narrator says,

> During my whole stay on the island I never witnessed a single quarrel, nor any thing that in the slightest degree approached even to a dispute. The natives appeared to form one household, whose members were bound together by the ties of strong affection. The love of kindred I did not so much perceive, for it seemed blended in the general love; and where all were treated as brothers and sisters, it was hard to tell who were actually related to each other by blood.

>   T 204

When the narrator escapes from this island of "general love," as he does at the end of *Typee*, his rescue, told in the sequel, *Omoo: A Narrative of Adventures in the South Seas* (1846–7), understandably stirs ambiguous feelings in him. He is "weighed down by a melancholy that could not be shaken off," and the sea that enables his rescue seems to him "a waste of waters" (O 7). In spite of the new "adventures" he goes to confront, a certain restiveness unsettles him, and the sea takes on a foreboding character. "On such a night, and all alone, reverie was inevitable. I leaned over the side, and could not help thinking of the strange objects we might be sailing over" (O 33). Whereas the surface seems an endless expanse of infinite repetition, there are surprises waiting below. The sea is already here what it will be for Ishmael, namely, the very element of the unknown and unknowable, frustrating all confident navigation toward a destination:

> From obvious prudential considerations the Pacific has been principally sailed over in known tracts, and this is the reason why new islands are still occasionally discovered, by exploring ships and adventurous whalers, notwithstanding the great number of vessels of all kinds of late navigating this vast ocean. Indeed, considerable portions still remain wholly unexplored; and there is doubt as to the actual existence of certain shoals, and reefs, and small clusters of islands vaguely laid down in the charts. The mere circumstance, therefore, of a ship like ours penetrating into these regions, was sufficient to cause any reflecting mind to feel at least a little uneasy. For my own part, the many stories I had heard of ships striking at midnight upon unknown rocks, with all sail set, and a slumbering crew, often recurred to me, especially, as from the absence of discipline, and our being so short-handed, the watches at night were careless in the extreme.
>
> O 35

When two of the crew die after illness and accident, they are buried at sea; the corpses, wrapped in their hammocks, become two of those "strange objects" one might soon be sailing over. "Behold here the fate of a sailor! They give him the last toss, and no one asks whose child he was" (O 46). Moreover, the fate of individual mariners mirrors the fate of entire peoples, in this case, the Tahitians. "Their prospects are hopeless," says the narrator:

> The islanders themselves, are mournfully watching their doom. Several years since, Pomaree II. said to Tyerman and Bennet, the deputies of the London Missionary Society, "You have come to see me at a very bad time. Your ancestors came in the time of men,

when Tahiti was inhabited: you are come to behold just the remnant of my people."

Of like import, was the prediction of Teearmoar, the high-priest of Paree; who lived over a hundred years ago. I have frequently heard it chanted, in a low, sad tone, by aged Tahitians:—

"A harree ta fow,
A toro ta farraro,
A mow ta tatarta."

The palm-tree shall grow,
The coral shall spread,
But man shall cease.

O 192

The narrator, were he hearing the "low, sad tone" of the chant today, when the islands are either plagued by plastic or consist entirely of plastic, would be further dejected by the fact that, to say the least, the coral shall *not* spread. How much deterioration of the seas has occurred since Melville wrote! Perhaps the hidden lesson of this second adventure book by Melville is that the sea, for all its dangers and for all its unknowability and immensity, opens possibilities of escape—and discovery—that are rapidly disappearing. Perhaps they were already disappearing for him. There is a note of sadness and nostalgia in the admission that, "weary somewhat of life in Imeeo, like all sailors ashore, I at last pined for the billows" (O 312). Even the bravado of the salty sailor talk does not quite manage to cover the sadness: "Crowding all sail, we braced the yards square; and, the breeze freshening, bowled straight away from the land. Once more the sailor's cradle rocked under me, and I found myself rolling in my gait" (O 316). Let ourselves be cradled, Melville's narrator seems to be saying, even if it must be on shipboard. And how long can it last for any mortal child?

In all fairness to the Duyckinck brothers it has to be noted that no one could have known what sorts of reading young Melville was stowing away in his sea chest. Nor could they have known the kind of personal library he began to put together once he returned to port. Melville's father had found Herman at age seven "backward in speech and somewhat slow in comprehension" (HP 1:35). But after writing *Typee* and *Omoo* Herman was turning it around and picking up speed. Already by age eleven he was doing better, his father admitted, "without being a bright scholar"; perhaps he would pursue a career in business, in which case he could "dispense with much book knowledge" (HP 1:48). Yet as Melville approached his thirties his library was expanding and deepening, and he was amassing considerable "book knowledge."

With *Mardi, and a Voyage Thither* (1847–9), we arrive at a new phase of Melville's career as a writer. He never doubted that in writing the second half of this two-volume novel he had discovered why he was writing. The "Historical Note" of the critical edition of the book, by Elizabeth S. Foster, says it well: although *Mardi* was meant to be a mere sequel to *Omoo*,

> Melville's book changed as he wrote it, but not so much or so momentously as the writing of the book changed Melville. It freed his imagination and his intellect to roam the universe from the silliest custom of man to Dantean heavens, to hobnob with the great writers and thinkers of the ages, to match wits with them and learn to speak their language. It stirred up demonic powers within him and gave him more than an inkling of his own genius. That is to say, it made possible *Moby-Dick*.

M 657

That is a powerful claim, and yet it seems exactly right. "We are off!" cry the first words of *Mardi*, and there is something about the opening that brings to mind the famous second choral ode of Sophocles' *Antigone*, which sings the prowess of an uncannily inventive humankind, plowing the earth and plying the waves:

> We are off! The courses and topsails are set: the coral-hung anchor swings from the bow: and together, the three royals are given to the breeze, that follows us out to sea like the baying of a hound. Out spreads the canvas—slow, aloft—boom-stretched, on both sides, with many a stun' sail; till like a hawk, with pinions poised, we shadow the sea with our sails, and reelingly cleave the brine.
>
> M 3

And yet, as we recall, Sophocles' choral ode adds those dire words near the end that pinpoint the vulnerability of those plucky mortals who are so uncanny: "Hades alone they have not managed to evade" (ll. 361–2).

The *writing* in *Mardi*, especially in its second volume, is so remarkably different from what has gone before. Close students of Melville are able to transform his prose into convincing blank verse merely by breaking up the lines along their natural joints; the exquisite vocabulary and the kinky syntax—two of Melville's great secrets—shine like Shakespeare.[2] In *Mardi*, the sea, "this phenomenon of the sea," is still a central figure—no, the central sun and moon—of Melville's system, but it receives new treatment. Chapters 2 and 16 portray the sea in a deadly calm, a calm that makes the mariner's

---

[2] True, Charles Olson regards such demonstrations as the *least* interesting aspect of Melville's debt to Shakespeare, and no doubt he is right. See Olson, "Lear and Moby Dick," in *Twice a Year*, vol. I (1938), 165–89. It is Olson who also gave me the astonishing quotation at the outset of the book from Keats's letter to Jane Reynolds.

cranium "a dome full of reverberations" and the hollows of his bones "whispering galleries"; the calm "revolutionizes his abdomen" and unsettles his mind" (M 9–10). Such a dead calm "tempts him to recant his belief in the eternal fitness of things; in short, almost makes an infidel of him" (ibid.). The awfulness of a calm is the awfulness of the nothing: "Thoughts of eternity thicken. He begins to feel anxious concerning his soul" (ibid.). Later, in "Benito Cereno," Melville's narrator will refer to the "tranced waters" of the sea in a calm, a calm that grants no calm, no repose or tranquillity (9:78). He adds, "The leaden ocean seemed laid out and leaded up, its course finished, soul gone, defunct" (ibid.). After the narrator of *Mardi* and a friend jump ship, having "borrowed" one of the lifeboats or "chamois," he finds himself once again stalemated by a calm. "On the eighth day there was a calm," chapter 16 begins, as though emending and subverting Genesis. For the Pacific in a calm is no paradise, but rather a chaos:

> But that morning, the two gray firmaments of sky and water seemed collapsed into a vague ellipsis. And alike, the Chamois seemed drifting in the atmosphere as in the sea. Every thing was fused into the calm: sky, air, water, and all. Not a fish was to be seen. The silence was that of a vacuum. No vitality lurked in the air. And this inert blending and brooding of all things seemed gray chaos in conception.
>
> M 48

When at last a breeze stirs, all is delight, and the chamois suddenly flits across "the sun-spangled, azure, rustling robe of the ocean, ermined with wave crests" (M 50). Yet the awful loneliness of the sea does not abate. Now that the narrator has jumped ship and will be regarded by his shipmates as not only missing but as good as dead, he has to wonder whether in fact he is still alive: "one feels like his own ghost unlawfully tenanting a defunct carcass" (M 29). The sea is no longer the steed ridden by "the genius of man," and the castaway is soon meditating on the varieties of shark that accompany their frail boat. It is foolish to hate them, he admits, and yet it is difficult to befriend them—especially the great White (M 40–1).

Mardi very soon becomes much more than an adventure story, however, as Elizabeth Foster has already noted. She continues: "As *Mardi* deepened, in the travelogue chapters, into an intermittent symposium on religion, philosophy, science, politics, and the poet's art, on faith and knowledge, on necessity and free will, on time and death and eternity, Melville's reading and also his writing were rushing him into such an intellectual expansion and exhilaration that his very being was ringing with the voices of the great dead" (M 661). For the first time the range and depth of Melville's prodigious self-education becomes clear—his formal education did not take him much beyond middle-school, and even that schooling was intermittent. In what follows, I will attempt to sample some of this education, focusing on three topics: (1) truth and art in the poet's craft; (2) belief, unbelief, the human body, and the gay science; and (3) time, finitude, and death.

1. Truth and art in the poet's craft

Whatever truths the narrator hopes to chase down, they will assuredly derive from what he calls "twilight revelations":

> In bright weather at sea, a sail, invisible in the full flood of noon, becomes perceptible toward sunset. It is the reverse in the morning. In sight at gray dawn, the distant vessel, though in reality approaching, recedes from view, as the sun rises higher and higher. This holds true, till its vicinity makes it readily fall within the ordinary scope of vision. And thus, too, here and there, with other distant things: the more light you throw on them, the more you obscure. Some revelations show best in a twilight.
>
> M 56

In the course of his adventures, the narrator befriends a poet, Yoomy, and a philosopher, Babbalanja. Many of Melville's twilight revelations come out of their mouths. The philosopher, for example, does not harp on protocol sentences. It is as though he has meditated on the Heidegger who writes "On the Essence of Truth" (W 73–97; BW 111–38). For Babbalanja declares that "truth is in things, and not in words: truth is voiceless" (M 283). The young poet, Yoomy, is of course a creature of words, and it is little wonder that he is so unsure of himself and his art. "'Often,'" he confesses, "'I so incline to a distrust of my powers, that I am far more keenly alive to censure, than to praise; and always deem it the more sincere of the two; and no praise so much elates me, as censure depresses'" (M 315). Himself occasionally manic, the narrator swells like the sea: "And like a frigate, I am full with a thousands souls," and the list of souls is formidable, including among others Homer, Anacreon, Hafiz, Petrarch, Genghis Kahn, Cambyses, Shakespeare, Milton, and many more (M 367–8). Nor are philosophers and religious writers excluded from the frigate's crew:

> In me, many worthies recline, and converse. I list to St. Paul who argues the doubts of Montaigne; Julian the Apostate cross-questions Augustine; and Thomas-a-Kempis unrolls his old black letters for all to decipher. Zeno murmurs maxims beneath the hoarse shout of Democritus; and though Democritus laugh loud and long, the sneer of Pyrrho be seen; yet, divine Plato, and Proclus, and Verulam are of my counsel; and Zoroaster whispered me before I was born.
>
> Ibid.

The philosopher Babbalanja appears to have as much buoyant self-confidence as the narrator, at least where inspirational company is concerned: "'I am intent upon the essence of things; the mystery that lieth beyond; the elements of the tear which much laughter provoketh;

that which is beneath the seeming; the precious pearl within the shaggy oyster. I probe the circle's center; I seek to evolve the inscrutable'" (M 352). That a South Sea islander should declaim in biblical English striketh the reader of *Mardi* as very strange, no doubt, and it helps to explain why this book, unlike its predecessors, did not sell. Melville's declamatory style, the high dudgeon of the Captain Ahab to come, dominates *Mardi*, and not always as convincingly as in the later novels. Here too for the first time, in chapter 180, we have a foretaste of several later chapters of *Moby-Dick*, composed and printed as dramas, or at least containing stage directions. Here too, and in the very next chapter of *Mardi*, we have for the first time one of Melville's catalogues and endless lists of people and things—sharks, mythological figures, political potentates—designed often for comic and satirical effect, very much in the tradition of Laurence Sterne and anticipating James Joyce. As Babbalanja at one point concedes, "'Genius is full of trash'" (M 595).

In the cases of both the poet and the philosopher, the writer is looking into the depths of self. Yoomy confesses that although he is not a woman, "'I feel in me a woman's soul'" (M 438). It is as though the poet rises to a higher potency of deity as Schelling describes it in his *Philosophy of Mythology*. Babbalanja quickly affirms the identity of poet and philosopher in this and in all things, except that for the philosopher "depth" is a dimension of the sea:

> "Yoomy: poets both, we differ but in seeming; thy airiest conceits are as the shadows of my deepest ponderings; though Yoomy soars, and Babbalanja dives, both meet at last. Not a song you sing, but I have thought its thought; and where dull Mardi sees but your rose, I unfold its petals, and disclose a pearl. Poets are we, Yoomy, in that we dwell without us; we live in grottoes, palms, and brooks; we ride the sea, we ride the sky; poets are omnipresent."
>
> Ibid.

Yet the omnipresent poet is not always ecstatic, not always buoyant. There is a moment, at the end of "Dreams" (chapter 119), when the narrator, a mere sailor, but now manacled to the writing desk as Prometheus to the rock, is very close to the later figure of *Pierre*, with which my own chapter began:

> My cheek blanches white while I write; I start at the scratch of my pen; my own mad brood of eagles devours me; fain would I unsay this audacity; but an iron-mailed hand clenches mine in a vice, and prints down every letter in my spite.... [M]y thoughts crush me down till I groan; in far fields I hear the song of the reaper, while I slave and faint in this cell. The fever runs through me like lava; my hot brain burns like a coal; and like many a monarch, I am less to be envied, than the veriest hind in the land.
>
> M 368

Melville's own impoverished family loudly desired that the writer quit his cell and get out there in the fields and do some real work. Let him sing the reaper's song and massacre the metaphors! Let him bring home the bacon!

2. Belief, unbelief, the human body, and the gay science

If Babbalanja anticipates Heidegger's truth essay, Melville himself anticipates in so many ways, and at so many moments, Nietzsche. For example, the Nietzsche of *la gaya scienza*. The narrator of *Mardi*, swathing unbelief in a broader and more generous belief, reflects on the afterlife of fish and the possibility of a heaven for whales, a reflection he does not take to be jejune:

> For, does it not appear a little unreasonable to imagine, that there is any creature, fish, flesh, or fowl, so little in love with life, as not to

21 *"Our souls belong to our bodies, not our bodies to our souls."*

cherish hopes of a future state? Why does man believe in it? One reason, reckoned cogent, is, that he desires it. Who shall say, then, that the leviathan this day harpooned on the coast of Japan, goes not straight to his ancestor, who rolled all Jonah, as a sweet morsel, under his tongue?

... As for the possible hereafter of the whales; a creature eighty feet long without stockings, and thirty feet round the waist before dinner, is not inconsiderately to be consigned to annihilation.

M 289

Babbalanja is less tolerant of such fancies and less whimsical about them than the narrator, however. He replies at length to the preachings of a native Mardian who believes in the prophet "Alma," a reply from which we may snatch this brief extract: "The prophet came to make us Mardians more virtuous and happy; but along with all previous good, the same wars, crimes, and miseries, which existed in Alma's day, under various modifications are yet extant" (M 349). The philosopher Babbalanja is surely a forerunner of Nietzsche's *Fröhliche Wissenschaft*, in which "The Madman" announces the death of God (aphorism 125; KSW 3:480–2); indeed, he appears to have been reading also in the works of Maurice Merleau-Ponty and reflecting on the human body in a startlingly novel way. Or, if not that, he has perhaps reflected on the spiritual plight of Homunculus in *Faust II*. It may even be that he has an inkling of Empedocles' pericardial thinking:

Our souls belong to our bodies, not our bodies to our souls. For which has the care of the other? which keeps house? which looks after the replenishing of the aorta and auricles, and stores away the secretions? Which toils and ticks while the other sleeps? Which is ever giving timely hints, and elderly warnings? Which is the most authoritative?—Our bodies, surely. At a hint, you must move; at a notice to quit, you depart. Simpletons show us, that a body can get along almost without a soul; but of a soul getting along without a body, we have no tangible and indisputable proof. My lord, the wisest of us breathe involuntarily. And how many millions there are who live from day to day by the incessant operation of subtle processes in them, of which they know nothing, and care less? Little ween they, of vessels lacteal and lymphatic, of arteries femoral and temporal; of pericranium or pericardium; lymph, chyle, fibrin, albumen, iron in the blood, and pudding in the head; they live by the charity of their bodies, to which they are but butlers. I say, my lord, our bodies are our betters. A soul so simple, that it prefers evil to good, is lodged in a frame, whose minutest action is full of unsearchable wisdom. Knowing this superiority of theirs, our bodies are inclined to be willful: our beards grow in spite of us; and as every one knows, they sometimes grow on dead men.

                                                                    M 505

When it comes to the soul, however, Babbalanja is no mean psychologist. Here the style of his response reminds us less of Nietzsche than of Emerson, whom Nietzsche so admired, and of Freud, just on the other side of Nietzsche. The subject in question is the host of specters that the soul carries within itself: "'We are full of ghosts and spirits; we are as grave-yards full of buried dead, that start to life before us. And all our dead sires, verily, are in us; *that* is their immortality. From sire to son, we go on multiplying corpses in ourselves; for all of which, are resurrections. Every thought's a soul of some past poet, hero, sage. We are fuller than a city'" (M 593–4).

Chapter 183, "Babbalanja at the Full of the Moon," stresses the gaiety of the gay science, but Melville's philosopher is no less earnest about the self-inflicted cruelty implicated in his task. Babbalanja thus anticipates Nietzsche's *Genealogy of Morals*. In section 9 of the third treatise of that work, Nietzsche portrays the genealogist as a "nutcracker of the soul," a merciless "vivisectionist of the self" (KSW 5:358). Even the laughter that might otherwise assuage the vivisectionist seems to stem from a divided heart. Here is Babbalanja advising his young friend Yoomy, the poet, who lists hard to melancholy:

> There is laughter in heaven, and laughter in hell. And a deep thought whose language is laughter. Though wisdom be wedded to woe, though the way thereto is by tears, yet all ends in a shout. . . . The wind strikes her dulcimers; the groves give a shout; the hurricane is only an hysterical laugh; and the lightning that blasts, blasts only in play. We must laugh or we die; to laugh is to live. Not to laugh is to have the tetanus. Will you weep? then laugh while you weep. For mirth and sorrow are kin; are published by identical nerves. Go, Yoomy: go study anatomy: there is much to be learned from the dead, more than you may learn from the living, and I am dead though I live; and as soon dissect myself as another: I curiously look into my secrets: and grope under my ribs. I have found that the heart is not whole, but divided. . . .
>
> M 613–14

3. Time, finitude, and death

Under this rubric, perhaps, appear Melville's profoundest paradoxes. Again it is Babbalanja who speaks: "'Ay, the dead are not to be found, even in their graves. Nor have they simply departed; for they willed not to go; they died not by choice; whithersoever they have gone, thither have they been dragged; and if so be, they are extinct, their nihilities went not more against their grain, than their forced quitting of Mardi. Either way, something has become of them that they sought not'" (M 237). In a remarkable chapter, the seventy-fifth, "Time and Temples," the narrator reflects on those "nihilities." (And what a word, *nihilities*, as though Melville is lavishing insights on the existentialists

of the century to come!) All the nothings of our past offer our present
whatever will endure: Homer's temple will continue to loom long after
Michelangelo's dome has collapsed. Melville's speculation takes him
to the very verge of Schelling's inquiry into "materialization," which is
the secret of the deity's "downgoing" or καταβολή into nature, the
mystery of *matter* and *mater* as such:

> And that which long endures full-fledged must have long lain in
> the germ. And duration is not of the future, but of the past; and
> eternity is eternal, because it has been; and though a strong new
> monument be builded to-day, it only is lasting because its blocks
> are old as the sun. It is not the Pyramids that are ancient, but the
> eternal granite whereof they are made; which had been equally
> ancient though yet in the quarry. For to make an eternity, we must
> build with eternities; whence, the vanity of the cry for any thing
> alike durable and new; and the folly of the reproach—Your granite
> hath come from the old-fashioned hills. For we are not gods and
> creators; and the controversialists have debated, whether indeed
> the All-Plastic Power itself can do more than mold.
>
> M 228–9

Much later in the novel, as the narrator and his motley crew head
west into the uncharted Pacific, we find an anticipation of one of the
most striking chapters of *Moby-Dick*, chapter 116, "The Dying Whale."
In *Mardi* there is mere mention of the west, "whitherward in mid-
ocean, the great whales turn to die" (M 551). If eternity clings to the
granite of the old-fashioned hills, it does not avail for flesh, not even
the flesh of this antediluvian demigod who is older than the Book. In
Moby-Dick Ahab observes "that strange spectacle observable in all
sperm whales dying—the turning sunwards of the head, and so
expiring," which introduces Ahab's most remarkable soliloquy, to be
presented later on in the chapter in full, but here in only a few extracts:

"He turns and turns him to it,—how slowly, but how steadfastly, his homage-rendering and invoking brow, with his last dying motions. . . . [H]ere, too, life dies sunwards full of faith; but see! no sooner dead, than death whirls round the corpse, and it heads some other way.— [. . .]

"Oh, trebly hooped and welded hip of power! Oh, high aspiring, rainbowed jet!—that one striveth, this one jetteth all in vain! In vain, oh whale, dost though seek intercedings with yon all-quickening sun, that only calls forth life, but gives it not again. Yet dost thou, darker half, rock me with a prouder, if a darker faith. All thy unnamable imminglings float beneath me here; I am buoyed by breaths of once living things, exhaled as air, but water now."

MD 496–7

Water, or rather brine, is full of gods once exhaled as air: Ahab's soliloquy is not only a recollection of pre-Platonic thinking but also an exergue to all those later tomes that will meditate on the mortal catastrophe, the disaster of human finitude. Albert Camus will say, and he will mean it as a celebration of the highest achievement imaginable, "I could, at least in the order of creative work, name some works that are truly absurd," and in a footnote to these *quelques oeuvres vraiment absurdes*, we find one single mention, "*Le* Moby Dick *de Melville par exemple.*"[3]

The culmination of *Mardi*'s long voyage toward absurdity comes as Babbalanja relates a "vision" he has had. He is brought to the mythic place whence the isle of Mardi itself emerged from the sea—the "voyage thither" is now coming to a close. His guide, about to fade, breathes the following words to Babbalanja. I imagine they are words that an ancient priest in the Hieron of the Great Gods on Schelling's

---

[3] Albert Camus, *Le mythe de Sisyphe* (Paris: Gallimard, 1942), 151.

Samothrace might have said to the initiates there, words that contain the very secret—the mortal secret—of the mysteries:

> 'Loved one, love on! But know, that heaven hath no roof. To know all is to be all. Beatitude there is none. And your only Mardian happiness is but exemption from great woes—no more. Great Love is sad; and heaven is Love. Sadness makes the silence throughout the realms of space; sadness is universal and eternal; but sadness is tranquillity; tranquillity the uttermost that souls may hope for.'
>
> M 636

Thus speaks a new breed of priest, a very unpriestly sort of priest, adrift on uncharted seas.

Of Melville's next two novels, *White-Jacket; or The World in a Man-of-War*, and *Redburn, His First Voyage*, both of them full-length novels written during a period of five months and published in 1849, I will say little here. Melville himself hated them, remembering them as desperate efforts to write a book that would sell and help him acquit his debts. Yet even though they have not the highfalutin diction and philosophical depth of *Mardi*, they show Melville learning a few new things—some of them about the sea, others about the humans who sail it.

A bit earlier I mentioned "snivelization." The word comes from one of Melville's wildest characters, "Larry" by name, whose tirade against all things civilized, because it is low comedy, enables Melville to say precisely what he wants to say. Here is nasal Larry, perhaps a remnant of Melville's earlier sea stories, who prefers "Madagasky" to "Ameriky" and "snivelization":

> "Why," said Larry, talking through his nose, as usual, "in *Madagasky* there, they don't wear any togs at all, nothing but a bowline round

the midships; they don't have no dinner, but keeps a dinin' all day off fat pigs and dogs; they don't go to bed any where, but keeps a noddin' all the time; and they gets drunk, too, from some first rate arrack they make from cocoa-nuts; and smokes plenty of 'baccy, too, I tell ye. Fine country, that! Blast Ameriky, I say!"

To tell the truth, this Larry dealt in some illiberal insinuations against civilization.

"And what's the use of bein' *snivelized*?" said he to me one night during our watch on deck; "snivelized chaps only learns the way to take on 'bout life, and snivel. . . . Snivelization has been the ruin on ye; and it's spiled me complete; I might have been a great man in Madagasky; it's too darned bad! Blast Ameriky, I say."

R 100–1

A less entertaining character is Jackson, foreshadowing *Billy Budd*'s Claggart. Whereas *Mardi* engages in philosophical speculation, *Redburn* develops a nuanced psychology of the sadistic type. Jackson and Claggart—these are Melville's Iago. Jackson is "a horrid desperado," but not in the sense of *Moby-Dick*'s "desperado philosophy." He evokes in the narrator feelings of abhorrence but also of pity: "there seemed even more woe than wickedness about the man," says Redburn, "and though there were moments when I almost hated this Jackson, yet I have pitied no man as I have pitied him" (R 105). Those instants of pity derive from the fact that Jackson seems as evil—and as ill—as Milton's Satan. Yet Jackson's dramatic death, recounted in chapter 59, a combination of the final stage of tuberculosis and a disastrous fall from a yard-arm into the sea, is one of Melville's most horrific depictions. One takes no comfort in it, finds no pleasure in it, except for that horrific pleasure we call *reading*.

Both *Redburn* and *White-Jacket* add some new aspects to Melville's critique of "snivelization." *Redburn* speaks out against cruelty to animals, especially the dray horses that work at the New York docks (R 197), and *White-Jacket* is eloquent against the navy's disciplinary practice of flogging its recalcitrant (or unlucky) sailors (W 113–14; 427). Finally, *Redburn* offers a judicious account of the better treatment received by black sailors in England than in the United States. This last is particularly worth citing:

> In Liverpool indeed the negro steps with a prouder pace, and lifts his head like a man; for here, no such exaggerated feeling exists in respect to him, as in America. Three or four times, I encountered our black steward, dressed very handsomely, and walking arm in arm with a good-looking English woman. In New York, such a couple would have been mobbed in three minutes; and the steward would have been lucky to escape with whole limbs. Owing to the friendly reception extended to them, and the unwonted immunities they enjoy in Liverpool, the black cooks and stewards of American ships are very much attached to the place and like to make voyages to it.
>
> Being so young and inexperienced then, and unconsciously swayed in some degree by those local and social prejudices, that are the marring of most men, and from which, for the mass, there seems no possible escape; at first I was surprised that a colored man should be treated as he is in this town; but a little reflection showed that, after all, it was but recognizing his claims to humanity and normal equality; so that, in some things, we Americans leave to other countries the carrying out of the principle that stands at the head of our Declaration of Independence.
>
> R 202

The quiet simplicity and clarity of young Redburn's meditation is what strikes me, perhaps especially now, at a time when racism and xenophobia, which we once thought to be in abeyance, are proudly proclaimed by populist heads of state and their mobs. "The marring of most men," indeed.[4]

I cannot abandon these two texts of Melville's, however, before citing one last remarkable passage. For at one point, late in *White-Jacket*, the narrator too falls from the top yard-arm—precisely as Jackson had plunged—into the sea. The writing is remarkable, and the fearful possibility of drowning, of sinking "into the speechless profound of the sea" (W 392), which is the fatality with which this chapter began, is painted here in unforgettable purples, azures, and greens:

> As I gushed into the sea, a thunder-boom sounded in my ear; my soul seemed flying from my mouth. The feeling of death flooded over me with the billows. The blow from the sea must have turned me, so that I sank almost feet foremost through a soft, seething, foamy lull. Some current seemed hurrying me away; in a trance I yielded, and sank deeper down with a glide. Purple and pathless was the deep calm now around me, flecked by summer lightnings in an azure afar. The horrible nausea was gone; the bloody, blind film turned a pale green; I wondered whether I was yet dead, or still dying. But of a sudden some fashionless form brushed my side— some inert, coiled fish of the sea; the thrill of being alive again tingled in my nerves, and the strong shunning of death shocked me through.
>
> For one instant an agonizing revulsion came over me as I found myself utterly sinking. Next moment the force of my fall was

---

[4] Melville's passage reminds me of an event in my own life in the United States. Among the students I led on a study tour to Greece—decades ago now—were two young African-Americans, one a graduate student of mine, the other an undergraduate I did not know well. We were engaging in easy conversation one afternoon, during which the younger of the two suddenly laughed and announced that he would not be returning to the United States with the group. "And why is that?" I asked. He replied, "For the first time in my life I feel free." "Free?" I asked. He hesitated and thought for a moment. Then he looked me in the eye, smiled, and said, "Here there are no *eyes* on me." It was very close to something W. E. B. Du Bois said about his years in Berlin, and I have never forgotten either remark.

22 *"This whole book is but a draught—nay, but the draught of a draught."*

expended; and there I hung, vibrating in the mid-deep. What wild sounds then rang in my ear! One was a soft moaning, as of low waves on the beach; the other wild and heartlessly jubilant, as of the sea in the height of a tempest. Oh soul! thou then heardest life and death: as he who stands upon the Corinthian shore hears both the Ionian and the Ægean waves. The life-and-death poise soon passed; and then I found myself slowly ascending, and caught a dim glimmering of light.

Quicker and quicker I mounted; till at last I bounded up like a buoy, and my whole head was bathed in the blessed air.

W 393

I know of only one other account of near drowning in the "speechless profound of the sea" as remarkable as this, and I will save it for the final chapter.

We arrive now at Melville's arguably two greatest works, *Moby-Dick* and *Pierre*, although this is not meant to slight *The Confidence-Man: His Masquerade*, the astonishingly varied short prose works, and the late masterpiece, *Billy Budd, Sailor.* And *Pierre* too I will have to reserve for another time and occasion. For most of us, I suspect, *Moby-Dick* is *the* novel of the sea. I have to wonder how many times I have read it, but in any case never enough. In this respect too the book is never quite finished; one hopes for a long life so that there will be time to read it again. In this portion of my encounter with the sea, I will restrain myself and mention only a few of the book's major miracles.[5]

---

[5] Allow me to insert a belated expression of gratitude to Ulrich Halfmann, who made it possible for me to read all of Melville once again, this time in the Northwestern-Newberry Library historical-critical edition. But the debt is greater than that. Whatever I have learned about literature, whether in theory or practice, I have learned from my friends Ulrich

Perhaps I am so immediately and directly addressed by this book simply because Melville introduces his "Etymology" of the word *whale* by saying that it has been supplied by "a late consumptive usher to a grammar school" (MD xv). The usher, "threadbare in coat, heart, body, and brain," loves to dust his old grammars because they "mildly reminded him of his mortality" (ibid.). A philosopher in our time who has read much of the Greeks, but who has also followed a steady regimen of Nietzsche and Heidegger, feels that he or she belongs to the uncanny house of Melville's usher. As for the "Extracts" that follow the "Etymology," they have been supplied by a sub-sub librarian, presumably a close colleague of the usher. At one point Melville addresses the entire tribe of subordinate librarians as follows: "Give it up, Sub-Subs! For by how much the more pains ye take to please the world, by so much the more shall ye for ever go thankless!" (MD xvii). In the following brief account of *Moby-Dick*, I dare not hope to please the world. My topics are all too predictable for that. They are: (1) the character of this masterpiece as a mere draft; (2) the sea; (3) the whale; and (4) Ahab.

1. A mere draft

Melville concludes his chapter on "Cetology" with this: "God keep me from ever completing anything. This whole book is but a draught— nay, but the draught of a draught. Oh, Time, Strength, Cash, and Patience!" (MD 145). The remark seems coy, but it is true that Melville felt constrained to send the earlier chapters off to the publisher before he had decided how to end the tale. That was the problem of Cash—or the lack of it. Well into the novel, in "The Affidavit," Melville admits

---

Halfmann, Helmbrecht Breinig, and Joseph Schöpp, along with the late Jochen Barkhausen, my colleagues at the University of Mannheim during the 1970s and 1980s. Neither my reading skills nor my generosity measure up to theirs.

that his story of the white whale and of Ahab's obsessive vengeance may meet with skepticism; he imagines that his critics "might scout at Moby-Dick as a monstrous fable, or still worse and more detestable, a hideous and intolerable allegory" (MD 205). Indeed, how much of the critical literature devotes itself to the allegory, the allegory of a draught of a draught, and how could a philosopher avoid searching for it—hideously and intolerably? As the hunter pursues the whale by following the latter's wake, so the writer—and after him the reader—puts all his stakes on "the proverbial evanescence of a thing writ in water, a wake" (MD 556). Years after he has written this sentence, Melville is in Rome. He is struck by John Keats's epitaph: "Here lies one whose name is writ in water" (HP 2:324–5). Perhaps that is the ambiguous allegory of a mere draft of a draft?

2. The sea

As the *Pequod* gains the open sea, Ishmael says this: I "turned me to admire the magnanimity of the sea which will permit no records" (MD 60). Writ in water, indeed. The sea, no longer an avenue of escape from Puritan America or a boulevard of colonial conquest, is now an enigma governed by no archon, suffering no archive, and having a mystery for its ἀρχή. The full awfulness of the sea and all its monsters to a helpless humanity is what soon strikes Ishmael:

> But though, to landsmen in general, the native inhabitants of the seas have ever been regarded with emotions unspeakably unsocial and repelling; though we know the sea to be an everlasting terra incognita, so that Columbus sailed over numberless unknown worlds to discover his one superficial western one; though, by vast odds, the most terrific of all mortal disasters have immemorially and indiscriminately befallen tens and hundreds of thousands of those who have gone upon the waters; though but a moment's

consideration will teach, that however baby man may brag of his science and skill, and however much, in a flattering future, that science and skill may augment; yet for ever and for ever, to the crack of doom, the sea will insult and murder him, and pulverize the stateliest, stiffest frigate he can make; nevertheless, by the continual repetition of these very impressions, man has lost the sense of the full awfulness of the sea which aboriginally belongs to it.

MD 273

Melville's masterpiece is designed to restore this lost sense. And one thing more, reminiscent of Hegel's gloomy view of the sea:

But not only is the sea such a foe to man who is alien to it, but it is also a fiend to its own offspring; worse than the Persian host who murdered his own guests; sparing not the creatures which itself hath spawned. Like a savage tigress that tossing in the jungle overlays her own cubs, so the sea dashes even the mightiest whales against the rocks, and leaves them there side by side with the split wrecks of ships. No mercy, no power but its own controls it. Panting and snorting like a mad battle steed that has lost its rider, the masterless ocean overruns the globe.

Consider the subtleness of the sea; how its most dreaded creatures glide under water, unapparent for the most part, and treacherously hidden beneath the loveliest tints of azure. Consider also the devilish brilliance and beauty of many of its most remorseless tribes, as the dainty embellished shape of many species of sharks. Consider, once more, the universal cannibalism of the sea; all whose creatures prey upon each other, carrying on eternal war since the world began.

Consider all this; and then turn to this green, gentle, and most docile earth; consider them both, the sea and the land; and do you not find a strange analogy to something in yourself? For as this appalling ocean surrounds the verdant land, so in the soul of man there lies one insular Tahiti, full of peace and joy, but encompassed by all the horrors of the half known life. God keep thee! Push not off from that isle, thou canst never return!

MD 274

In the course of this encounter we have learned that the human being is by no means "alien" to the sea, and that we too are precisely the sea's "offspring." And if Melville's entire career demonstrates one thing, it is that he scorns the lee shore and seeks the open seas, for all their peril. Yet the sea is above all else a burial ground, a Potters' Field of drowned mariners who have obeyed the summons of the thalassic regressive undertow. In the chapter called "The Pacific," Ishmael shows how unappeased, how restive, this ostensibly pacific ocean is:

There is, one knows not what sweet mystery about this sea, whose gently awful stirrings seem to speak of some hidden soul beneath; like those fabled undulations of the Ephesian sod over the buried Evangelist St. John. And meet it is, that over these sea-pastures, wide-rolling watery prairies and Potters' Fields of all four continents, the waves should rise and fall, and ebb and flow unceasingly; for here, millions of mixed shades and shadows, drowned dreams, somnambulisms, reveries; all that we call lives and souls, lie dreaming, dreaming, still; tossing like slumberers in their beds; the ever-rolling waves but made so by their restlessness.

MD 482

These would be the gods or *manes* that, as Thales says, are in all things, above all in water. And like true gods, they are not appeased, not even in the "Pacific." Which makes of that ocean something two-faced, duplicitous, or deceitful, especially at times when the sea is calm. Echoing Lucretius, Melville writes:

At such times, under an abated sun; afloat all day upon smooth, slow heaving swells; seated in his boat, light as a birch canoe; and so sociably mixing with the soft waves themselves, that like hearth-stone cats they purr against the gunwale; these are the times of dreamy quietude, when beholding the tranquil beauty and brilliancy of the ocean's skin, one forgets the tiger heart that pants beneath it; and would not willingly remember, that this velvet paw but conceals a remorseless fang.

MD 491

The ambivalence that marks Melville's response to the sea—better, the *ambiguity* of the sea itself—is the cornerstone of Melville's metaphysics—if one may be allowed to drag him into the maelstroms of metaphysics, which he both avoids and, trying to skirt them, fails to avoid. Let the following passages from the very first chapter, "Loomings," do their work without much commentary from me.

But why, incidentally, "Loomings"? Would not "Drolleries" be a more fitting title? Such rollicking good humor! At least in these initial chapters, although the humor is sustained by Stubb in the later chapters. Surely, Melville has his outlandish humor from Laurence Sterne. There is something extravagant about that humor, as there is with people who joke at funerals. Or, as Thoreau would say, there is something *extra-vagant*, something meandering yet far-reaching and far-flung, something extra *vagrant* about it. Ishmael is bound to go whaling on the broad expanse of the high seas; yet he, like the rest of humankind, is in search of a simple element, *water*. Why?

There is magic in it. Let the most absent-minded of men be plunged in his deepest reveries—stand that man on his legs, set his feet a-going, and he will infallibly lead you to water, if water there be in all that region. Should you ever be athirst in the great American desert, try this experiment, if your caravan happen to be supplied with a metaphysical professor. Yes, as every one knows, meditation and water are wedded for ever.

MD 4

It is as though Melville's Ishmael, "unlettered Ishmael" as he calls himself, has absorbed the lessons of all the early Greek thinkers mentioned earlier, has understood Kant on sublimity, has recently audited Schelling's lectures on Poseidon, and has contemplated the theories of psychoanalysis and bioanalysis:

> Why did the old Persians hold the sea holy? Why did the Greeks give it a separate deity, and make him the own brother of Jove? Surely all this is not without meaning. And still deeper the meaning of that story of Narcissus, who because he could not grasp the tormenting, mild image he saw in the fountain, plunged into it and was drowned. But that same image, we ourselves see in all rivers and oceans. It is the image of the ungraspable phantom of life; and this is the key to it all.

MD 5

After this sudden encounter with the "ungraspable phantom," the drollery returns with Ishmael's account of his choice of a whaling vessel and his desire to sail as a simple seaman. Such a desire means that he will have to submit to rough handling from his superiors, "some old hunks of a sea-captain" (MD 6). Yet in the midst of the drollery there is something like the basis for an ethics—perhaps the only possible ethics, which we might call the ethics of the universal thump:

> Who aint a slave? Tell me that. Well, then, however the old sea-captains may order me about—however they may thump and punch me about, I have the satisfaction of knowing that it is all right; that everybody else is one way or other served in much the

same way—either in a physical or metaphysical point of view, that is; and so the universal thump is passed round, and all hands should rub each other's shoulder-blades, and be content.

Ibid.

At the end of Melville's opening chapter the reader is allowed a glimpse of what is looming in the distance, hundreds of pages and thousands of nautical miles farther on: "By reason of these things, then, the whaling voyage was welcome; the great flood-gates of the wonder-world swung open, and in the wild conceits that swayed me to my purpose, two and two there floated into my inmost soul, endless processions of the whale, and, midmost of them all, one grand hooded phantom, like a snow hill in the air" (MD 7).

3. The whale

Two of Melville's "Extracts" strike me with particular force, one affirming that the whale is the "sovereignest thing on earth" (MD xix), the other recounting a detail from a dissection of the whale (MD xxiii). Together they call to mind an incredible scene described by Jacques Derrida in the tenth and eleventh sessions of the first year of his course on *The Beast and the Sovereign*. Derrida portrays the Sun King, Louis XIV, observing the dissection of an elephant by the court doctors. In the rising stench of the surgical theater, we come to understand that it is one sovereign pitted against another, the largest land animal under the knife of the most powerful sovereign of Europe. An even more striking confrontation would have pitted the Sun King against the spermaceti whale, which towers over its land rival. Moreover, since the whale is antediluvian, there is something expressly divine about it—it is surely as old as the hovering Elohim themselves, perhaps as old as Urania, the earliest "materialization" of spirit. And if both Urania and the Elohim are the inventions of a people, then the whale, eschewing the geotropic tendency of other sea mammals, entirely at home in waters that are always already there when gods and mortals arrive, is certainly much older. Late in his novel, Melville pictures the white whale as a white bull emerging from the sea—Zeus himself, inviting Europa to mount. During the first day of the chase, Ishmael reflects:

> A gentle joyousness—a mighty mildness of repose in swiftness, invested the gliding whale. Not the white bull Jupiter swimming away with ravished Europa clinging to his graceful horns; his lovely, leering eyes sideways intent upon the maid; with smooth bewitching fleetness, rippling straight for the nuptial bower in Crete; not Jove, not that great majesty Supreme! did surpass the glorified White Whale as he so divinely swam.
>
> MD 548

Arguably, however, it is not this image of the "glorified" whale that best manifests its divinity. A more divinely domestic scene than that of the rape of Europa is painted in Melville's chapter called "The Grand Armada." Here the glory and the power of the whale, as though softening in response to Schelling's (and Clement's) expectations, are elevated to the potency of tender mystery. And, as Ferenczi and Rank would alike affirm, the mystery is one of mothers and their infants— perhaps also of Leukothea, nurse of Dionysos:

> But far beneath this wondrous world upon the surface, another and still stranger world met our eyes as we gazed over the side. For, suspended in those watery vaults, floated the forms of the nursing mothers of the whales, and those that by their enormous girth seemed shortly to become mothers. The lake, as I have hinted, was to a considerable depth exceedingly transparent; and as human infants while suckling will calmly and fixedly gaze away from the

23 "*Oh, trebly hooped and welded hip of power!*"

breast, as if leading two different lives at the time; and while yet drawing mortal nourishment, be still spiritually feasting upon some unearthly reminiscence;—even so did the young of these whales seem looking up towards us, but not at us, as if we were but a bit of Gulf-weed in their new-born sight. Floating on their sides, the mothers also seemed quietly eyeing us. One of these little infants, that from certain queer tokens seemed hardly a day old, might have measured some fourteen feet in length, and some six feet in girth. He was a little frisky; though as yet his body seemed scarce yet recovered from that irksome position it had so lately occupied in the maternal reticule; where, tail to head, and all ready for the final spring, the unborn whale lies bent like a Tartar's bow. The delicate side-fins, and the palms of his flukes, still freshly retained the plaited crumpled appearance of a baby's ears newly arrived from foreign parts.

MD 387–8

The tenderness of Melville's depiction of the scene is all in the details: the mothers floating on their sides, the nursing calves looking away into infinity ("The whale calves trying the light," as W. S. Merwin puts it so beautifully in "For a Coming Extinction"[6]), one nursling

---

[6] I am indebted to the interpretation of "The Grand Armada" offered by Helmbrecht Breinig, who brings W. S. Merwin's poem into direct connection with it. See Helmbrecht Breinig, "Wa(h)lverwandtschaften: Zweifelhafte Beziehungen zwischen Menschen und anderen Tieren bei Herman Melville und W. S. Merwin," in *Der philologische Zweifel: Ein Buch für Dietmar Peschel* (Vienna: Fassbaender, 2016), 1–26. Merwin's poem (from *The Lice*, 1967) is to be found in W. S. Merwin, *The Second Four Books of Poems* (Port Townsend, Washington: Copper Canyon Press, 1993), 122–3. The word *Wa(h)lverwandtschaften* in Breinig's title brings Goethe's *Elective Affinities* (*Die Wahlverwandtschaften*) into affinity with the whale, *der Wal*. W. S. Merwin's poem also appears in the beautiful dual-language collection of English-language poems on animals by Helmbrecht Breinig and Wolfram Donat, eds., *Das auge des raben schwarz: Tiergedichte aus der englischprachigen Welt* (Gelnhausen, Germany: Libronauti, 2016), 148–9, with a translation of Merwin's poem into German by Susanne Opfermann.

particularly frisky, fresh from "the maternal reticule," the still-crumpled appearance of the palms of the flukes or the ears of the baby, depending on whose baby or calf it is. The scene convinces us that Melville himself, the son of an impoverished father, whatever difficulties he may have had as yet another impoverished father repeating the catastrophe of his own upbringing, was perfectly capable of suffering *couvade*.[7]

Such tenderness awaits us in the chapter called, for reasons that never become clear, "The Symphony." There, to our astonishment, it is a tenderness shown by Captain Ahab.

4. Ahab

The first indications of the phenomenon of Ahab appear in the novel before the personage himself enters on the scene. Ishmael refers to "a man of greatly superior natural force, with a globular brain and a ponderous heart," clearly the pondering heart of a pericardial thinker; such a man is ready "to learn a bold and nervous lofty language," which is perhaps the best description we have of Ahab's soliloquies to come; such a man would be "a mighty pageant creature, formed for noble tragedies" (MD 73).[8] It will not detract from such a figure "if either by birth or other circumstances, he have what seems a half wilful over-ruling morbidness at the bottom of his nature. For all men

---

[7] If I may refer the reader to a work of fiction, see Krell, "Melville's Couvade," in *The Oxford Literary Review*, 32:2 (2010), 271–89. The story offers an account of this strange French word, *couvade*, and the wondrous phenomenon (regarded by some as pathological) of fathers in labor that it names.

[8] George R. Stewart regards this as the "Insight Passage," that is, the passage that marks the moment when Melville begins to transform the *Ur-Moby-Dick* into the novel in which Ahab—not Queequeg, not Bulkington, and not even Ishmael—is the central character. See Stewart, "The Two Moby Dicks," in *American Literature*, vol. 25 (1953/54), 417–48; reprinted in *Wege der Forschung CCXCIV*, ed. Paul Gerhard Buchloh and Hartmut Krüger (Darmstadt: Wissenschaftliche Buchgesellschaft, 1974), esp. 266–7 and 277.

tragically great are made so through a certain morbidness. Be sure of this, O young ambition, all mortal greatness is but disease" (MD 74). "Half wilful" may be but half the adequate estimation of Captain Ahab's willfulness; yet the melancholy reminds us of Sophocles' insistence that the hero is never long secure from destruction. Only for the briefest time is such a man or woman ἐκτὸς Ἄτας, "beyond [the reach of] Doom." One might say the same thing of the hunted whale—that only for the moment is he or she beyond the reach of the flying harpoon. But that would suggest something like the uncanny identity of the white whale and Captain Ahab.

In chapter 44, "The Chart," we find Ahab bent over his charts, trying to calculate the white whale's path through the seas and the seasons. Note the word *wrinkled* in the following passage:

> While thus employed, the heavy pewter lamp suspended in chains over his head, continually rocked with the motion of the ship, and for ever threw shifting gleams and shadows of lines upon his wrinkled brow, till it almost seemed that while he himself was marking out lines and courses on the wrinkled charts, some invisible pencil was also tracing lines and courses upon the deeply marked chart of his forehead.
>
> MD 198

Two pages later, Ishmael wonders whether the white whale "should turn up his wrinkled brow off the Persian Gulf" (MD 201). When Ishmael contrasts the right whale's and the sperm whale's foreheads, he does not fail to note the latter's "wrinkles in the forehead" (MD 335). Wrinkled brows on both sides, the whale's and Ahab's. If the whale's wrinkles derive from his having read Plato and then later Spinoza, as Ishmael supposes, Ahab's come from his unread Augustine—he seeks in vain to "tranquillize his unquiet heart" (MD 201). Obsessed by his quest, Ahab is no longer Ahab: "God help thee, old man, thy thoughts have created a creature in thee; and he whose intense thinking thus makes him a Prometheus; a vulture feeds upon that heart for ever; that vulture the very creature he creates" (MD 202). Some pages later Ishmael generalizes the diagnosis: "But in pursuit of those far mysteries we dream of, or in tormented chase of that demon phantom that, some time or other, swims before all human hearts; while chasing such over this round globe, they either lead us on in barren mazes or midway leave us whelmed" (MD 237). "Whelmed," a word that Melville may have found in Milton's "Lycidas": neither overwhelmed nor underwhelmed, but simply "whelmed." That is the action of the sea on these drowning men—who do drown.

Earlier on I presented Ahab's meditation on the dying whale in only a few extracts. Allow me to fill in the blanks. Ahab has seen the dying whale expiring sunwards full of faith; once dead, however, the sea spins the whale where it will—"death whirls round the corpse" (MD 497). At that point Ahab exclaims:

> "Oh, thou dark Hindoo half of nature, who of drowned bones hast builded thy separate throne somewhere in the heart of these unverdured seas; thou art an infidel, thou queen, and too truly speakest to me in the wide-slaughtering Typhoon, and the hushed burial of its after calm. Nor has this thy whale sunwards turned his dying head, and then gone round again, without a lesson to me.
>
> "Oh, trebly hooped and welded hip of power! Oh, high aspiring, rainbowed jet!—that one striveth, this one jetteth all in vain! In vain, oh whale, dost thou seek intercedings with yon all-quickening sun, that only calls forth life, but gives it not again. Yet dost thou, darker half, rock me with a prouder, if a darker faith. All thy unnamable imminglings float beneath me here; I am buoyed by breaths of once living things, exhaled as air, but water now.

"Then hail, for ever hail, O sea, in whose eternal tossings the wild fowl finds his only rest. Born of the earth, yet suckled by the sea; though hill and valley mothered me, ye billows are my foster-brothers!"

Ibid.

Ahab seems to have accepted the full impact of the thalassic regressive undertow—a prouder if a darker faith. (Darker at least for Freud, slightly less so for Nietzsche and Ferenczi.) Ahab is buoyed by that faith, at least for the moment. He freely abandons the earth that gives birth to him and accepts the sea as his nurse and the waves as his foster-brothers. Does Ahab believe that he can reenact the phylogenetic achievement of the whale, which resists the geotropic pull that moves sea lions and seals, in order himself to become a member of the wrinkle-browed cetaceans, wholly given over to the family of the sea? He does not claim so much for himself, of course. When he commits himself to the billows, his foster-brothers, such fraternity reminds us of young Redburn's first reaction to the sea, seeing in it "my little brother's face, when he was sleeping an infant in the cradle."[9]

Yet before Ahab commits himself to the waves, let us consider one more soliloquy, from one of the oddest of Melville's many odd chapters, chapter 132, "The Symphony." It is surely not a stormy Beethoven symphony; perhaps it is closest to Sibelius's Sixth. It opens with the air and sea in a kind of marital union, "the pensive air . . . with

---

[9] Fraternity with the sea and its waves is also an important theme in Romain Gary's *La promesse de l'aube*. The exhausted narrator lies on the sand within sight and sound of the Pacific as he delivers his long tale, and he confesses to feeling a certain brotherly affinity with the sea: "Sometimes I lift my head and look at my brother the Ocean in friendship: he pretends to be infinite, but I know that he too thrusts himself against his limits everywhere, and that is no doubt the cause of all this tumult, all these crashing waves" (RG 438–9). We never learn how close Gary's narrator will get to the waves; as for Ahab, we know that in the end his foster-brothers will embrace him, his nurse engulf him.

a woman's look" and the sea heaving "with long, strong, lingering swells, as Samson's chest in his sleep" (MD 542). The distribution of genders strikes us as odd, although it is consistent with the brotherhood of the billows, if not with the sea as suckling nurse. "Unspeckled birds" are the "gentle thoughts of the feminine air," while, "far down in the bottomless blue, rushed mighty leviathans, sword-fish, and sharks; and these were the strong, troubled, murderous thinkings of the masculine sea" (ibid.). And yet the two azures seem but one: the sun oversees this marriage of heaven and earth, or of air and sea, or of the sea with itself, observing with evident pleasure "the throbbing trust, the loving alarms, with which the poor bride gave her bosom away" (MD 542). Yet if the oldest images of heaven and earth that we have, including for example those of Ouranos and Gaia, take the sky to be masculine and the earth and her seas to be female, then Melville's marriage of heaven and earth is not the usual one, not the usual symphony.

Be that as it may, onto this idyllic conjugal scene Ahab now enters like the second movement of Mahler's Fifth, *Stürmisch bewegt, mit grösster Vehemenz*: "Tied up and twisted; gnarled and knotted with wrinkles [again those birthmarks of Leviathan!]; haggardly firm and unyielding; his eyes glowing like coals, that still glow in the ashes of ruin; untottering Ahab stood forth in the clearness of the morn; lifting his splintered helmet of a brow to the fair girl's forehead of heaven" (MD 542–3). The breezes frolic about Ahab's woe. Ishmael, however, now offers a strange comparison—a reference to "Miriam and Martha," who may be biblical figures, but who sound as though they are Ahab's daughters. Yet how would Ishmael know about Ahab's possible daughters, whom he never can have seen? At all events, our narrator says, "But so I have seen little Miriam and Martha, laughing-eyed elves, heedlessly gambol around their old sire; sporting with the circle of singed locks which grew on the marge of that burnt-out crater of his brain" (MD 543). Miriam—Aaron's sister, the prophetess? Mary and Martha, the sisters of Lazarus? But who, then, is their "old sire," he with a crater for a brain? Not the Lord, surely. At any rate, the feminine airs frolic while the mysteries multiply, and so we have our brief *scherzo*. The next movement of the symphony would have to be marked *lamentoso*, or perhaps, as Mahler would put it, leaving nothing to chance, *adagio: sehr langsam und noch zurückhaltend*, "very slow and, moreover, altogether reticent":

> Slowly crossing the deck from the scuttle, Ahab leaned over the side, and watched how his shadow in the water sank and sank to his gaze, the more that he strove to pierce the profundity. But the lovely aromas in that enchanted air did at last seem to dispel, for a moment, the cankerous thing in his soul. That glad, happy air, that winsome sky, did at last stroke and caress him; the step-mother world, so long cruel—forbidding—now threw affectionate arms round his stubborn neck, and did seem to joyously sob over him, as if over one, that however wilful and erring, she could yet find it in her heart to save and to bless. From beneath his slouched hat Ahab dropped a tear in the sea; nor did all the Pacific contain such wealth as that one wee drop.
>
> Ibid.

Ahab's woe is not that of Jackson, nor will it be that of Claggart. Ahab's woe, expressed in that one wee drop, is fine hammered steel. Such a combination of intrepidity and vulnerability has not been seen before or after in literature, such a desire to pierce (yet not mindlessly and not unfeelingly) the impenetrable profundity. Starbuck approaches Ahab but is careful not to disturb him. Ahab turns, sees him: "'Oh, Starbuck! it is a mild, mild wind, and a mild looking sky. On such a day—very much such a sweetness as this—I struck my first whale—a boy-harpooner of eighteen! Forty—forty—forty years ago!—ago!'" (ibid.). The punctuation—all hiatuses and exclamation marks!—produces some odd effects: when Ahab talks of harpooning his first whale, a mere hiatus separates this from the phrase "a boy-harpooner of eighteen," as though boy and whale were the same, or as though the harpoon had recoiled. Then three times "forty" and a double "ago," as though Ahab's youth belongs to mythic time. Ahab now outlines for Starbuck the solitude of his life:

> "Forty years of continual whaling! forty years of privation, and peril, and storm-time! forty years on the pitiless sea! for forty years has Ahab forsaken the peaceful land, for forty years to make war on the horrors of the deep! Aye and yes, Starbuck, out of those forty years I have not spent three ashore. When I think of this life I have led; the desolation of solitude it has been; the masoned, walled-town of a Captain's exclusiveness, which admits but small entrance to any sympathy from the green country without—oh, weariness! heaviness! Guinea-coast slavery of solitary command!—when I think of all this; only half-suspected, not so keenly known to me before—and how for forty years I have fed upon dry salted fare—fit emblem of the dry nourishment of my soul!—when the poorest landsman has had fresh fruit to his daily hand, and broken the world's fresh bread, to my mouldy crusts—away, whole oceans away, from that young girl-wife I wedded past fifty, and sailed for Cape Horn the next day, leaving but one dent in my marriage pillow—wife? wife?—rather a widow with her husband alive! Aye, I widowed that poor girl when I married her, Starbuck. . . ."
>
> MD 543–4

At this point a thousand commentators have stopped to do the math. Eighteen (the age of the "boy-harpooner") plus forty (the years of "continual whaling") equals fifty-eight. Married at fifty, or "past" fifty. Therefore a maximum of eight years of marriage. When exactly did the white whale wound Captain Ahab? The leg, the missing leg, is cause enough for vengeance; however, shortly after leaving Nantucket, the *Pequod*'s captain receives another wound, precisely from the ivory leg that has served as his prosthesis, that ivory leg—but is it not of whalebone?—inexplicably splintering, and, as he falls, wounding him somewhere in the vicinity of the groin? The calculation is close, confusions can arise. Can Ahab have been chasing the same whale for eight years? No reader should doubt it. Can the second wound have had an impact on the marriage? No reader should even suspect it— the wounding to the groin has occurred quite recently, on the present voyage of the *Pequod*.

Yet it is not a matter of doing the math; it is a matter of Ahab's acknowledging his vulnerability. In the eighth sketch of "The Encantadas," the narrator says of Hunilla, the Chola widow, "Humanity, thou strong thing, I worship thee, not in the laurelled victor, but in this vanquished one" (9:157).

Whence the universal vulnerability of humankind, which Melville or his narrator is constrained to worship? Ishmael's meditation on Ahab's second accident in the chapter on "Ahab's Leg" yields one of his own most extended and most profound meditations, and it culminates in one of Melville's most striking formulations, one that would last a Nietzschean genealogist and a reader of Hölderlin or Schelling—and perhaps even a psychoanalyst hot on the castration trail—a lifetime: "To trail the genealogies of these high mortal miseries, carries us at last among the sourceless primogenitures of the gods; so that, in the face of all the glad, hay-making suns, and soft-cymbaling, round harvest moons, we must needs give in to this: that the gods themselves are not for ever glad. The ineffaceable, sad birth-mark in the brow of man, is but the stamp of sorrow in the signers" (MD 464).

Melville's intimation of the sadness of the universe and its gods reminds us of Hölderlin's most radical insights. In his novel *Hyperion*,

Hölderlin writes, "I am calm, for I want nothing better than what the gods have. Must not everything suffer? And the more splendid a being is, the deeper its suffering. Does not holy nature suffer? O my godhead! that you were able to mourn to the extent that you were blessed—that is something I was long unable to grasp. Yet the delight that does not suffer is sleep, and without death there is no life" (CHV 1:751).

Ahab feels no compassion for the unglad gods. He is no initiate at Samothrace—or so we might at first think. He is the last of the line of Lycurgus and Ino. Yet Hölderlin would reply that precisely for this reason the words that come out of Ahab's mouth open the space for deity; precisely because Ahab's words fall just short of curse and blasphemy, any deity worthy of the name would have to take them seriously:

> "... and then, the madness, the frenzy, the boiling blood and the smoking brow, with which, for a thousand lowerings old Ahab has furiously, foamingly chased his prey—more a demon than a man!—aye, aye! what a forty years' fool—fool—old fool has old Ahab been! Why this strife of the chase? why weary, and palsy the arm at the oar, and the iron, and the lance? how the richer or better is Ahab now?"
>
> MD 544

Ahab bemoans the loss of his leg; he laments his squandered life; he appears to be weeping. He confesses that he feels "deadly faint, bowed, and humped, as though I were Adam, staggering beneath the piled centuries since Paradise" (ibid.). He begs Starbuck to stand close so that he can look into his eyes, confessing that the human eye is a more worthy object than sea or sky, indeed, "better than to gaze upon God" (ibid.). Starbuck's eye reveals to Ahab what his own life has cost him: "By the green land; by the bright hearth-stone! this is the magic glass, man; I see my wife and my child in thy eye" (ibid.). One child, not two. In any case, he commands Starbuck to remain on board, not to lower after Moby-Dick: "'No, no; stay on board, on board! lower not when I do; when branded Ahab gives chase to Moby Dick. That hazard shall not be thine. No, no! not with the far away home I see in thy eye!'" (ibid.)

Starbuck now pleads that the *Pequod* and all her crew and captain head for home. "The Symphony" now floats a second *scherzo*, but it is the shortest movement of the work, marked *schattenhaft*, "umbrous": "But Ahab's glance was averted; like a blighted fruit tree he shook, and cast his last, cindered apple to the soil" (MD 545). "The Symphony," marked *crescendo*, now produces what Melville somewhere calls "Beethoven sounds":

> "What is it, what nameless, inscrutable, unearthly thing is it; what cozening, hidden lord and master, and cruel, remorseless emperor commands me; that against all natural lovings and longings, I so keep pushing, and crowding, and jamming myself on all the time; recklessly making me ready to do what in my own proper, natural heart, I durst not so much as dare? Is Ahab, Ahab? Is it I, God, or who, that lifts this arm? But if the great sun move not of himself; but is as an errand-boy in heaven; nor one single star can revolve, but by some invisible power; how then can this one small heart beat; this one small brain think thoughts; unless God does that beating, does that thinking, does that living, and not I. By heaven, man, we are turned round and round in this world, like yonder windlass, and Fate is the handspike. And all the time, lo! that smiling sky, and this unsounded sea! Look! see yon Albacore! who put it in him to chase and fang that flying-fish? Where do murderers go, man! Who's to doom, when the judge himself is dragged to the bar?"
>
> Ibid.

That is perhaps as close as Ahab comes to curse and blasphemy, the *defiance* that opens a space for uncanny deity. There is of course more, much more, to this "Symphony," this *Moby-Dick*, and this Melville. Yet already my chapter is bulging—like one of those mothers whose term is imminent. I am aware, painfully aware, embarrassed even, that it has been nothing more than a string of passages from Melville's works, a loving reader's pastiche or bricolage. The chapter itself is no *Pequod*, no mighty whaler, but a swaying skiff, a bobbing barque, a dinghy. As my German friends might quip, it is *ein sehr geringes dinghy*. Yet who would dare to paraphrase Melville, the author who managed to write in water? Certainly not the usher to a grammar school or a sub-sub-librarian, even if they too, like Ahab, try to gaze into the impenetrable profundity—into the "speechless profound of the sea."

24 *"The ocean brims with natural griefs and tragedies."*

7

Waves and Drops of Time

A hermitage in the forest is the refuge of the narrow-minded misanthrope; a hammock on the ocean is the asylum for the generous distressed. The ocean brims with natural griefs and tragedies; and into that watery immensity of terror, man's private grief is lost like a drop.

HERMAN MELVILLE, *ISRAEL POTTER*

Infinity sometimes flows in drops. . . . And yet human life flows too rapidly for us to be able to hear all of life's voices and to find responses to them.

ROBERT MUSIL, "TONKA"

Indeed, in certain caves, water drips down.

XENOPHANES OF COLOPHON (DK B37)

Allow me to begin this final chapter with a kind of preface, a second preface. Whenever I am reading Heidegger's interpretation of ecstatic temporality in sections 65 and 68 of *Being and Time*, which I do over and over again, I think of time as passing by *suddenly*. The "ecstases" of time—future, having-been, and present—seem to spin in a kind of whirlwind, each ecstasy funneling swiftly into the other two and the entire system of funnels dashing onward like a cyclone. Perhaps that is because Heidegger calls the ecstases *Entrückungen*, "raptures," and we remember that the Latin *raptim* gives us our word *rapidly*. Augustine speaks of the future "flying by" into the past: *transvolat* is his word. There is also something about the morphology of the two Greek words, ἔκστασις and ἐξαίφνης, the latter meaning "all of a sudden" or "imperceptibly quickly," that makes me think of ecstatic temporality as moving swiftly.

Yet there seems to be another kind of temporality, one that moves much more slowly. I will call it *stalactitic temporality*, after the Greek σταλάσσω, "to drip," even though the word *stalactitic* does not glide trippingly o'er the tongue. By it I mean the slow dripping of drops from the stalactites in some cavern or other, perhaps in the caves of Evvia or Crete, or those near Taxco, Mexico, that have so impressed me. Here I take them to be caverns of the human body itself—not merely the cave of the psychoanalyst's *Höhlenerotik*, but all the hollows of the body male and female. It is Virginia Woolf's novel, *The Waves*, that suggests to me this notion of a very slow temporality, dripping its drops in a hidden cave as ecstatic temporality whirls by on the surface of the earth.

Back in chapter 3, while discussing Charles Lyell's *continuist* view of earth history, I remarked that for him the only catastrophe in that history is *time*. In a sense, the time of an individual life, "which will have been so short," and the vast periods of the time of phylogenetic development, along with the even longer eons of earth history, have been our subject all along. There was talk, back in chapter 3, of the "ontological import" of time in both psychoanalysis and bioanalysis. The role of time in what Ferenczi calls "depth biology," but also in Freud's notion of the "timelessness" of the unconscious, needs to be confronted.

Heidegger would not sanction a reading of Woolf's *The Waves* as a way of broaching the question of time. Probably no one would. Yet whether it is the regular lapping of the waves on the shore throughout her novel, and sometimes the crashing of those waves, or the rising and setting of the sun, or our orbiting around the sun during the changing seasons, or the slow dripping of the drops of time on and in Woolf's cavernous characters, it was *time* that hovered over my first encounter with this wonderful book. Let me proceed now to a reading of it.

The novel is thin as far as events are concerned. Six children, close to one another yet apparently not of the same family, play together in the garden of a house near the sea. The novel follows the six through their lives from early school days to old age, doing so solely by way of interior monologue and stream of consciousness. "The surface of my mind," says Bernard, "slips along like a pale-grey stream reflecting what passes" (96).[1] The nine sections of the book are preceded by italicized pages that tell of the waves "themselves," if one may say so.

Among the very few reported events are these: Jinny kisses Louis in the garden; the children go to school, where they are all enamored of Percival, who is their Golden Lad, their young Apollo, that is to say, a sporty boy who seems to be everything they desire to be and to have but are not and have not (Bernard says of Percival, "He is conventional; he is a hero" [104]); at the end of their secondary school studies, after which the group disperses, they enjoy a dinner party with Percival, who is about to leave for India to join the colonial army; soon

---

[1] The edition I have used throughout, and to which I will refer by page number in the body of my text, is: Virginia Woolf, *The Waves*, ed. Sam Gilpin (London: Collector's Library, CRW Publishing, 2005). The novel was first published in 1931.

thereafter, in a horse-racing accident in India, young Percival is killed; many years later, the six, now well into maturity, celebrate a kind of memorial dinner for Percival at Hampton Court; at a certain undisclosed point, one of the six, Rhoda, takes her life, apparently by leaping into the sea; another of the six, Bernard, who is an inveterate storyteller, begins to occupy an increasing number of pages of the novel as it draws to a close, even though, or perhaps precisely because, he finds that his stories are faltering and cannot find their proper endings. One other character, unnamed, appears at various moments throughout the novel, namely, "a lady who is writing."

Various figures of time and of the passing of time are woven into the novel: (1) the temporality of everydayness, which eventually seems to whelm the lives of all the characters, a temporality marked by the incessant and repetitive pounding or the regular lapping of waves on the shore; (2) the time marked by the path of the sun across the sky, from pre-dawn to nightfall, a time Heidegger quite late in *Being and Time* calls *die Weltzeit*, "cosmic" or "world" time; cosmic time also derives from the orbit of the Earth around the sun, which yields the months ("from January to December," as the novel declares more than once) and the seasons; finally (3) the temporality of the time that it takes for a drop to drip. This last figure occupies the final hundred pages of the book, the final third of the text. It is the strangest of the figures for time, this "stalactitic" temporality. It is the time that, pendent, takes its time to drip and that, once the drop has fallen, sometimes leaves a sediment, a deposit, some build-up below; or perhaps the drop merely produces a pool or a puddle that will eventually evaporate or drain away and leave no lasting monument.

Allow me now a more detailed word concerning the six characters. Among the six young children playing in the garden within sound of the sea, the six being Bernard, Rhoda, Neville, Jinny, Susan, and Louis,

Jinny kisses Louis on the nape of the neck. She will continue to kiss boys for the rest of her life. "I dance," says Jinny, "I ripple. I am thrown over you like a net of light. I lie quivering flung over you" (10). We have seen this *quivering* earlier on, in Empedocles' "limbs of the god," as Strife gains the center, and in Heidegger's "last god." Whereas Jinny is happy in her osculations, their first recipient, young Louis, is not: "She has found me. I am struck on the nape of the neck. She has kissed me. All is shattered" (10). Susan, who has seen the amorous event, is even more irate than Louis, however. "I saw them, Jinny and Louis, kissing. Now I will wrap my agony inside my pocket handkerchief" (11; cf. 85, 162). Later, at boarding school, Louis will be happier. "There is no crudity here, no sudden kisses," he says (29). Indeed, there will be little crudity and very few kisses (other than that remembered one) in the novel, except in the case of Jinny, the only character capable of rapture with and in her body: "I can imagine nothing beyond the circle cast by my body. My body goes before me, like a lantern down a dark lane, bringing one thing after another out of darkness into a ring of light. I dazzle you; I make you believe that this is all" (109).

Jinny is so remarkably different in this respect from the terrified, faceless Rhoda and even from the sullen Susan, as well as from all three boys, that it is worth hearing from her in greater detail. She speaks of her rashness or her courage vis-à-vis the others: "And being rash, and much more courageous than you are, I do not temper my beauty with meanness lest it should scorch me. I gulp it down entire. It is made of flesh; it is made of stuff. My imagination is the body's" (188). In the following passage she invokes the word *rapture*, which, for Heidegger and for others after him, is a word for ecstatic temporality. For Jinny the temporalizing word *rapture* has to do with an intense focus on the aura surrounding her body. For example, at one point she is on a train; as the train enters a tunnel a man lowers his newspaper and stares at her reflection in the window:

My body instantly of its own accord puts forth a frill under his gaze. My body lives a life of its own. . . . There is then a great society of bodies, and mine is introduced. . . . And I lie back; I give myself up to rapture; I think that at the end of the tunnel I enter a lamp-lit room with chairs, into one of which I sink, much admired, my dress billowing round me. But behold, looking up, I meet the eyes of a sour woman, who suspects me of rapture. My body shuts in her face, impertinently, like a parasol. I open my body, I shut my body at my will. Life is beginning. I now break into my hoard of life.

53

Such confidence in the "hoard of life" is shared only by Bernard.

The reader soon realizes that Woolf establishes the character and prevailing mood of each of her personages by means of repeated phrases in their respective monologues: "hoard of life" belongs to Jinny, "telling stories" and "making phrases" to Bernard. Woolf herself suggests that all six characters are really one, however, and not separate persons at all: a note in her diary for October 8, 1931, responding to a review in *The Times* that praised her characterizations of the six, Woolf writes, "Odd that they should praise my characters when I meant to have none."[2]

The following brief account of the six may reveal how difficult it was to be a single gathered Virginia. Neville, the poet, gives us the first *drop* of the novel: " 'I see a globe,' said Neville, 'hanging down in a drop against the enormous flanks of some hill' " (7). At chapel, Neville declares his contempt for ecclesiastical and scholastic authority:

---

[2] The editor of my edition of *The Waves*, Sam Gilpin, cites Woolf's diaries in his afterword at 259. Yet one need not revert to the diaries for evidence of the unity of all six of Woolf's characters. For the ninth and final section of the novel finds them all dissolving one-by-one, leaving nothing but a sense of fragmentation of the self. "Am I all of them?" the text asks itself, and replies, "Am I one and distinct? I do not know. . . . There is no division between me and them" (247).

"The words of authority are corrupted by those who speak them. I gibe and mock at this sad religion, at these tremulous, grief-stricken figures advancing, cadaverous and wounded, down a white road shadowed by fig trees where boys sprawl in the dust—naked boys; and goatskins distended with wine hang at the tavern door" (29). Neville reads Catullus and Shakespeare, whom the cricketer Percival cannot comprehend, but Neville also loves Percival precisely for his vapidity:

> Yet I could not live with him and suffer his stupidity. He will coarsen and snore. He will marry and there will be scenes of tenderness at breakfast. But now he is young. Not a thread, not a sheet of paper lies between him and the sun, between him and the rain, between him and the moon as he lies naked, tumbled, hot, on his bed.
>
> 40

He also loves Percival because he, Neville, means nothing to the star cricketer:

> There is Percival in his billycock hat. He will forget me. He will leave my letters lying about among guns and dogs unanswered. I shall send him poems and he will perhaps reply with a picture postcard. But it is for that that I love him. I shall propose meeting— under a clock by some Cross; and shall wait, and he will not come. It is for that that I love him. Oblivious, almost entirely ignorant, he will pass from my life.
>
> 50

The rich vein of mordant reproof that the poet repeatedly taps— Bernard describes Neville's effect on him as "a roll of heavy waters" and a "devastating presence" (75)—also contains a healthy streak of self-criticism. That streak achieves levels of unhealthy intensity a therapist would call masochistic, whereas the lady writing would be more likely to think such self-critique quite natural even at its most devastating intensity. Neville says of himself, in the third section of the book:

> There is some flaw in me—some fatal hesitancy, which, if I pass it over, turns to foam and falsity. Yet it is incredible that I should not be a great poet. What did I write last night if it was not poetry? Am I too fast, too facile? I do not know. I do not know myself sometimes, or how to measure and name and count out the grains that make me what I am.
>
> 70

Yet of all the characters, it is Neville who is best prepared for surprises, for new catastrophes, when "suddenly the waves gape and up shoulders a monster" (169).

Susan, anguished when she sees Jinny kissing Louis in the garden, loves only her father, a farmer, and she longs to return home from boarding school. "I cannot be divided, or kept apart," she says (82). She is fated to see others kissing—she soon sees two servants, the scullery maid Florrie and the boot-boy Ernest, kissing amid the wind-blown laundry sheets (20, 105); always the others are kissing, and she is forced to watch. She hates her school: "My eyes swell; my eyes prick with tears. I hate the smell of pine and linoleum. I hate the wind-bitten shrubs and the sanitary tiles. I hate the cheerful jokes and glazed look of everyone" (27). As the months pass she tears off the sheets from her calendar and crumples them: "I have torn them off and screwed them up so that they no longer exist, save as a weight in my side" (44). She looks forward to nothing but her return to the farm. "Then my freedom will unfurl, and all these restrictions that wrinkle and shrivel—hours and order and discipline, and being here and there exactly at the right moment—will crack asunder" (45). Her years of study abroad do nothing for her—schools always have the same flooring: "I was sent to Switzerland to finish my education. I hate linoleum; I hate fir trees and mountains" (82). And even if she is fated to see the others kiss and to hate Jinny with a fearsome jealousy, she makes up her mind: "I shall have children" (83). Susan commits herself furiously to maternity: "My children will carry me on; their teething, their crying, their going to school and coming back will be like the waves of the sea under me" (111). Indeed, when the babies come, she wraps the sea of her entire being around them; she is "all spun to a fine thread round the cradle, wrapping in a cocoon made of my own blood the delicate limbs of my baby ... making of my own body a hollow, a warm shelter for my child to sleep in" (146). Sometimes the drops of time seem to her the promise of ripening and maturity: "The pear fills itself and drops from the tree" (145). Drops of moisture are often simply prisms for beauty, "the purple drops in the cabbage leaves; the red drops in the roses" (147). "I am glutted with natural happiness," she declares (ibid.). Yet she is not always content with the cocoon or the sea of her maternal body: "I am sick of the body, I am sick of my own craft, industry and cunning, of the unscrupulous ways of the mother who protects, who collects under her jealous eyes at one long table her own children, always her own" (163). Finally, this compromise: "My body has been used daily, rightly, like a tool by a good workman, all over. The blade is clean, sharp, worn in the centre" (183). Yet Louis soon quotes her as also saying, " 'My ruined life, my wasted life' " (195). In the same vein, she herself says, "Still I gape ... like a young bird, unsatisfied, for something that has escaped me" (199).

Louis is the son of a Brisbane banker, a "colonial" with an accent that the others will mock. He excels at school but will never perform up to the standard he sets for himself. In his ears the sea's waves are always pounding, stamping. Here is the first word we have from him: "A great beast's foot is chained. It stamps, and stamps, and stamps" (7). And then: "All tremors shake me, and the weight of the earth is pressed to my ribs" (9). His anxiety is such that, at school, Louis attaches himself to Bernard, "because he [Bernard] is not afraid" (25). Louis is a kind of Empedoclean, in the sense that he is a child of Strife: "I, Louis, I, who shall walk the earth these seventy years, am born entire, out of hatred, out of discord" (33). These very passions, however, are what he most fears and despises: "passions that lay in wait down there in the dark weeds which grow at the bottom rise and pound us with their waves" (120). Later in his life, quite successful in business, Louis forms a brief relationship with Rhoda; he watches Susan and Bernard, Jinny and Neville vainly attempting to do the same. He remarks, "Illusion returns as they approach down the avenue. Rippling and questioning begin. What do I think of you—what do you think of me? Who are you? Who am I?—that quivers again in its uneasy air over us, and the pulse quickens and the eye brightens and all the insanity of personal existence without which life would fall flat and die, begins again" (198). Again the quivering, but without the sensual quality and the showmanship that it has in Jinny.

Bernard is the storyteller, forever entertaining or boring his young fellows. He is the phrasemaker, jotting down in his alphabetized notebook (alphabetized for speedy retrieval) his aperçus for the novel he will someday write. He uses the word *waves* quite often, and he is the second, after Neville, to give us the word *drop*, here in the plural: " 'Look at the spider's web on the corner of the balcony,' said Bernard. 'It has beads of water on it, drops of white light' " (7). He will be the theorist of stalactitic temporality, the drops of time, even though his "drops" sometimes seem odd: whereas other people *fall* asleep, Bernard "drops" asleep at night (159). He is the character who is most involved with the others, most dependent on their company, devoting much of his time to reporting this or that about them. "I see Louis, stone-carved, sculpturesque; Neville, scissor-cutting, exact; Susan with eyes like lumps of crystal; Jinny dancing like a flame, febrile, hot,

over dry earth; and Rhoda the nymph of the fountain always wet"
(99). Bernard is also the one (though not the only one: note Susan at
164) who descries, in the house near the sea and its waves, a lady who
is writing: "The lady sits between the two long windows, writing" (14).
Bernard also admires Dr. Crane, the headmaster, whom the other
children despise on account of his bathos and empty rhetoric. As
Bernard catalogues his own insights, he expresses his solidarity with
the world: "I do not believe in separation. We are not single. Also I
wish to add to my collection of valuable observations upon the true
nature of human life. My book will certainly run to many volumes,
embracing every known variety of man and woman" (57). Yet the very
presence of Neville, the poet, is enough to prick the balloon of
Bernard's egotism: "Hence he will reach perfection, and I shall fail and
shall leave nothing behind me but imperfect phrases littered with
sand" (77). Even though *The Waves* ultimately leaves everything in
Bernard's hands—for the ninth and final section is his own lonely
stream—Bernard begins to lose himself already in midstream. In the
fourth of the nine sections of the book he laments, "I do not remember
my special gifts, or idiosyncrasy, or the marks I bear on my person;
eyes, nose or mouth. I am not, at this moment, myself" (97). At times
he drifts happily on the clouds of his phrases: "how lovely the smoke
of my phrase is"; but when the smoke clears, "observe how meretricious
the phrase is—made up of what evasions and old lies" (112–13).

Rhoda plays with flower petals she drops into a basin of water. "I
have a fleet now swimming from shore to shore. I will drop a twig in
as a raft for a drowning sailor. I will drop a stone in and see bubbles
rise from the depths of the sea" (15). Yet Rhoda is not Leukothea. She
is herself the stone, herself the drowning sailor, and there is no rescuer
for her. "Meaning has gone. The clock ticks" (17). At school she studies
a geometric figure on the board that she does not understand: "Look,
the loop of the figure is beginning to fill with time; it holds the world

in it. I begin to draw a figure and the world is looped in it, and I myself am outside the loop; which I now join—so—and seal up, and make entire. The world is entire, and I am outside of it, crying, 'Oh save me, from being blown for ever outside the loop of time!'" (17–18). In bed, trying to drop off to sleep, she says, "Let me pull myself out of these waters. But they heap themselves on me; they sweep me between their great shoulders; I am turned; I am tumbled; I am stretched, among these long lights, these long waves, these endless paths, with people pursuing, pursuing" (23). And then:

> The door opens; the tiger leaps. The door opens; terror rushes in; terror upon terror, pursuing me.... But here the door opens and people come; they come towards me. Throwing faint smiles to mask their cruelty, their indifference, they seize me.... I must take his hand; I must answer. But what answer shall I give? I am thrust back to stand burning in this clumsy, this ill-fitting body, to receive the shafts of his indifference and his scorn.... The tiger leaps. Tongues with their whips are upon me.
>
> 88–9

Near the end she says, "Oh, life, how I have dreaded you, oh, human beings, how I have hated you! How you have nudged, how you have interrupted, how hideous you have looked in Oxford Street, how squalid sitting opposite each other staring in the Tube!" (173–4). And then, on the very verge of the end,

> Who then comes with me? Flowers only.... We launch out now over the precipice. Beneath us lie the lights of the herring fleet. The cliffs vanish. Rippling small, rippling grey, innumerable waves spread beneath us. I touch nothing. I see nothing. We may sink and settle on the waves. The sea will drum in my ears. The white petals will be darkened with sea water. They will float for a moment and

then sink. Rolling me over the waves will shoulder me under. Everything falls in a tremendous shower, dissolving me.

176

A remark by Neville late in the book exposes something of the Wordsworthian character of *The Waves*, with the difference that emotion—and the emotion in question is *sorrow* or *grief,* even a *mourning* beyond sadness—is not recollected in tranquillity but tasted as gall and bitterness: "But there was another glory once, when we watched for the door to open, and Percival came" (183). The name Percival begins to sound like *Parsifal,* in this case himself the very grail they all seek. Late in the novel, Bernard tries to account for the effects of that terrible death—without mentioning Percival by name. "We saw for a moment laid out among us the body of the complete human being whom we have failed to be, but at the same time cannot forget. All that we might have been we saw; all that we had missed; and we grudged for a moment the other's claim, as children when the cake is cut, the one cake, the only cake, watch their slice diminishing" (237). This central event, Percival's death, which means nothing to the reader inasmuch as the character "Percival" is without profile or contours of any kind except for the cricket, the self-confidence, the poor performance at school, and the reported rakish beauty. His death is mirrored in a distorted way by the barely recorded event of Rhoda's death. For the reader comes to know Rhoda well because of her bizarre and even terrifying self-destructive monologues. "I have no face," she says repeatedly (28, 36). Why the facelessness? "This is part of the emerging monster to whom we are attached" (55). Late in the novel Bernard "evokes the figure of Rhoda" in his imagination, and then, in a clause set in the past perfect or pluperfect tense and elaborated by no further detail or comment, he tells us that "she had killed herself" (241). Later he feels "the rush of wind of her flight when

25 *"... the water-coloured jewels with sparks of fire in them ..."*

she leapt" (248). The reader can scarcely avoid speculating that it is into the waves of the sea that she leapt, somewhere in Spain perhaps, somewhere near Gibraltar, in sight of Africa. It is also difficult for commentators and biographers not to identify Rhoda with Virginia Woolf herself, who died in waves of sweet water a decade after writing *The Waves*. And it is clear that Bernard too has a special relation to the narrator, if not to the author herself.

Yet surely it is the lady who is writing, the lady whom the children see from the garden, the woman in the house with the long windows, who most readily suggests herself as the famous author. (She is all six children, to repeat, and all the children are one.) The haunting presence of the lady who is writing, like the haunting absence of Rhoda after her suicide, is elaborated by nothing at all; it is merely repeated by one assertive wave after another: "The lady sits between the two long windows, writing" (14); " 'and the woman sat at a table writing,' said Bernard" (105); Susan too "saw the lady writing" (164); "The lady sat writing" (206); "and the lady sits writing" (213); "the lady writing" (230); and then at the end, again Bernard, but this time somewhat oddly, almost abstractly and in the plural, "women writing" (244).

What is the lady writing? If we assume that she is writing the italicized passages that open each of the nine sections, then she is writing of the waves and the sun's action on the waves, of the birds busy in the trees and shrubs of the garden, and of the sun's illuminations of the interior of the house. Each of her selves possesses an extraordinary vocabulary, and she herself is able to write, concerning the birds, "lovelily they came descending" (61). There is much dripping of drops in these italicized passages, many of them seemingly random and weightless. "*In the bucket near the house the tap stopped dripping, as if the bucket were full, and then the tap dripped one, two, three separate drops in succession*" (140). Seeing with the eyes of the birds, as it were, she gives us on the same page two very different drops: "*Or *they saw the rain drop on the hedge, pendent but not falling, with a whole house bent in it, and towering elms"*; and then this: "*Down there among the roots where the flowers decayed, gusts of dead smells were wafted; drops formed on the bloated sides of swollen things"* (62). This same italicized passage, however, opens with an idyll:

> *The sun rose. Bars of yellow and green fell on the shore, gilding the ribs of the eaten-out boat and making the sea-holly and its mailed leaves gleam blue as steel. Light almost pierced the thin swift waves as they raced fan-shaped over the beach. The girl who had shaken her head and made all the jewels, the topaz, the aquamarine, the water-coloured jewels with sparks of fire in them, dance, now bared her brows and with wide-opened eyes drove a straight pathway over the waves. Their quivering mackerel sparkling was darkened; they massed themselves; their green hollows deepened and darkened and might be traversed by shoals of wandering fish.*
>
> 61

Who is this girl who drives a straight pathway over the waves? This is her first and last appearance in the novel. We know nothing about her. She is Sea Sparkle.[3] But then, to close, this: "*The wind rose. The waves drummed on the shore, like turbaned warriors, like turbaned men with poisoned assegais who, whirling their arms on high, advance upon the feeding flocks, the white sheep"* (63). It is difficult not to hear Rhoda's voice in these last lines.

To repeat, Bernard clearly bears a special relation to the lady who is writing, and often he appears as the more insufferable aspects of her

---

[3] An astute reviewer of my manuscript suggests that this "girl" is in fact the figure that appears on the opening page of the novel, when the early dawn brightens "as if the arm of a woman couched beneath the horizon had raised a lamp" (5). She would be not the Greek *Helios* or the Latin *sol*, invariably masculine figures, but the German *die Sonne*. Or perhaps, remembering Roberto Calasso's account in chapter 5 of Ino Leukothea, the radiant goddess, this veiled "girl" is in fact "the slow upward spreading of the light as the hidden is made plain in the dawn."

self. Early on in the novel Bernard self-describes as follows: "But 'joined to the sensibility of a woman' (I am here quoting my own biographer), 'Bernard possessed the logical sobriety of a man' " (64). And two pages later: "Who am I thinking of? Byron of course. I am, in some ways, like Byron. Perhaps a sip of Byron will help to put me in the vein. Let me read a page" (66). Yet the lady who is writing—writing perhaps the italicized passages of *The Waves*—writes less self-consciously, less narcissistically, less pompously than this.

The reader of the novel is struck by the possibility that the lady herself, in the seventh of the nine sections of the book, the very section that introduces the stalactitic temporality of the drop, comes to speak as a character. In this seventh section Bernard is again doubting the efficacy of storytelling, despairing of his own unremitting phrase-making, long after all the other characters have expressed their impatience with it. Now an unidentified monologist interrupts Bernard's grumble, feeding him the name of an otherwise colorless school chum, "Larpent," known heretofore only as one of "the chubby little boys" back at school (32; cf. 39, 50, 55, 56), as a new name for the possible continuation of the story. She—if we may identify her as a she, for it is only a nameless, unidentified voice—interrupts Bernard as he is listening to "a fatal sound of ruining worlds and waters falling to destruction" (162). She says, "So, Bernard (I recall you, you the usual partner in my enterprises), let us begin this new chapter, and observe the formation of this new, this unknown, strange, altogether unidentified and terrifying experience—the new drop—which is about to shape itself. Larpent is that man's name" (ibid.).

Now, Bernard is at that moment in a restaurant in Rome. He is startled to see a man he went to school with decades earlier sitting at a nearby table. What was his name? Should Bernard approach him? No, wait. At that instant a "pretty woman" enters the restaurant. As she walks toward Bernard's table he hears a voice—perhaps the pretty woman's imagined voice, or perhaps the voice of the lady who is writing—telling him that the man is Larpent. Perhaps there is a new story here, contained in the droplet of this strange coincidence, two school chums meeting by chance decades later in Rome; perhaps a new drop of storyline is about to fall? Perhaps it will yield the precipitated marble of a monumental tale, perhaps another truly absurd novel? However, the name Larpent disappears from the remaining pages of the book. There is in fact no new drop for the story.

Bernard, the usual partner in the enterprise of storytelling, is often the mouthpiece of the drop. During the third section of the book he says, "It has been on the whole a good day. The drop that forms on the roof of the soul in the evening is round, many-coloured" (68). Such a drop would surely refract the radiant light that otherwise streams through the dome of eternity. Yet Bernard's drop takes on a more somber hue as the novel proceeds. Bernard begins the seventh section, in which the lady who is writing seems to come to speak, with this:

"And time," said Bernard, "lets fall its drop. The drop that has formed on the roof of the soul falls. On the roof of my mind time, forming, lets fall its drop. Last week, as I stood shaving, the drop fell. I, standing with my razor in my hand, became suddenly aware of the merely habitual nature of my action (this is the drop forming) and congratulated my hands, ironically, for keeping at it. Shave, shave, shave, I said. Go on shaving. The drop fell. All through the day's work, at intervals, my mind went to an empty place, saying, 'What is lost? What is over?' And 'Over and done with,' I muttered, 'over and done with,' solacing myself with words. People noticed the vacuity of my face and the aimlessness of my conversation. The last words of my sentence trailed away. And as I buttoned on my coat to go home I said more dramatically, 'I have lost my youth.'

"It is curious how, at every crisis, some phrase which does not fit insists upon coming to the rescue—the penalty of living in an old civilisation with a notebook. This drop falling has nothing to do with losing my youth. This drop falling is time tapering to a point. Time, which is a sunny pasture covered with a dancing light, time, which is widespread as a field at midday, becomes pendent. Time tapers to a point. As a drop falls from a glass heavy with some sediment, time falls. These are the true cycles, these are the true events. Then as if all the luminosity of the atmosphere were withdrawn I see to the bare bottom. I see what habit covers. I lie sluggish in bed for days. I dine out and gape like a codfish."

157–8

It is unfair to stop citing the passage here—the writing is so uncannily powerful in its desperate quietude. But let us concern ourselves with this drop that forms out of the widespread meadow of time. It falls so suddenly, so precipitously, so unexpectedly, that we are tempted to invoke the suddenness of ecstatic temporality, the ἐξαίφνης of ἔκστασις. Yet how long must one wait for the drop to form, remain pendent, taper, and only then, taking its own sweet or bitter time, to drop? Apparently as long as one must wait for the penny to drop. And that can mean eternities, or at least eons, lifetimes.

Time tapering to a point, or else failing to do so, time as either sharpening or dulling the point of existence, is a principal figure of the first half of Heidegger's 1929–30 lecture course, *The Fundamental Concepts of Metaphysics: World, Finitude, Solitude.*[4] There it is a question of whether the boredom we suffer—we and each of Woolf's

---

[4] See 29/30, especially sections 31–3 for the following.

six characters—invariably dulls the point of time. And what is the point of time? The point of time is what pricks us, you should forgive the expression, but it is Susan's word. Why the need for pricking? Because otherwise Dasein dawdles, Dasein diddles, Dasein fudges, Dasein fiddles.

The idea of the pricking point of time is fundamentally Kierkegaardian, Lutheran, Augustinian, and Pauline: something—and these four might call that something *grace*—needs to startle us out of our lethargy and torpor; something needs to lift us out of our inherited, inveterate fallenness. Some fundamental attunement, whether it be anxiety or joy or profound boredom, needs to burst all the balloons floated by our dispersed and distracted everydayness. Even after Percival's death, when everything should be changed forever, Bernard notes, "The sequence returns; one thing leads to another—the usual order.... There is little time left to answer the question; my powers flag; I become torpid" (132). The difficulty concerning Heidegger's understanding of profound boredom, however, is that nothing beyond the boredom itself does the pricking, no grace, no prophecy, no preachment, no call, unless it is a call from nowhere and no one. The needling *of* time *by* time occurs—or fails to occur—precisely when all beings and we ourselves drift into insipid indifference.[5]

Two figures dominate Heidegger's discussion in 1929–30. The first is the paradoxical figure he calls *die Bannung der Zeit*, which designates

---

[5] I should at this point re-read Charles Scott's *Living with Indifference* (Bloomington: Indiana University Press, 2007), in order to note the differences between Scott's "indifference" and Heidegger's *Gleichgültigkeit* and *Indifferenz*. If I remember well, there is no needling in or about Scott's "indifference," so that the chiliastic rhetoric of Heidegger's "fundamental attunement," "decision," and "resoluteness," disappears altogether from Scott's thinking and writing. Which does not mean that Scott fails to make his points. And if *resolve* is not Scott's word for living with indifference, perhaps the word *resilience* serves. I refer the reader to Krell, "Narrative as Trauma and Resilience in Charles Scott's *Living with Indifference*," in *Epoché*, 17:1 (Fall 2012), 75–88. A bit later in the chapter, I will cite one or two passages from Scott's remarkable book.

the way in which, when we are bored, time both *bans* us from beings as a whole and *binds* us in the blink of an eye to our proper being mortal. Both banishment and binding are said by the same word, *bannen*. We might translate it as *spellbinding*, thinking of the mesmerizing spell that excludes every extraneous object from our attention and the fascination that will allow no interference. Heidegger would no doubt reject the language of mesmerism here, since it is the language of consciousness (or unconsciousness, which for him comes to the same) and subjectivity. For him *die Bannung der Zeit* is nothing less than the temporalizing of *Entschlossenheit*, our resolve to confront the essential possibility of mortal existence, to wit, our finitude and our death.

The second figure is that of the tip or point of time, *die Spitze der Zeit*. Much later in his career, in his second essay (written in 1953) on the poetry of Georg Trakl, Heidegger will invoke the point of a spear, *die Spitze des Speers*, which he takes to be the meaning of not time but place or locale, *der Ort* or *die Ortschaft* of Trakl's single unsung poem. In 1929–30 the tip or point of time, time at its extreme in profound boredom, time *zugespitzt*, time driving its point home, makes it possible for Dasein to find and hold onto the moment of its resolve. There is therefore something eschatological about profound boredom, "eschatological" in the sense Heidegger elaborates in his remarkable reading of "Anaximander's Saying" (H 301–2; EGT 18). Profound boredom, driven to the extreme, at the very tip of its paradoxical banning and binding, enables Dasein to see itself as finite possibility-being and to be resolutely open to mortal existence. The tip or point of time makes it possible for Dasein to be *attuned to* both a finite self and a self-revealing, self-concealing world. Thus the two figures are in fact one. "Indeed," says Heidegger, "this *banning time* [*diese* bannende Zeit] is the *point* [*diese* Spitze] itself, the point that essentially makes Dasein possible" (29/30:223).

Yet is Dasein, being-here, properly possible? Does time have a pricking point? If so, it is not as frivolous as it sounds to wonder whether the characters of Woolf's *The Waves* get the point. They are not in any obvious way pricked by the point of time, the point that ought to startle them out of their profound boredom. They *are* in search—futile search, as it turns out—of some fundamental attunement to their world. Not one of the six finds it. Each is, as Rhoda says, "hoping for a wave to lift us" (137), or at least, as Louis says, seeking "the protective waves of the ordinary" (79). Yet they all find that the waves of the ordinary in fact "shoulder them under." The tsunami of Percival's death whelms them, as Melville would say, and they flounder, then founder, seeking refuge in the ordinary. Well enough they know the boredom of their lives; well enough they sense that they are banished. Yet the binding power of time in the moment and in resolve eludes them. Theirs is the boredom not of profundity but of triviality; it is the boredom of Eliot's "Cocktail Party," of "Prufrock," and of "The Wasteland." Theirs is the hollowness of "The Hollow Men." Moreover, each of them, but especially Neville, would be suspicious of the very desire (Heidegger's desire) for a temporal pricking, for a tip or a point to burst the bubble of everydayness. For does not the "factical ideal" (SZ 310) that lies concealed in the call of conscience, the plea for authenticity, the demand for resolute decision, and, yes, the pricking *point* of time arise from the all-too-familiar needling of the ascetic priest, who attains power precisely by prescribing for all who exist the prickly hairshirt? Would not a genealogy of Heidegger's *Spitze* lead us to what Nietzsche's Zarathustra, in his speech "On Redemption," calls revenge against time and time's "It *was*" (KSW 4:180), no matter how perspicuous about Nietzsche Heidegger tries to be?

At all events, the temporality of the dripping drop does not offer any of Woolf's six a prism for possible insight, an *Augenblick* in

Heidegger's sense. Temporal banning in the novel finds no binding, no ligature; there is no tip or tipping point, but only the pendent drop and the waiting, along with the unraveling of all stories—shades of Maurice Blanchot's *l'attente* and Samuel Beckett's *en attendant*. If there is a discovery of mortality in the novel—and *mortality* or *finitude* still might be words for what the six do uncover—that discovery has nothing to do with a resoluteness that takes hold and bravely swims ahead through the oncoming waves of life.

No, a different order of time, a different temporality, is at work here. It does not run ahead. It lingers behind; it limps. It does not swirl in an ecstasy of raptures; it drips.

When the drop finally drips for Bernard, when everydayness falls away at the point when he happens to be shaving, which he does every day, something does precipitate. Perhaps the drops, then, constitute stages on life's way? Bernard says, "But let me consider. The drop falls; another stage has been reached. Stage upon stage. And why should there be an end of stages? And where do they lead? To what conclusion? For they come wearing robes of solemnity" (159). Yet drops are not stages. What precipitates is something more disturbing than a recognizable stage of development in a predictable evolution or a solemn and edifying salvation story. What precipitates, rather, is a series of parlous, volatile, uncertain insights. To begin with, Bernard, the storyteller and life-long fashioner of phrases, says, "I am not so gifted as at one time seemed likely" (159). An understatement perhaps, but perhaps also an excessively harsh judgment, yet one that in either case does subversive work. Early on in the novel, Neville, the poet, foresees the difficulty: "Among the tortures and devastations of life is this then—our friends are not able to finish their stories" (32). That is in the second of the nine sections, with Bernard having opened the section with bravado: "'Now,' said Bernard, 'the time has come. The day has come. The cab is at the door'" (25). At the dinner with Percival, something seems to drop, and it is something brilliant, resplendent: Bernard senses "the last drop and the brightest that we let fall like some supernal quicksilver into the swelling and splendid moment created by us from Percival" (123). The words that end the sentence, "by us from," are odd, as must be the chemistry of supernal quicksilver. Perhaps they reflect the doubt that Bernard only now has suffered: "I could make a dozen stories of what he said, of what she said—I can see a dozen pictures. But what are stories? Toys I twist, bubbles I blow, one ring passing through another. And sometimes I begin to doubt if there are stories" (122). After learning of Percival's death, Bernard's doubts deepen, and yet, in what might have been a moment of insight, as the drop falls, Bernard dines out and gapes at Melvillean nihilities like the codfish on his plate.

And so time, in stalactitic temporality, drips its drop. Yet nothing is less certain than that a stalagmite forms from the dripping. In the seventh section Bernard says, "I have made up thousands of stories; I have filled innumerable notebooks with phrases to be used when I have found the true story, the one story to which all these phrases refer. But I have never yet found that story. And I begin to ask, Are there stories?" (160). It is at this moment that the unidentified voice, perhaps that of the lady writing, interrupts Bernard's doleful reverie, tossing him the bait of the chubby "Larpent" redivivus in a Roman restaurant. To no avail. Bernard senses that his phrases are "imperfect," as imperfect as the "It *was*" of time, and that they ring hollow (185), so that the story cannot and will not find its end. The sea urchin will in some mysterious way "use" its own necrotic tissue in order to regenerate itself, yet, as we noted earlier, this stratagem succeeds only for the time being. At some point necrosis becomes true to its name, and the bloated drop either falls or evaporates.

Within that hollow or hollowing out of phrases, some of the other characters experience the falling of the stalactitic drop. Louis says, in a tone one might call Mephisphelean were it not for its apparent serenity, "I do not see how you can say that it is fortunate to have lived" (187). By contrast, Jinny has her own way of letting the droplet drop in the dribs and drabs of her hoard of life, and without waiting for eons to pass: "My imagination is the body's," she tells us again, and even though her escapades have not always gone well ("My traffics have led me into strange places"), she adds the following as her ultimate justification: "The torments, the divisions of your lives have been solved for me night after night, sometimes only by the touch of a finger under the tablecloth as we sat dining—so fluid has my body become, forming even at the touch of a finger into one full drop, which fills itself, which quivers, which flashes, which falls into ecstasy" (188–9). With Jinny, alone among the six, stalactitic and ecstatic temporalities seem to elide—at least for a time, for the time being. In sharp contrast, Rhoda observes how the others stand "embedded in a substance made of repeated moments run together" (190), as though the others were stalagmites with faces, whereas she is all dissolution and drainage.

Bernard's stalagmitic meltdown and the evaporation of his stories continues. " 'Drop upon drop,' said Bernard, 'silence falls. It forms on the roof of the mind and falls into pools beneath. For ever alone, alone, alone, alone—hear silence fall and sweep its rings to the farthest edges. Gorged and replete, solid with middle-aged content, I, whom loneliness destroys, let silence fall, drop by drop' " (191). This silence, however, is hyperacidic, so that, to repeat, no monumental stalagmite forms below: "But now silence falling pits my face, wastes my nose like a snowman stood out in a yard in the rain. As silence falls I am dissolved utterly and become featureless and scarcely to be distinguished from another. It does not matter. What matters? We have dined well. The fish, the veal cutlets, the wine have blunted the sharp tooth of egotism. Anxiety is at rest" (ibid.).

Rhoda will soon counter Bernard's lassitude by noting that "it is not often that one has no anxiety" (195), and Louis joins the dismal chorus: "Our separate drops are dissolved; we are extinct, lost in the abysses of time, in the darkness" (192). And Bernard ultimately has to agree: "Our lives too stream away, down the unlighted avenues, past the strip of time, unidentified" (194). And once again Rhoda: "'A weight has dropped into the night,' said Rhoda, 'dragging it down'" (196).

In the novel's final section, the ninth, it becomes clear to Bernard that for a temporality that beads and drops, that is, for stalactitic temporality, where you would think there must be solid limestone residues and columnar monuments below, with each drop contributing a layer to glistening monoliths of memory, the illusion that there can be stories evanesces. Whatever it is that one might have wanted to incise into the monolith as though it were a marble column of St. Mark's in Venice or St. Peter's in Rome, is precisely what is melting away into a puddle. "The illusion is upon me that something adheres for a moment, has roundness, weight, depth, is completed," says Bernard (204). Yet the illusion of stalagmitic cohesion is defeated by his exhaustion: "How tired I am of stories, how tired I am of phrases that come down beautifully with all their feet on the ground!" (ibid.). No stalagmites, then, but mere puddles and pools. Drainage. Seepage. Eventually the erstwhile storyteller comes to recognize the cowardice and cruelty of his tales: "On the outskirts of every agony sits some observant fellow who points" (213). Storytelling is ostensive but also ostentatious. Storytelling is (in) vain.

All agree that there is comfort in stories. "I was always going to the bookcase for another sip of the divine specific," says Bernard (214), who is nostalgic for textual, scriptural divinity, the wholeness and holiness of the book. "Let us again pretend that life is a solid substance, shaped like a globe, which we turn about in our fingers. Let us pretend that we can make out a plain and logical story, so that when one matter is dispatched—love for instance—we go on, in an orderly manner, to the next" (215). Love—for instance? The illusion that "some sediment" has "formed" is at times quite strong: "I formed; a drop fell; I fell—that is, from some completed experience I had emerged" (217). Completed experience? What would that be? Who could tell its story, upon completion, in an orderly manner? Bernard eventually grows sober and asks, "Should this be the end of the story? a kind of sigh? a last ripple of the wave? A trickle of water to some gutter where, burbling, it dies away? . . . But if there are no stories, what end can there be or what beginning?" (ibid.). An understatement, almost banal, now says it all: "Life is not susceptible perhaps to the treatment we give it when we try to tell it" (ibid.). Others may think that such defeatism is merely an effect of old age, the onset of the storyteller's dotage, the silent herald of senescence. Bernard counters, "It is not age; it is that a drop has fallen; another drop. Time has given the arrangement another shake" (233). But can this new arrangement, this novel agitation, be told? Will it shake down into narrative?

Not only is there no narrative, however; there is not even an enduring image.[6] The italicized preamble of section seven invokes a "wave of light" that flashes "as if a fin cut the green glass of a lake" (155). However, as the narrative "I" begins already in this section to abandon Bernard, the image of the fin turns and returns: "A fin turns . . . the fin of a porpoise . . . 'Fin in a waste of waters'" (161). In the ninth and final section, the fin falters once and for all: "Nothing, nothing, nothing broke with its fin that leaden waste of waters. Nothing would happen to lift that weight of intolerable boredom" (210–11). The fin will have turned with special significance for Bernard the storyteller, who is stymied by

---

[6] The present paragraph was suggested to me by that same astute (unfortunately anonymous) reviewer of my manuscript, who reminded me of the image of the "fin," the fin of a porpoise, as a figure of finite time in *The Waves*. That figure eventually falters. My gratitude to the reviewer for this and other suggestions.

Neville the poet: the two at one point share an insight that then "sank into one of those silences which are now and again broken by a few words, as if a fin rose in the wastes of silence; and then the fin, the thought, sinks back into the depths, spreading round it a little ripple of satisfaction, content" (234). That contentment, however, is interrupted by a ticking clock, as the two suddenly become genuinely aware of one another: "It was Neville who changed our time" (ibid.). And in the end Bernard too, the "usual" accomplice of the narrator, fades away to silence: "No fin breaks the waste of this immeasurable sea" (243).

As for the drop itself, it falls at thirty-two feet per second per second. That would be fast enough to qualify as ecstatic. However, recall the slowness of stalactitic temporality, precipitate time in its formation. Precipitate time is not precipitous. Its passivity weighs on it and causes it to bead gradually and to swell painfully slowly. Its colloidal dispersion of water-soluble minerals, its suspension of amberat, silica, and calcium carbonate seems *even when it falls* to suspend ecstatic temporality and to disperse in slow motion. True, we live in a fast-motion time in which our pronounced everydayness, the dictatorship of the "they," *das Man*, encourages us to think we can do with our lives and our bodies whatever we will and as quickly as we want. It all moves very fast, mindlessly fast.

Yet the consequences of all our inanities belong to precipitate, stalactitic temporality, which may move very slowly. The consequences unfold in another order of time, in another embodied temporality— embodied for the time being. Percival's unforeseen accident, Rhoda's foreseeable yet unforeseen suicide, Susan's high-wire act of natural contentment over an abyss of dark despair, Louis's self-mocked success in business, Jinny's increasingly desperate faith in her romantic "traffics," Neville's exhaustion, Bernard's gradual dissolution, the eventual fate of the lady writing, a fate that takes a decade to play itself out—these things too pertain to a different order of time, neither cosmic time nor ecstatic temporality, and yet in that order of stalactitic temporality we will have had the future anterior time of our lives. Which—and it was Derrida who made the remark—will have been so short.

The Waves is not a cheering book. The pleasure granted by its rich descriptions and its astonishing vocabulary does not palliate the cruelties and the outrages that engulf each of the six or seven characters in it. Perhaps that is why one may consider the book to be "philosophical."

Surely, one may rejoin, not every precipitate is catastrophic. See how slowly the miraculous fetus forms in the amnion. Susan's response to this miracle? "I shall be debased and hidebound by the bestial and beautiful passion of maternity" (112). Well, at least the word *beautiful* falls. Stalactites and stalagmites themselves are sublime, if not beautiful, and they measure out their lives in millennia, as we do not. True, they too are vulnerable to the human touch, which stains and degrades them, but we are far more vulnerable and evanescent than they. As for beauty, the rapturous Jinny, now well beyond middle age, eventually has this to say:

> But look—there is my body in that looking-glass. How solitary, how shrunk, how aged! I am no longer young. I am no longer part of the procession. Millions descend those stairs in a terrible descent. Great wheels churn inexorably urging them downwards. Millions have died. Percival died. I still move. But who will come if I signal?
>
> 165

What seems to fail in *The Waves*, whether or not the characters marry and have families and whether or not they have relationships, is the intimacy of love and love-making, about which the novel remains taciturn. "Love for instance," says the storyteller, as though there would be anything else to go on to "in an orderly manner." Neville the poet does say at one point, "Meanwhile, let us abolish the ticking of time's clock with one blow. Come closer" (154). Perhaps it is Bernard to whom he is speaking or of whom he is silently thinking. Some pages later, however, he says, "Swept away by the old hallucination, I cry, 'Come closer, closer'" (170). Yet it is Neville who also accepts the consequences of the hallucination: "There can be no doubt … that our mean lives, unsightly as they are, put on splendour and have meaning only under the eyes of love" (151). Still later, when exhaustion dulls the splendor, Neville confirms an earlier judgment by Bernard: "We are in that passive and exhausted frame of mind when we only wish to rejoin the body of our mother from whom we have been severed" (198). Earlier on, Bernard has identified the first day of school as a "second severance from the body of our mother" (106). Ferenczi and Rank would call it the third severance, birth and weaning being the first and second.

Each drop of stalactitic temporality seems to be but a repetition of that severance, the drying up of the seas. The dripping of the drop, which, despite the pounding of the waves, is all that is left of the oceans, is a moment not of insight and resolve but of separation and abandonment, not a point pricking us to wakefulness but a truncation, a cutting of the cord, as we say. Four times *alone*, as Bernard says. Irigaray reminds us in her *L'oubli de l'air* that our rejoining the matrix of the mother and thus annealing severance is impossible, even if she holds out a certain stubborn hope for "the only tenderness there is," *la seule tendresse*, which she recognizes and understands as a noun of the feminine gender.[7] She is not the only one to do so. The very

---

[7] See Luce Irigaray, *L'oubli de l'air chez Martin Heidegger* (Paris: Minuit, 1983), 108–9. During the mid-1980s, when I was writing *Daimon Life: Heidegger and Life-Philosophy*, and ever afterward, Luce Irigaray's thought concerning "the sole tenderness" has been with me. As for the book itself, she told me that she began to write it in late May 1976, at the moment she learned of Heidegger's death. Thus *L'oubli*, however critical of Heidegger it is, and it *is* critical, must be considered a work of mourning. It has been translated into English by Mary Beth Mader and published by the University of Texas Press (Austin, 1999).

promise of dawn, in Romain Gary's *La promesse de l'aube*, is what he calls at the outset *quelque tendresse essentielle*, and it is represented by none other than his raucous, impossible mother; much later in his *récit* the narrator speaks of *quelque tendresse providentielle féminine*, mixing up providential deity with womankind, as Schelling would surely have him do (RG 13, 350).

Sometimes the sea, for all its pounding waves, seems to embody such tenderness, and I will turn to this possibility of tenderness—all but absent from *The Waves*—at the end. For the end of *The Waves* itself is dark. The final waves described in the italicized passage that opens section nine, the last, are "waves of darkness":

> *As if there were waves of darkness in the air, darkness moved on, covering houses, hills, trees, as waves of water wash round the sides of some sunken ship. Darkness washed down streets, eddying round single figures, engulfing them; blotting out couples clasped under the showery darkness of elm trees in full summer foliage. Darkness rolled its waves along grassy rides and over the wrinkled skin of the turf, enveloping the solitary thorn tree and the empty snail shells at its foot. Mounting higher, darkness blew along the bare upland slopes, and met the fretted and abraded pinnacles of the mountain where the snow lodges for ever on the hard rock, even when the valleys are full of running streams and yellow vine leaves, and girls, sitting on verandahs, look up at the snow, shading their faces with their fans. Them, too, darkness covered.*

> 202–3

There is some brave talk at the end—from Bernard, of course—about "eternal renewal" and about death as "the enemy" against which the hero, imitating Percival, will "fling himself" (254). Phrases. And then comes the final *italicized* phrase of the book—the only italicized phrase to appear at the *end* of a section, the last: "*The waves broke on*

26 *"As if there were waves of darkness in the air . . ."*

the shore." The word *broke*, in the simple past, the "imperfect," gives a new and foreboding meaning to the breaking waves.

"Fear death by drowning." I did not shy from citing Eliot's words earlier on in the book, without mentioning their source. Yet Rhoda's death by drowning, reported by Bernard in the most abstract way, along with Redburn's plunge from the top yard-arm into the sea, remind us that an encounter with the sea has to confront the danger not only of shark and stonefish but also of possible drowning. I interrupt this reflection on Woolf's *The Waves* in order to focus for an instant on these drowning women and men who do drown. Charles Scott's *Living with Indifference* will help me here.

Scott meditates on the role of the limbic system in traumatic experiences such as near-drowning. His descriptions of the limbic system, one of the most primitive and most important of our systems when it comes to trauma, while not themselves the literature of fiction, do what literature at its best does—they leave us both spellbound and perhaps even traumatized, *gebannt* perhaps, but also anxious to hear more and understand better. In his chapter on trauma Scott writes:

> Some of those who have undergone intense trauma speak of watching it happen to them as though they were outside of it—safely distanced—and as though they were articulating a vast indifference to themselves in the traumatic occurrence. That occurrence is there—I see it. (Strangely, it's happening to my body but not to me-seeing-it-happen. Who is that man drowning? Looks like me. I believe he's stopped breathing.) But that occurrence is not I. I'm elsewhere.
>
> LI 130

Such is perhaps the very distance that our best writers are able to open and sustain in their narratives. Recall Melville, coolly opening the distance in and for his hero, Pierre, who has come to see that his writing is murdering his lungs, but who is helpless to prevent his slow demise. I repeat Melville's words: "For in tremendous extremities human souls are like drowning men; well enough they know they are in peril; well enough they know the causes of that peril;—nevertheless, the sea is the sea, and these drowning men do drown." Scott shows how trauma dulls the edge of Melville's "well enough they know," and yet his account elaborates the peril and the terrible *rescue* from peril with an edge that would have caused Melville himself to marvel. Scott writes:

> This distance of I from the trauma's immediacy has its survival value, I assume, in many situations. Or, if not survival, its value in a cerebral release from trauma's power. It allows a distance, in the drowning, for example, from the feel of the water entering my lungs, the terror of the heart's fluttering, pounding, and slowing, the effects of strangulation. Indeed the blue of the water and the filtered rays of light, the increasingly slow motion of the body, the stilling of the water where there had been so much thrashing, the white sand rising up to the sinking thing, the light streaming down to darkness—there is something beautiful in the indifference of drowning. But now imagine a dark figure plunging in the water. Something jarring happens. Like a rude awakening. The distance collapses into terrible chest pain, heaving efforts to cough. The affections of vomiting, sucking air, water stinging and congesting air passages, flowing out. Unbearable pressure in my head. Agonizing light. I, having drowned, am now here.
>
> LI 130

What reader can survive this cruel inversion of doom and rescue? A page later, after the reader has either coughed up enough brine to come-to or has breathed in enough water finally to let go and submit to being "the sinking thing," the thing caught at last in the thalassic tug

Waves and Drops of Time

that has been steadily pursuing it a life long, Scott enters a footnote to assure us that he did not actually drown. Almost, but not quite. And he reports the accounts of two persons who did drown, if one can say such a thing, but then were lugged back to life (131n. 5). What grips Scott in all this is the relation between "the limbic hit" of trauma, which leaves us speechless and indifferent to narrative, cut off from "the procedures of control that are necessary for a narrative" (133), and the *ensuing* narrative, the *recounting* of trauma itself, *après coup*. What is it that can give the writing both its intimacy with and distance from "the limbic hit"? Not all writing needs this, of course, since there can be whimsy. But the sort of writing that a meditation on the sea must find and must practice? When does the penny finally drop? And the drop itself? How long must the drop remain pendent?

Let me advance toward my conclusion by remembering the "stamping beast" of the waves that Louis repeatedly hears and fears, the surging surf that often roars in Woolf's *The Waves*. Not only Louis fears the furious surf, however, for so does the writer of those italicized passages:

> *The waves broke and spread their waters swiftly over the shore. One after another they massed themselves and fell; the spray tossed itself back with the energy of their fall. The waves were steeped deep-blue save for a pattern of diamond-pointed light on their backs which rippled as the backs of great horses ripple with muscles as they move. The waves fell; withdrew and fell again, like the thud of a great beast stamping.*

> 127

> *The waves massed themselves, curved their backs and crashed. Up spurted stones and shingle. They swept round the rocks, and the spray,*

leaping high, spattered the walls of a cave that had been dry before,
and left pools inland, where some fish stranded lashed its tail as the
wave drew back.

141

How can we not be reminded of one of Nietzsche's most remarkable passages? It is the passage promised back in chapter 1, namely, number 60 in *The Gay Science,* and if chronology did not get in the way we might well think that Nietzsche had lifted it from Virginia Woolf. Here is the passage, the title of which I will suppress for a moment:

Do I still have ears? Am I only an ear and nothing more? Here I stand in the midst of the furious surf [*inmitten des Brandes der Brandung,* literally, in the midst of the surf's conflagration], whose white flames lick their way up to my feet:—on every side it howls, threatens, screams shrilly at me, while in the deepest depths the old Earth-shaker sings his aria like a deep-voiced bellowing bull: he stamps out such an Earth-shaker's beat that even these monstrous, weathered boulders feel their hearts trembling in their bodies. Then, suddenly, as though born out of nothing, beyond the gateway of this hellish labyrinth, only a few leagues away—appears a great sailing ship gliding along as silent as a ghost. Oh, this ghostly beauty! With what magic it grips me! How, now? Has all the stillness and silence in the world boarded this ship? Does my happiness itself reside in this quiet place, my happier ego, my second, eternalized self? To be not dead and yet also no longer living? As a ghostlike, silent, gazing, gliding, hovering daimon? Something very like the ship that with its white sails glides across the dark ocean like a gigantic butterfly! Yes! To glide over existence! That's it! That would be it! [*Ueber das Dasein hinlaufen! Das ist es! Das wäre es!*] — — It seems the noise here has turned me into a fantasist? All loud noise causes us to posit our happiness in stillness and remoteness. When a man stands in the midst of his noise, in the surf of his chances and his choices [*seine Würfe und Entwürfe*], he then also sees a silent and magical creature gliding by; he longs for the happiness and the seclusion of that creature—it's the women [*es sind die Frauen*]. He well-nigh believes that his better self dwells with the women: at these quiet sites even the loudest surf becomes as still as death and life itself a dream about life. And yet! And yet! My noble enthusiast, even on the loveliest sailing ship there is so much noise, so much fuss, and unfortunately so much wretchedly petty fuss! The magic and the mightiest effect of women, to speak the language of the philosophers, is action at a distance, *actio in distans*: but what pertains to it first of all and above all is—distance!

KSW 3:424–5

The passage is called *Die Frauen und ihre Wirkung in die Ferne*, "Women and their action at a distance," and it is not difficult to imagine the wrath it may evoke. Yet I have always felt that the gender identity of the ship's crew and passengers, as well as that of the speaker who is embroiled in the surf of his own noise, his own plots and ploys, could be altered every which way, the roles reversed and even entirely reconfigured, entirely remade, at which point the outcome would remain precisely the same. Action at a distance is the action of desire— not of the specific desired "thing" but of *la Chose* itself, as Lacan would say, namely, desire. Schelling calls it *Sehnsucht*, "languor" and "languishing." Melville might see it in Ahab's "one wee drop." Nietzsche appears to be espying Jinny (or Novalis's Djinnistan, after whom Jinny may have been named) in the distance, at least the Jinny that the young Jinny herself sees in the rings rippling outward from her imagined and felt body. But could it not also be Jinny who is standing *inmitten des Brandes der Brandung*, Jinny in search of her young man gliding across the horizon, or Susan in search of her otherwise landlocked farmer, or Rhoda in search of a fiery column in the desert? Each of Woolf's six monologists, whether man or woman, would, I think, agree: where desire, love, intimacy, hate—emotion and passion of any kind—are concerned, action is always action at a distance, never in full presence, never subject to our control and command.

"That's it!" exclaims the narrator, in the indicative mood, but then, "That would be it!" in the subjunctive-contrary-to-fact, followed by a double hiatus and an alteration in the voice. A second alteration occurs with the double "And yet! And yet!" Now the voice calls for a *maintenance* of the distance. The desire to maintain the distance, however, which is evident in the arch and condescending response to the *Phantast* and "enthusiast," is itself caught in desirous turmoil: no matter how coyly and cleverly the critic chides the Lutheran dreamer ("Here I stand"), his own desire to maintain the distance is a disingenuous expression of the distance itself, not of the thinker's assumed urbanity and autonomy. Both the *Phantast* and the critic ultimately succumb to the self-produced noise that deafens them. He, or she, or both of them miss the boat, after all, and they miss it in more senses than one. At least to the extent that one counts on a particular object's being on the boat, one is merely making more noise when one begs for distance from the closeness that causes such confusion and heartbreak and, yes, "fuss," in the first place. What he or she or they have a chance to discern across those leagues of remoteness is that she or he or they have indeed missed the boat; they have not the heart to break out into a swim, however, driving "a straight pathway over the waves," so that what is left to them is the furious surf of their unrelieved aloneness.

It's the women? Or is it, more precisely, as Buck Mulligan says of the sea, paraphrasing Algernon Swinburne, "our great sweet mother," to whom we yearn to return? Or, finally, is it what the characters of *The Waves* are unable to recount or celebrate, namely, festivals of remembrance—remembrance of love, for instance? If the surf were less furious in its surge, the characters might let themselves be cradled. But that too—the fury of the surging surf—does not lie within their power.

The temporalizing figures of sun, wave, and drop in Woolf's *The Waves*—do they come to the same—in the sense of the eternal recurrence of the same? The sun, from pre-dawn till nightfall, advances across the sky, describing the one and only meridian of a lifetime, from childhood to demise, the one and only life that is granted to each human being. The path is solitary and terminal, even if the waves continue their lapping or pounding, and even if the earth continues to twirl around the sun. For, as another great writer (we have heard from him already) once put it, lineages that are mortal are granted but one opportunity on the earth—*"porque las estirpes condenadas a cien años de soledad no tenían una segunda oportunidad sobre la tierra"* (GM 351).

The waves, stamping like a beast or lapping with steady regularity on the shore, figure the incessant surge of the unstoppable sea. They figure, if we can coin a word, *incessancy*. At one point they figure nature as pure upsurgence, φύσις, at another the pounding that mortals take from both earth and world. The drop, as from a stalactite, for some of the characters at least and for some of the time, signifies the formation and the growing pressure of civilization, from ancient Egypt and far-off India through imperial Rome to the shores of a boastful yet weary Britannia. For Rhoda, who is the one who talks of stalactites, the droplets of time—even early on in her life—fall as the witnesses to her mortality:

> And I will now rock the brown basin from side to side so that my ships may ride the waves. Some will founder. Some will dash themselves against the cliffs. One sails alone. That is my ship. It sails

into icy caverns where the sea-bear barks and stalactites swing
green chains. The waves rise; their crests curl; look at the lights on
the mastheads. They have scattered, they have foundered, all except
my ship, which mounts the wave and sweeps before the gale and
reaches the islands where the parrots chatter and the creepers . . .

15

The ellipsis points indicate the dwindling of Rhoda's fantasy, the
fantasy of her surviving ship. In spite of the promise of the corpusants
("look at the lights on the mastheads"), some ships "will dash
themselves against the cliffs."

For the storyteller, for Bernard and for the lady who is writing, the
drop means the decisive formations and releases of a life: birth,
weaning, childhood, schooling, marriage, failed affairs, a consuming
profession, the births of children, senescence, and death. Yet the
spherical pressure of the droplet, succumbing to gravity and forming
the delicate skin of the water into its pear shape, does not hold; the
globular drop does not become a globe one can turn in one's fingers in
order to locate on it some definite site. The drop is not round but
elliptical, bulbous, tear-shaped, and when it finally drops it leaves no
limestone monument but merely splatters on the floor and disperses.

When you photograph a breaking wave at two-thousandth's of a
second, what strikes you in the resulting image are the drops, frozen
as crystals or pearls, perfect adamantine drops in profusion through
the sunlight. The naked eye of a mortal never sees these drops,
however, so that the camera captures the seeming unreal, or the real
that lies beyond the mortals' reality probe. What you see of the waves
on the shore is the splash, the spume, the forming pool, the slow
seepage into the sand, the withdrawal. The lady writing finds it
important to record the surging surf, the noise, the seepages and
withdrawals, even if they should come to nothing for her six characters.

She finds it important to record and to write until the pressure of the final droplet—releasing, falling, dispersing in the disequilibrium she fears will never be righted—sends her to the river.

Yet this is no way to end a chapter on *The Waves*, the waves of the sea, even if we cannot take Bernard's brave phrase-making at the end ("O Death!") as anything more than bluff. And it is no way to end a philosophical encounter with the sea. For the sea, as furious as its surf can be, can also grow calm, though not through any power, will, or defiance of ours.

Recalling Melville's *Mardi*, I think of the final fading words of the Mardian priest, the priest I imagine to be in the Hieron of ancient Samothrace. Heeding the calm of the night sea, its silence and its sadness, the sadness that is "universal and eternal," seeing that heaven has no roof and that "exemption from great woes" is the best a dweller on Mardi can hope for, he says that "sadness is tranquillity" and tranquillity "the uttermost that souls may hope for." Even so, he has already greeted all the initiates—perhaps there are six or seven of them—with the not entirely tranquil invitation, "Loved one, love on!"

27 *"But much is / To be kept close." Wild lily at Balos Bay.*

A Concluding Word

I looked at the sea: something happened in me. I don't know what:
a boundless peace, the impression of having arrived. Since then
the sea has always been for me a humble yet sufficient metaphysics.
I don't know how to talk about the sea. All I know is that it
suddenly releases me from all my obligations. Each time
I look at it I become a man happily drowned.

ROMAIN GARY, *LA PROMESSE DE L'AUBE*

The sea takes and gives memory, we heard Hölderlin say. Presumably
he was thinking of those placid days or nights when the silent sea
seems a barely breathing animal. Recall those lines from Hölderlin's
"Mnemosyne" that I cited at the outset of the book and that became a
kind of refrain for it. They are Hölderlin's hymn to the waves, sung in
a rhythm made famous by Chopin, the rhythm of a barcarolle:

> . . . And always
> Our longing soars into the unbounded. But much is
> To be kept close. We need loyalty.
> But forwards and backwards we will not want
> To look. Let ourselves be cradled, as
> On the swaying skiff of sea.

Back in chapter 1, such letting ourselves be cradled was interpreted as a "giving-over," the German *Hingebung* or *Hingabe*. In order to achieve it we have to succumb to the hallucination Neville entertains for an instant when he begs, "Come closer, closer." Letting ourselves be cradled is as close as close can get. Perhaps Jinny, alone of the six monologists, is the one who at least early in her life lets herself be cradled in this way, precisely because she *is* a body, rather than merely *having* one as an encumbrance. "And I lie back; I give myself up to rapture." Such giving-over will not keep the drop of stalactitic temporality from forming and falling; it will not keep the thug Old Age from dropping to the floor of her life.[1] Yet it may give her stories, indeed, the best of stories—love stories, for instance—even if both she and we do not know how to end such stories in an orderly manner. To bring stories to a fitting end requires that an author look ahead, look behind, and look ahead again, always on the lookout. "But forwards and backwards we will not want / To look." Instead, "Let ourselves be cradled, as / On the swaying skiff of sea."

Great works of fiction cradle us as poems do, especially poems out of the cradle endlessly rocking. Once again I will refrain from citing that great long poem of Whitman's, with its low and delicious word, a word the sea whispers him, but I will cite another poem more befitting the temporality of the drop. And Whitman, for all his ecstasies, is a poet of drops and droplets, from "Trickle Drops" to "Lingering Last Drops." Here is Whitman's "Out of the Rolling Ocean the Crowd":

> Out of the rolling ocean the crowd came a drop gently to me,
> Whispering *I love you, before long I die,*
> *I have travel'd a long way merely to look on you to touch you,*

---

[1] On the thug Old Age, see the Greek myth of Tithonos, as retold in my short story, "Timorous, Tumescent, and Toothless: The True Story of Tithonos, Prince of Troy," which, along with others of my stories, are available online at www.davidfarrellkrell.com

For I could not die till I once look'd on you,
For I fear'd I might afterward lose you.

Now we have met, we have look'd, we are safe,
Return in peace to the ocean my love,
I too am part of that ocean my love, we are not so much
  separated,
Behold the great rondure, the cohesion of all, how perfect!
But as for me, for you, the irresistible sea is to separate us,
As for an hour carrying us diverse, yet cannot carry us diverse
  forever;
Be not impatient—a little space—know you I salute the air, the
  ocean and the land,
Every day at sundown for your dear sake my love.

WW 106–7

The ocean, even if Ὠκεανός is a fresh-water stream, may be defined as a *body* of water. Perhaps one body can cradle another, though certainly not through *actio in distans*, nor as perfect presence, nor even as sheer proximity; rather, there may be a cradling of *intimi*, rising on the swells of an *amicitia intima*. Friendship may be what forms during those festivals of memory invoked by Ferenczi and hoped for by Neville when he makes his request. Such memorable friendships, however ecstatic betimes, might have to unfold on the temporality of the drop, whether the drop be of saliva, semen, or the sometimes reluctant and sometimes abundantly flowing stream of mother-of-pearl. Or drops of pericardial blood and ink, as Whitman hints in "Trickle Drops":

Trickle drops! my blue veins leaving!
O drops of me! trickle, slow drops,
Candid from me falling, drip, bleeding drops,
From wounds made to free you when you were prison'd,

From my face, from my forehead and lips,
From my breast, from within where I was conceal'd, press forth
   red drops, confession drops,
Stain every page, stain every song I sing, every word I say, bloody
   drops,
Let them know your scarlet heat, let them glisten,
Saturate them with yourself all ashamed and wet,
Glow upon all I have written or shall write, bleeding drops,
Let it all be seen in your light, blushing drops.

WW 125

Or may not the drops be even and especially of tears, which is another saline solution? And are we not always seeking solutions?

A final word, if I may, not on the terms *encounter* or *meditation*, which I still find puffed-up and incomprehensible except as desperate efforts to find an alternative to calculative thinking, but on the word and the thing I have been calling *cradling*. A very beautiful woman I know, an experienced diver, once said to me that she had no fear of drowning.

—For me it would be the most natural thing in the world just to stay down there and to give up breathing, she said.

There was no doubting she meant what she said.

No brag, no bluff.

I worried about her.

She worried about my lack of confidence in the sea.

When I float on my back at Ormos Balos now, letting myself be cradled, I play a little game. I close my eyes, breathe as easily as I can under the circumstances, and let myself drift on the rippling waves for as long as I can. The sun is bright orange through my porous eyelids, the sea calm and entirely reassuring. Now it is not levitation that I feel, not elevation into the aerian; I feel now that I am being slowly turned like the hands on a clock face. I suspect too that the impalpable current will carry me slowly eastward toward that pyramidal rock that juts out of the sea where the bay comes to an abrupt end. The indigo beneath me is no longer color but sheer depth, and the deep is populated by the unknown, even if most of that unknown is in my imagination, not in the Aegean.

All too soon I have to open my eyes. I believe that it has been thirty minutes since I closed them, but I know that it is more like two. Maybe thirty seconds? The sun is where I left it. The hands of the clock have scarcely moved. That pyramidal rock is still safely distant, almost as far away as it was when my eyes gave up on vision.

I think of that beautiful woman who has vanished from my life. I imagine her smiling a smile that fluctuates between irony and benediction. I head for the sheepish shore.

Index

activity, xxxiv, 8, 52, 63, 69, 81, 91–2,
    97, 99, 208
Aegean Sea, xxxii, xxxvi, 2–5, 12, 19,
    69, 164, 193, 301
Ahab, xl, 26, 118–19, 218, 224–5,
    232–3, 242–52, 291
Akrotiri, Thira, 22–3, 88, 135
ambiguity, 166, 170, 174, 199, 210, 233,
    236
ambivalence, 47, 49, 145, 236
amnion, amniotic fluid, xxxv, 37, 45–7,
    49, 54–7, 78, 111, 113, 115,
    129–30, 172–3, 183
amphibians, 10, 39–40, 49, 53–6, 60,
    62, 76, 105, 129, 159, 172–3
amphimixis, 63–4, 67, 96, 112
Anaximander of Miletus,
    xxxvii–xxxviii, 5, 39–40, 88–9,
    117, 120, 126, 132, 135, 137–43
antediluvian, 47, 60, 224, 238; see also
    cetaceans, flood, whales
anxiety, 24, 31, 49, 73, 85, 169, 215,
    264, 274, 279–80; see also
    terror
Ἀπάτη, see deceit, deception
ἄπειρον, 137–8, 154; see also
    Anaximander, infinite,
    unbounded
Aphrodite, Kypris, 4, 99, 143, 148, 157,
    160, 166, 177–9, 192

Aral Sea, xxxvi, 51, 69; see also
    desiccation
Ararat, Mount, 47, 69, 72, 120, 126
Aristophanes, 70–1, 159
Aristotle, xxxvi, 88–9, 117, 123–5, 127,
    129, 132, 134, 138–9, 157–8, 169
Atlantic Ocean, xxxiii–xxxiv, 11, 21,
    29–30, 204
Atlantis, 21
Augustine, 57, 64, 196, 217, 243, 256,
    274
autotomy, 72–3, 84, 98, 100, 105, 181

barcarolle, xxxiii–xxxiv, 15, 17–19,
    297; see also Chopin, music
Bemächtigung (overpowering), 60–1;
    see also will to power
Bible, the, 62–3, 126–7, 163–4, 166,
    185, 215, 218, 246; see also
    Christianity, God, religion
bioanalysis, xxxi, 33, 43–4, 69, 79–81,
    83, 92, 96, 101–8, 115, 237, 256
birth, xxxv, 43–4, 47, 49, 54–60, 65, 67,
    75–80, 85, 92, 106, 112, 114,
    141, 144, 152–3, 165, 171, 173,
    175, 180, 185, 189–90, 193,
    241–2, 246, 249, 285, 294; see
    also trauma
blood, xxxviii, 7, 16, 40, 50, 60–1, 66,
    99, 103, 129, 143, 145, 149, 159,

192, 202, 210, 222, 229, 250, 263,
    299–300; *see also* pericardial
    thinking
body, the human, xxx, xxxii, xl, 2–4,
    10, 13–14, 37–8, 44, 49, 54–7,
    60, 65–6, 69–70, 73–4, 84, 102,
    105, 125, 128–9, 133, 154, 169,
    181, 193, 216, 219–23, 232, 241,
    256, 259–60, 263, 266–7, 279,
    284–5, 287–8, 291, 298–9
Bölsche, Wilhelm, 45–6, 63, 72, 85–7,
    108
boredom, 273–6, 281; *see also*
    everydayness

Calasso, Roberto, 136, 163, 182–3,
    186–92, 195
calculative thinking, 131, 249, 300
Camus, Albert, 225
castration, 166, 180–1, 249
catastrophe, catastrophism,
    xxxiii–xxxviii, 22, 25, 42–4, 47,
    49, 53–4, 60, 62, 67, 69–77,
    80–1, 83–93, 96–109, 112, 115,
    120, 125–6, 139, 142, 182–3,
    189, 225, 242, 256, 262, 283;
    see also desiccation
cetaceans, xxxv, 172, 175, 245; *see also*
    whales
Christianity, 164–6, 196, 200–1, 206;
    see also Bible, God, religion
civilization, 21, 90, 98–100, 201–6, 209,
    226–7, 293
Clement of Alexandria, xxxix, 165–8,
    239
cloaca, 53, 61–2, 64, 74, 85
colonialism, 121, 135, 200–3, 233, 257,
    263
corals, 21, 26–7, 31–4, 196, 212, 214
cradle, cradling, xxxi–xxxiv, xli,
    1–2, 11–18, 23, 25, 32, 51,

57–8, 81, 212, 245, 263, 293,
    297–300
Crete, 19–21, 23, 239, 256
Cuvier, Georges, xxxvi, 86–90
cycles, 89, 119–20, 139, 145, 157, 183,
    273

Darwin, Charles, 51, 56, 62–3, 69
Dasein (being–here), xli, 40, 274–6, 290
death, 31, 39, 42–3, 47, 58, 60, 72, 77,
    80, 84–5, 102, 104–9, 111–15,
    170, 173, 178, 183, 189, 193, 204,
    216, 221, 223–7, 229, 231, 244,
    250, 267, 274–8, 285, 287, 291,
    294–5
deceit, deception (Ἀπάτη), 8, 149,
    177–80, 187, 235
Demeter, 54, 166, 182
Derrida, Jacques, 60, 90–3, 238, 283
desiccation, drying up of the seas,
    xxxv–xxxvi, 62, 67–72, 84–5, 88,
    90, 104, 120, 139, 182; *see also*
    catastrophe
destruction-and-death drives, xxxv,
    xxxvii, 33–4, 43, 51, 92, 101,
    105, 108, 112, 147
Devonian Age, 39, 88
Dionysos, xxxviii, 54, 57, 166–8, 180,
    183, 186, 188–94, 239
diving, 33–5, 117, 159, 180, 187, 218, 300
divinity, 89, 133–4, 137–8, 156, 165–9,
    177, 180, 185, 190–7, 217,
    238–9, 280; *see also* God,
    religion
downgoing, καταβολή, 166–7, 182,
    184–6, 224; *see also* material,
    materialization
drowning, 15, 32, 39, 41, 47, 74, 111,
    126, 190, 192, 199–200, 229,
    231, 235, 237, 244, 265, 287–9,
    297, 300

duality, duplicity, *dyás*, 51–3, 144–7,
159, 177–8, 182, 184, 186, 235
Duras, Marguerite, 74

Earth, xxx, xxxviii, 21, 41–2, 46–7,
49–50, 54–5, 57–8, 74–8, 84–7,
89–90, 103, 113, 118–21,
123–7, 129, 136, 141, 144,
148–9, 151, 157, 160, 163,
165–6, 169–72, 182–3, 192,
203–4, 214, 234, 238, 241,
245–6, 251, 256, 258, 263–5,
290, 293
earthquake, xxxiii, 18–19, 22, 32
ecstasy, ἔκστασις, xl, 77, 154, 219,
255–6, 259, 273, 277, 279,
282–3, 298–9; *see also*
temporality, tragedy
Egypt, 19, 121, 128–9, 151, 164, 166, 293
Empedocles of Acragas, xxxvii–xxxviii,
5, 111, 114, 117–19, 143–54,
157–60, 178, 221, 259, 264
encounter, xii, xxxi, xxxiii–xxxiv, xli,
117, 142–3, 153, 159, 164, 196,
200, 228, 231, 235, 237, 257, 287,
295, 300; *see also* meditative
thinking
Eros, erotic drive, xxxviii, 4, 33–4, 51,
56, 59, 61, 63–6, 73, 78–9, 84,
99–100, 106, 108, 112, 136, 147,
178, 188, 201, 210, 256
eternal recurrence, xxxvii–xxxviii, 27,
72, 91, 111, 114, 139, 145–6,
155–7, 164, 189, 224, 226, 285,
290, 293, 295
Euripides, 183, 189
everydayness, 258, 274, 276–7, 282; *see*
also boredom

fancy, fantasy, 51, 57, 62, 132; *see also*
imagination

fathers, xxxviii–xxxix, 31, 57, 61, 74,
76, 85, 142, 151, 165–7, 169,
180, 204, 213, 242, 262
female, xxxv, xxxix, 42, 45–6, 53,
57–67, 70, 85, 99, 128, 157–9,
166, 169, 172, 180, 183–9, 201,
207, 246–7, 256, 284–5
Ferenczi, Sándor, xxxi, xxxiv–xxxvii, 7,
31, 33, 42–81, 83–115, 131, 139,
142, 168–9, 173, 181, 188, 239,
245, 256, 284, 299
festivals, 3, 74–6, 85, 92, 114–15, 136,
177, 292–3, 299
fiction, xxxv, 43, 66, 79, 287, 298; *see*
also storytelling, writing
finitude, xxxix–xl, 183, 216, 223–6,
273, 275–7
fire, xxx–xxxi, xxxviii, 4, 22, 117–19,
139, 148, 157, 172–4, 189, 270;
see also Logos, sun
fish, xxxiv–xxxvi, 2, 5, 17, 29–30, 32–4,
39–40, 42, 44–6, 49, 51, 55–6,
59, 69, 83, 109, 113, 117–18,
120, 125–8, 139, 141–3, 149,
159, 168, 173–4, 186–7, 215,
219–21, 229, 246, 251, 270, 273,
278–9, 287, 290
float, floating, xxxi–xxxii, xxxix, xli,
1–2, 13–14, 49, 83, 124–7, 208,
225, 236, 238–9, 241, 244, 251,
266–7, 274, 300
flood, 47, 59, 69, 86, 89, 104, 120,
124–7, 171, 185, 216, 229, 238
Foster, Elizabeth S., 213, 216
freshwater, xxxvi, 5, 16, 29, 85, 127–8,
137, 143–4, 299; *see also* rain,
rivers
Freud, Sigmund, xxxiv–xxxv, xxxvii, 4,
8, 23–4, 33, 42–3, 45, 51–3,
57–8, 60–1, 63–5, 67, 70–2, 75,
77–9, 93, 97–101, 105–6, 108–9,

111, 113, 130, 145–7, 184, 201,
    222, 245, 256

García-Márquez, Gabriel, 91
Gary, Romain, 245, 285, 297
genitality, xxxv, 31, 39, 42, 47, 52–5,
    57–8, 62, 64–6, 70–1, 73–4, 76,
    79, 83–5, 92, 96–7, 100, 102–4.
    108, 112–13, 131, 172, 178; *see
    also* sex
germ, germ cells, 67, 70–6, 84–5, 109, 224
gestation, *see* pregnancy
Gilgamesh, 104, 125–6
giving-over (*Hingebung*), 14–15, 298
God, gods, goddesses, xxxi,
    xxxvii–xxxix, 2–3, 5, 17, 25,
    46–7, 61, 77, 89, 98, 117, 119,
    125–6, 128, 134–7, 142, 144,
    146, 148–9, 151–3, 156, 159–61,
    163–70, 175, 177–80, 183–7,
    189–90, 192–3, 195–7, 221,
    224–5, 232, 235, 239, 243–4,
    249–51, 259; *see also* divinity,
    religion
Goethe, Johann von, xxxii, 2–4, 46, 63,
    114–15
Graves, Robert, 190
Grimaud, Hélène, 17–18
Guthrie, W. K. C., 4, 193

Hades, xxxviii, 144, 165, 167, 180, 184,
    214
Haeckel, Ernst, 45, 51
hate (Νεῖκος), 15, 111, 145, 164, 202–3,
    216, 226–7, 262–3, 266, 292
Hegel, G. W. F., xxxi, 14–15, 44, 51, 63,
    66, 77, 107, 113, 169–75, 186,
    234
Heidegger, Martin, xl–xli, 25, 40–2, 95,
    105, 122, 136, 138, 152–3, 179,
    195, 217, 219, 232, 255–9, 273–7

Hera, xxix, 144, 178–9, 187, 189–90
Heraclitus of Ephesus, xxxvii–xxxviii,
    7, 83, 89, 117–19, 131–2, 149,
    154–5, 172
heredity, 75, 84
heroes, 2, 12, 41, 90, 126, 135, 139, 152,
    154, 167, 179, 195–6, 203, 222,
    243, 257, 285, 288
Hölderlin, Friedrich, xxxi–xxxiii,
    xxxviii, xli, 1–2, 9, 11–15, 17–18,
    90, 136, 143, 151–4, 169, 171,
    195–6, 210, 249–50, 297–8
Homer, 26, 89, 120, 127, 170, 184, 217,
    224
homunculus, xxxvii–xxxviii, 2–4,
    114–15, 221

Ice Ages, 76, 78
imagination, 11, 17, 50, 63, 114, 121–2,
    132, 143, 151, 169, 207, 213, 219,
    225, 233, 259, 267, 272, 279, 288,
    291, 295, 301; *see also* fancy
infancy, 13, 141, 180
infinite, xxxii, 8, 12–13, 41, 117, 127,
    137, 145–6, 174, 210, 241, 255;
    see also ἄπειρον, unbounded
inhibition, 63, 105
Ino, *see* Leukothea
inorganic, 41, 44, 71–2, 84, 101, 105,
    107–9, 111, 113; *see also*
    material, matter
intimacy, 7, 103, 131, 153, 210, 283,
    289, 292, 299–301
introjection, 56–8, 62, 67, 85, 173
Irigaray, Luce, 67, 188, 284

Joyce, James, 167, 218

Kant, Immanuel, xxxvi, 49–51, 69–70,
    106, 111, 174, 237
καταβολή, *see* downgoing

Keats, John, viii, 18, 214, 233
Kirk, G. S., Raven, J. R., and Schofield,
    M., 126, 128, 139
Kronos, xxxvii–xxxix, 160, 163, 165,
    168–70, 175, 178, 183, 197

Lamarck, Jean-Baptiste, 45, 51, 53, 56,
    69, 86–7, 108
latency, 76, 78–9, 141–2, 185
Lesky, Albin, 4–5, 135
Leukothea, xxxi, xxxviii–xxxix, 25, 47,
    54, 164, 167, 170, 186, 189–97,
    239, 265
Leviathan, 126, 142, 221, 246
life, *see* origins of
lifedeath, 77, 93, 107; *see also* finitude,
    mortality
Lingis, Alphonso, xxxiv, 13, 31–5, 37,
    158–9
literature, *see* fiction, poetry,
    storytelling
Logos, the, 118, 123; *see also*
    Heraclitus of Ephesus
love (φιλία), 12, 27, 38–41, 47, 60, 66,
    70, 73, 85, 90, 111, 143–8, 151,
    157, 159–60, 165–6, 175, 178–9,
    188, 199, 201–2, 205, 210, 219,
    226, 261–2, 281, 283–4, 292–3,
    295, 298–9
Lucretius, 83, 169, 235
Lyell, Charles, 87, 256

male, 39, 42, 44, 46, 49, 53, 60–7, 70,
    122, 128, 148, 159, 178, 183, 186,
    188, 256
mammals, xxxiv–xxxv, 37, 39–44, 47,
    49, 53, 56, 58–9, 67, 76, 129, 159,
    172–3, 239
mater, maternity, xxxviii, 44, 49,
    71–3, 77–8, 81, 165, 241–2,
    263, 283

material, materialization, 19, 59, 73,
    77–8, 84, 95, 117, 125, 147,
    165–8, 224, 238; *see also*
    downgoing, καταβολή
matter, 22, 26, 50, 58, 71–2, 77–8, 80,
    108–9, 117, 124, 165–6, 224; *see
    also* inorganic
meditative thinking, xi–xii, xxxiii, xl, 2,
    15, 27, 31, 109, 121, 131–3, 143,
    154–7, 175, 216–17, 225, 228,
    237, 244, 249, 287, 289, 300; *see
    also* encounter
Mediterranean Sea, 4, 69, 127, 153
Melville, Herman, xii, xxxi, xxxiii,
    xxxv, xxxix, 15–18, 30, 61, 74,
    118, 196, 199–252, 255, 276,
    278, 287–8, 291, 295
memory, xxxiv, 12–14, 16, 18, 75–6,
    79–81, 85, 92, 101, 114–15,
    122, 153, 180–2, 233, 258, 280,
    297, 299
Merleau-Ponty, Maurice, 13, 26, 170–1,
    181–2, 221
metaphysics, 93, 107–8, 117, 124, 131,
    236–8, 273, 297; *see also*
    ontology
Milton, John, xl, 217, 227, 244
moisture, 47, 54–6, 61
moon, the, 32, 34, 47, 59, 89, 108, 156,
    171, 181, 208, 214, 222, 249, 261
mortality, xxxix, 83, 136–7, 144–5,
    148–9, 165, 177, 179–80, 190,
    192, 197, 212, 214, 225–6,
    232–3, 239, 241, 243, 249, 275,
    277, 293–4; *see also* death,
    finitude, lifedeath
mothers, 8, 13, 37, 46, 51, 54, 56–8, 65,
    67, 71, 74, 77, 85, 92, 102, 119,
    122, 142, 165–8, 171, 180,
    182–3, 186, 189, 196, 201, 239,
    241, 245, 247, 252, 263, 284–5,

292; *see also mater*, material, maternity, pregnancy
music, 9, 17–18, 111, 133, 242, 245–52
Musil, Robert, xxx, 199, 255
mysteries, the, xxxv, 18, 31, 42, 50, 57–8, 62, 67, 70, 74, 85, 89, 97, 134, 136–7, 168, 175, 182–5, 188–97, 217, 224, 226, 233, 235, 239, 244, 247, 278; *see also* gods, religion
myth, mythology, xxxi, xxxviii–xxxix, 21, 47, 57, 62, 74, 85, 91, 95, 126–7, 130, 132, 152, 159–60, 163–97, 218, 225, 248

nature (φύσις), xxxix–xl, 8, 26, 42, 50–3, 63, 70, 86–7, 90–2, 108, 124–5, 129–30, 132, 146, 166–75, 203, 209, 224, 244, 250, 293
neurosis, 53, 64, 66, 96, 100, 103
Nietzsche, Friedrich, xxxi, xxxiii, xxxviii, xl, 7–10, 14, 17, 27, 37–8, 77, 91, 93, 98, 102, 109, 111, 113–15, 129, 131–4, 136, 138–9, 143, 145, 153–8, 174, 179, 184, 206, 219, 221–3, 232, 245, 249, 276, 290–1
Novalis (Friedrich von Hardenberg), 43, 108, 291
nursing, xxxviii–xxxix, 46–7, 54, 59–60, 141, 172, 186, 189–93, 239, 241–2, 245–6

oceanic feeling, xxxiv, 8–9, 23–5, 136, 185
odor, 59, 170–5, 186–9
ontogeny, 60–3, 69, 76–8, 84–5, 103, 112
ontology, xli, 92–3, 102–3, 108, 195, 256; *see also* metaphysics

organism, 3, 50–3, 63–4, 76, 87, 96, 98–100, 103–7, 109, 111, 113, 172
origins, x, xxxv, 4, 66, 90–2, 125, 128–30, 135, 138, 155, 185–6
of language, xxxiii, 90–2
of life, x, xxxv, 63–4, 71–2, 76, 84, 109, 115, 142
of society, 90–2, 159–60

Pacific Ocean, 19, 29–30, 196, 200, 204, 211, 215, 224, 235, 247
Parmenides of Elea, 143
passivity, xi, xxxi–xxxii, xxxiv, 2, 61, 66, 77, 99, 113, 181, 187, 196, 282, 284
paternity, *see* fathers
pericardial thinking, xxxviii, 143, 148–9, 153, 157, 159, 221–2, 242, 299
Persephone, xxxviii, 164–6, 180–6
Persia, 5, 164, 166, 234, 237, 243
Phantasie, see fancy
phantasms, phantoms, xxxv, xl, 66–7, 70, 132, 146, 173, 186, 237–8, 244, 292
phylogenesis, x, xxxiv–xxxvi, 42–6, 60–2, 66–7, 69–78, 83–5, 98, 101, 103, 105–6, 112, 131, 188, 245, 256
Pip, xxxix, 26, 196–7
Plato, xxxvii, 21, 54, 58, 70, 95, 108, 121–3, 136, 143, 159, 217, 225, 243
play, 3, 31, 64–5, 74–5, 91–2, 133, 151, 154, 177, 188, 223, 257–8, 265, 300
pleasure, unpleasure (*Lust, Unlust*), xxxvi–xxxvii, 42, 44, 49, 52–3, 62–3, 66–70, 72–6, 81, 84–5, 92, 96–106, 109, 112, 156, 175, 187–8, 227, 246, 283

poetry, x–xiii, xxxiii, xxxix, 12, 15–17, 46, 57–8, 71, 89, 127, 152–3, 168, 216–19, 222–3, 260–2, 265, 275, 277, 282–4, 298
politics, 146, 210, 216, 218; *see also* society
Poseidon, xxxi, xxxviii–xxxix, 5, 25, 47, 160, 164–70, 175, 192, 237
pregnancy, 2, 55, 144, 172–3, 186, 189, 263; *see also mater*, maternity, mothers
Pre-Platonic thinkers, 123, 143, 225
priests, xl, 76, 151–2, 164, 186, 212, 225–6, 276, 295
prosopopoeia, 14, 104
psychoanalysis, *see* Ferenczi, Freud, Rank
psychotherapy, *see* therapy
purposiveness in nature, 50, 52–3, 106; *see also* teleology

racism, 228–9
rain, xiii, xxxvi–xxxvii, 89, 119–20, 125–6, 139, 157, 171, 182–3, 261, 270, 279; *see also* freshwater
Rank, Otto, xxxv, 43, 47, 129–30, 166, 185, 239, 284
rapidity, rapture (ἐχαιφνης), xxxiv, 31–5, 40, 118, 158, 196, 212, 255–6, 259–60, 277, 283, 298
regression, xxxv–xxxvii, 7, 39, 53, 70, 90, 100–3, 105–7, 113
religion, xi, xxxiv, xxxix, 23–5, 136, 168, 185, 203, 216–17, 261; *see also* divinity, God, mysteries
repression, 64, 98–100, 129–30, 188
reptiles, 49, 53–6, 159, 172–3
Rhea, xxxviii, 165, 167
rhythm, 57, 133, 155, 297

rivers, xxx, xxxiii, 10, 39, 56, 89, 104, 120, 127, 130, 171, 237, 295; *see also* freshwater
Rousseau, Jean-Jacques, 77, 90–2, 112, 205–6

salinity, salt, x, xii, xxxiii, xxxv–xxxvi, xxxviii–xxxix, 4, 16, 25, 37, 54–5, 69, 113, 120, 126–8, 137, 143–4, 168–9, 171–2, 192, 212, 248, 300
Sallis, John, 123
Samothrace, xxxix, 2–3, 47, 134, 164, 186, 192–3, 226, 250, 295
Schelling, F. W. J., xxxi, xxxviii–xxxix, 3, 26, 45, 57–8, 63, 78, 102, 108, 132, 136, 160, 163–90, 195, 197, 218, 224–6, 237, 239, 249, 285, 291
Schopenhauer, Arthur, 9, 14, 77, 113
science, xxx, xxxv–xxxvi, 2, 9, 16, 32, 38–41, 43, 55, 83, 85–8, 91, 93–6, 101, 103, 108–9, 133, 135, 156, 168–9, 209, 216, 219, 222, 234, 290–1
Scott, Charles, 274, 287–9
seasons, the, 21, 32, 243, 257–8
Sehnsucht (languor, languishing, longing), 1, 3–4, 12, 18, 58, 71, 185, 251, 291, 297
separation, severance, 40, 77, 87, 108, 144–5, 147–8, 157, 178–80, 237, 244, 248, 260, 265, 269, 280, 284, 299
sex, sexuality, x, xxxv, 42–6, 49–53, 56, 60–1, 63, 65–7, 69–70, 74–7, 83–5, 97–100, 104, 108, 114–15, 165, 172–3, 181, 188, 201; *see also* genitality
Shakespeare, William, xl, 31, 214, 217, 261
sharks, 32, 34–5, 142, 216, 218, 234, 246, 287

ships, 3, 16, 23, 25–6, 29–30, 34–5, 47,
    121, 125, 136, 170, 179, 193,
    211–12, 215, 228, 234, 243, 285,
    290–1, 293–4
shipwreck, 170, 185, 192, 234
silence, xxxiii, 7–9, 13, 29, 80, 118, 153,
    183, 215, 226, 279, 281–2, 284,
    290–1, 295, 297
sleep, x, 15, 35, 47, 56, 65, 79–81,
    100–1, 105, 113, 179, 208, 221,
    245–6, 250, 263–4, 266
smell, *see* odor
society, 78–9, 90–2, 95, 142, 201,
    203–9, 228–9, 260; *see also*
    origins of, politics
Socrates, 122–3
Sophocles, 47, 189, 195, 214, 243
sperm and egg, *see* germ
Sterne, Laurence, xl, 218, 236
storytelling, 9–10, 23–4, 27, 34–5,
    38–42, 46, 62–3, 117, 121–3,
    126–7, 149, 165–6, 180, 183,
    186–93, 195, 204, 208–9, 233,
    237, 258, 264, 271–3, 277–83,
    294; *see also* fiction
strife, *see* hate (Νεῖκος)
sun, the, xxxi, 7, 10, 15, 23, 26, 29, 58,
    68–9, 89, 108, 119, 140–1,
    149–50, 157, 170, 179, 208,
    214–16, 224–5, 230, 236, 238,
    244, 246, 249, 251, 257–8, 261,
    269–70, 273, 286, 293–4,
    299–301; *see also* fire
supplementarity, xxxvi, 56, 90–2, 96,
    107
swimming, xxxii, 1–2, 9–10, 35, 38, 42,
    55, 118, 174, 192, 208, 239, 244,
    265, 277, 292

teleology, 33, 50–1, 111–12; *see also*
    purposiveness in nature

temporality, xxxi, xxxv, xxxvii, xl–xli,
    155, 222, 255–60, 264, 271,
    273–84, 293, 298–9; *see also*
    time
tenderness, 169–70, 190, 210, 239,
    241–2, 261, 284–5
tension (*Spannung*), 69, 72–4, 84–5,
    97–8, 100, 131–2, 167–8
terror, 38, 127, 169–70, 188, 255, 266,
    288; *see also* anxiety
θάλασσα, θάλαττα, xxxiii, 4–5, 117–18
thalassic regressive tendency, x,
    xxxv–xxxvii, 7, 52–63, 67, 83,
    92, 106–9, 111, 235, 245, 288–9
Thales of Miletus, xxxii–xxxiii, xxxvii,
    3, 5, 25, 30, 89, 117, 121–38, 154,
    168, 175, 185, 187, 235
therapy, 44, 64, 115, 261–2
thinking, *see* calculative, meditative,
    pericardial
Thira (Santorini), xxxii–xxxiii, 1, 5,
    18–23, 88, 121, 135, 160
time, xxxv, xxxvii, xl–xli, 3–4, 25, 42, 52,
    72, 86–7, 89, 92, 101–2, 106, 113,
    117, 126, 136, 138–44, 148–9,
    152, 155–8, 182–3, 211–12, 216,
    223–6, 232, 243, 248, 255–95; *see*
    also temporality
Tournier, Michel, 47, 80–1
tragedy, the tragic, xxxvii–xxxix, 9, 75,
    111, 113, 115, 121, 129–32, 138,
    148–57, 182–3, 188–9, 208,
    242–3, 255
trash vortices, xxxiv, 27, 29–30, 204, 218
trauma, xxxv, 43, 47, 74–6, 80, 92, 96,
    287–9
trimethylamine, 59, 79, 100, 186; *see*
    also odor
truth, 8, 33, 46, 66–7, 130–1, 147, 164,
    182, 185, 188, 216–19
tsunami, 18–19, 21, 276

unbounded, the, 1, 12, 22, 24, 33–4,
  138–9, 154–5, 297; *see also*
  Anaximander, ἄπειρον,
  Hölderlin, infinite
uncanny, the, 31–2, 40, 47, 90, 137,
  184–5, 195, 214, 232, 243, 252,
  273
undertow, x, xii, xxxv, xxxvii, 7, 9,
  52–3, 56–7, 60, 67, 83, 92, 106,
  111, 141, 151, 183, 235, 245; *see
  also* thalassic regressive
  tendency
unpleasure (*Unlust*), *see* pleasure
Urania, 166–8, 170, 182, 186, 238; *see
  also* Dionysos, Leukothea,
  Persephone, Rhea
utraquism, 93, 95–6, 169

vertebrates, 42, 44, 56–7, 78
volcanoes, xxxiii, xxxvi, 18–23, 30, 32,
  87, 145; *see also* earthquake,
  tsunami

whales, xl, 16, 37–8, 59–60, 172–3, 175,
  219–21, 224–5, 232–52; *see also*
  cetaceans

Whitman, Walt, 13, 15, 58, 298–300
will to power, 113–14; *see also*
  Bemächtigung
woman, xxxix, 10, 54, 61–7, 80, 122,
  165–6, 172, 177–93, 196, 208,
  218, 228, 243, 246, 260, 265, 269,
  271–2, 285, 292–3, 300–1; *see
  also* female
Woolf, Virginia, xii, xxxi, xl–xli, 15,
  152, 256–95
writing, viii, xi–xii, xxxi, xxxiv,
  xxxix–xl, 1, 15, 18, 24–5, 30,
  43, 90, 98, 104, 131, 137, 152,
  199–200, 213–14, 216, 219, 226,
  229, 233, 252, 258, 265, 269–73,
  278, 282, 288–9, 294–5

Xenophanes of Colophon,
  xxxvii–xxxviii, 88–9, 117,
  119–21, 139, 255

Yeats, W. B., 127

Zeus, xxxviii, 47, 57, 62, 71, 74, 85, 144,
  151, 160, 165, 175, 177–80,
  182–5, 189, 191, 239